What if I had never tried it

VALENTINO ROSSI

THE AUTOBIOGRAPHY

What if I had never tried it

VALENTINO ROSSI

THE AUTOBIOGRAPHY

With Enrico Borghi

Translated by Gabriele Marcotti

CENTURY

This edition first published in 2006 by Motorbooks, an imprint
of MBI Publishing Company, Galtier Plaza, Suite 200,
380 Jackson Street, St. Paul, MN 55101-3885 USA

First published in the United Kingdom in 2005 by Century

MBI Publishing Company titles are also available at discounts in
bulk quantity for industrial or sales-promotional use. For
details write to Special Sales Manager at MBI Publishing
Company, Galtier Plaza, Suite 200, 380 Jackson Street,
St. Paul, MN 55101-3885 USA

For a free catalog, call 1-800-826-6600, or visit
our website at www.motorbooks.com.

ISBN-13: 978-0-7603-2682-4
ISBN-10: 0-7603-2682-7

Designed by Peter Ward
All photographs copyright © Milagro,
except as stated otherwise

Printed in the United States of America

What if I had never tried it

ONE

CAPITOLO UNO

When we swerved to the left, bent right over, fully in third gear, at 170 kilometres per hour, from my Honda all I could see were the upper exhaust pipes of his Yamaha. He was still ahead of me, just as we came into the turn at the top of the hill, right where the horizon ends and you begin to disappear behind it. I was glued to him. It was the dying moments of an open shoot-out which began with eight riders and was now down to two. The two of us. Me and Max Biaggi.

The final reckoning of the 2001 championship. Last lap. Last tough spot. Last point of attack. Last chance . . . for me.

That turn is on a stretch of asphalt spread like butter over a shallow, green hill. It clings to the hill tightly, following every contour. It's like a long "S", first left, then right, and the apex is the top of the hill. Before you get there, you're going uphill. After that, it's all downhill.

When you go in to the corner, you can't see what's on the other side. You have to ride from memory. You have no idea when you can brake, you only begin to understand when you're on the other side and if you haven't picked the right spot, it's too late, there's nothing you can do about it.

I planned an outside trajectory, so that I could be on his right in the brief downhill stretch and then on the inside on the following turn. There is only one way to get through that turn, in first gear, after downshifting from fourth.

If you are first coming out of there, it's over. You've won. I felt my elbow brush up against his Yamaha, first his exhaust pipe, then his rear tyre. I was taking a huge risk of course, I was. But I had to. It was the only way to get ahead of him when it came to brake. And that's what I did. When he realised what was happening, I was right there, next to him, on the outside. And suddenly it was too late for him to react. We came down side by side, and I went into the tight right turn first, and stayed ahead in the long left turn that followed, crossing the finish line ahead of him.

And that was how I won the 2001 Australian Grand Prix and became the new 500cc World Champion.

Three years later, Sete Gibernau and I found ourselves in the exact same spot on the same track. He was expecting me to attack him, just as I had attacked Biaggi. He knew what was coming – it was the last lap and I had already tried to attack him a few turns earlier, but then I had made a crucial mistake and had allowed Gibernau to regain the lead. This time, I decided to go inside, at the entrance of the uphill turn, so that I'd be ahead just as we went downhill. I wanted to seal the victory early, before the long downhill stretch, so I went for it, just as we came into the long turn and the elevation changed.

"I did it!" I thought to myself. But my elation lasted a mere instant. It was a false dawn. Gibernau came off his brakes and closed my path, and we reached the top of the hill together, with his Honda nudging the front wheel of my Yamaha. But then, suddenly, I saw him going wide, too wide. He couldn't close the trajectory, he was blowing the turn.

"Oh, you're going wide, aren't you . . . yeah, you're going wide . . . yes, yes, you can't do it . . . you're too wide . . . I'm coming through!" The thought dashed through my mind as I hit the gas and accelerated past him.

In that part of the track, you're going very fast and you're bent right over. You can't touch your brakes and you can't get up. Once you're in, you're in. If you made the slightest mistake, if your speed isn't right, you're out.

Gibernau came into the turn too fast, while I had exactly the right speed. I passed him, going ahead into the last, slow right turn – just as I had done three years earlier.

And that was how I won the 2004 Australian Grand Prix.

I won with the Yamaha. I beat the Honda. And I retained my MotoGP world title.

Those were two glorious moves, coming as they did at the climax of two outstanding races in two intense seasons. The first in 500cc, the second in MotoGP.

I thought of the coincidences. They occurred in the exact same spot, three years apart. And I thought there was something magical about them. The 2001 and 2004 titles were not only the most hard-fought, but also the most significant among those I have won. I won them on the same track, Philip Island, making two incredible manoeuvres, in the same spot, in the same crucial moment of the season. And in each case I wanted to put the final nail in the coffin and secure the title.

That long left turn where I made two of the overtaking moves I enjoyed the most in my entire career, is probably the most exciting stretch of a fantastic track that will forever be close to my heart. At Philip Island, there is the long initial straightaway, and following that you reach the ocean after a series of turns – some wide, some tight, with changes in speed and elevation. You reach the ocean and then you leave it behind, twice, before joining a long ramp which takes you straight up to the famous long left turn. But just before that, there is a very fast chicane: you arrive in fourth gear, at 200kph, go down to third gear and 170kph to negotiate the "right–left" change in direction and, finally, you take on that long uphill curve. On that long turn, you spend what seems like an eternity bent over, flying along at very high speeds, unable to see what's ahead. It is one of the most beautiful, fastest and difficult turns in the whole MotoGP tour. You have to be extremely accurate and sensitive to negotiate your way through it, and it's one of those spots where the quality of the rider makes all the difference. Just as, to me, it makes all the difference if it's the last lap or not.

I love beating my opponents on the last lap. It's the most exciting way to win a race. Sure, sometimes it would probably be best to avoid problems, rush out ahead and build up a huge lead, but there are times when you realise you can't build a gap with the others, and at those times it's best if you wait for the last lap. It's the ultimate showdown. You've prepared, lap after lap. You've studied your main opponent's trajectories, the way he takes every turn; you know where he's strongest and where his weaknesses are, you know where he's vulnerable if you attack him. It's the ultimate rush. On that last lap, you may be able to surprise your opponent once, at best, but that's it. He won't fall for anything after that. Everything becomes tougher.

I think back to 2001 and 2004 and I know that Biaggi and Gibernau gave everything they had. I know, because I did the same. It was the crucial moment, the stakes were huge, it wasn't just about the world title; at stake were the future paths of our racing careers.

In 2001, Biaggi and I were competing to win what would be not just our first title in the 500cc, but also the final title ever in that category. The following season, of course, the MotoGP era kicked off, replacing the 500cc category. At the time, I had only been racing 500cc for one season and so, for me, this was my first and only chance to win the title I had always dreamed about. I only had the one chance to win it and that chance was now. Biaggi was in the exact same boat as me, but I desperately wanted to be the last ever 500cc world champion.

The stakes were very high in 2004 as well, given what happened the year before: I had left Honda and gone to Yamaha, in search of new challenges. I was determined to prove that I could win even without a bike, the Honda, which everyone thought was invincible.

I chose Yamaha, a team which was in serious difficulty, which only made the challenge that much greater. This wasn't just about winning another title, it was about resentment and pride, rancour and honour. I knew that the 2004 season could put an end to an entirely different issue and therefore there was so much more pressure. I knew that if I could win right away, with a Yamaha, in my first season, it would change the face of motorcycling for ever. And that's what happened in Australia, on the hills of Philip Island, where I put the finishing touches on an adventure which had begun in South Africa.

Yes, South Africa. Welkom, the young city located in Free State. The date was 18 April 2004, a day which will long live in the history of motorcycle racing. I won my very first race with Yamaha. It was also the very first race of the 2004 World Championship. It was something absolutely unthinkable, even for me.

You may have seen me stop at the edge of the track, getting off my beautiful Yamaha, and watched as I sat down next to her, wrapping my arms around my knees and lowering my head. You may have wondered what I was doing; perhaps you thought I was overcome with emotion and was having a quiet sob of relief. In fact, I wasn't. Not at all. Behind my black visor, I was laughing. Laughing heartily at that. In that moment, huddled next to my bike on the grass, resting against her tyres, just me and my Yamaha, I was laughing. Laughing because of the incredible feeling of pride, relief and happiness which had overcome me.

"And so in the end I was right!" I thought to myself. "I can't believe it, I screwed them all . . . what a show!"

I remember the time I said I needed a bike to win at Welkom. It was during a meeting with Davide Brivio, team director of Yamaha MotoGP, and Lin Jarvis, managing director of Yamaha Motor Racing, where I first decided that I was going to race on the Yamaha for the 2004 season. I told them I wanted a bike that could win in South Africa. In other words – win right away. They were all rather at a loss. Sometimes, during our meetings with the Yamaha guys, towards the end of 2003, I'd come up with phrases that left them confused, surprised, maybe even scared them a little. I did it to motivate them.

Masao Furusawa, Jarvis and Brivio always explained what Yamaha's plans were and what they were going to do, as if to reassure me. I remember them telling me about changes in the racing department, back in Japan. How they were going to hire new engineers, this guy, that guy. They'd always repeat themselves and insist: "Don't worry, we can make this bike go, we can make it work!"

I listened quietly and, to be fair, they did have an ambitious project. At the time, though, I simply couldn't be sure it was going to work. This was still 2003. The MotoGP landscape was very different. The very best Yamaha was still a second per lap behind on the Honda. If you're a second a lap slower at this level, you might as well be a whole year behind . . .

So I'd sit there and think about things, and then once in a while, just to shake them up, I'd turn to Brivio and say: "You do realise, don't you, that if this bike is no good I'm going to blame you and you alone? Because I know you. I don't know Jarvis and Furusawa – you're the one I know and you're the one who's going to get it!"

He'd sit quietly and listen.

"If this bike doesn't go, it's going to be your arse on the line!" I'd say and he'd look at me with this strange expression, somewhere between worry and terror.

To be fair, we were all worried before we started working together, but it was his job to be the optimist. Certainly, he had to be more of an optimist than me.

Looking back, what I said about wanting a bike that could win at Welkom, well, that was a way of boosting morale, an attempt at wishful thinking. You can't demand something like that. And, even if you get it, there's no certainty you'll win. But then again, we riders always say all sorts of things. Sometimes we believe what we say, even when it sounds crazy, other times we're just being hopeful and, still at other times, it's all an exercise in self-delusion. We try to convince ourselves of something, because ultimately, every time you step on to the track, words don't matter, and it's just you, the bike and your opponents.

In fact, that's the only time you really have a clear picture of things. When you're actually on the track, racing against your opponents. That's when you know where you are and where the others stand. You know how your bike is doing and how those of your opponents are faring. That's the moment of clarity. Then, you can say whatever you like to everyone else: your chief mechanic, your mum, your girlfriend, the press . . . but, deep down, you know the truth and you know it with crystal-clear clarity. You can tell people you fell because the bike didn't follow the trajectory it was supposed to follow, or tell them that you're actually really fast, but the bike simply isn't. Inside you, however, you know the truth. You know you fell off because you made a mistake, or because your opponent is simply faster than you.

And the opposite is also true. Deep down, you know whether your victories were deserved. You know if you won races on the turns, when it's down to your ability as a rider, or on the straightaways, when it's all about the power of the engine. You know the others are looking to make excuses when they say you beat them just because the bike was better. I always knew the truth behind each of my victories, and behind each of my defeats, too. I knew exactly why and how I won or lost. And so, at the end of 2003, after winning everything in sight with the Honda, I was certain I could win with another bike. But, of course, until I actually did it, I couldn't be truly certain. Thus, I set off on my journey, in search of that place where certainty meets truth.

Everybody said that in 2004 I would rack up a series of disappointments with Yamaha. The mere notion that I could win the world title with one race to spare seemed exceptionally far-fetched.

A friend of mine told me that, in one of the final races of 2003, when my move to Yamaha was the favourite talking point all over the paddock, he ran into Gibernau, who was watching footage of me laughing on a video monitor.

"You'll see, next year when he's on Yamaha and the bike is slipping all over the place and he's landing on his rear end, he won't be laughing quite so much," my friend heard Gibernau say.

When this story was told to me, I had no idea that I would actually win the same number of races – nine – that I won the previous year on the Honda. I couldn't imagine that we would spend the whole year at the head of the pack, pulling away.

But I did know something for sure: I would do something that would make history in this sport.

That's why that first race at Welkom was the most important of my career. Because it was my first with Yamaha. Because I battled until the last turn with Biaggi. Because he and I were so fast that Gibernau, who finished third, might as well have been racing another championship.

As for the guy who finished fourth, well, he had virtually disappeared. Ultimately, I had proved what I had set out to prove: the importance of man over machine. That's what it was all about and my win at Welkom confirmed this.

We left the track and the town of Welkom, a few hours after the race, headed for the airport to catch the British Airways flight that would take us back to London. We had planned for some time that I would leave straight away, so that I could be in Europe on Monday. The trip from Welkom to Johannesburg takes about three hours by car. We were in a Volkswagen minivan. I was stretched out over the back seats. With me were the driver, my manager Gibo (whose real name is Luigino Badioli) and my best friend Alessio Salucci, whom everyone calls Uccio.

I was lying there, relaxing, enjoying what I had just achieved. The phone kept ringing, as I continued to field congratulatory calls from Italy. I could tell in my friends' voices that something had changed. They were somehow different. They had to stop themselves every so often because they almost could not breathe. They couldn't express everything they wanted to tell me.

I felt shivers run down my back and I had goosebumps along my back and my arms. I could sense their amazement, their joy, their empathy. I had lived through so many emotional moments, but that afternoon, sensing my friends' reactions, I understood that I had achieved something truly important. And that was when I began to realise that I had produced a seminal moment in the history of motor-cycling.

In some ways, motorcycling has never been the same.

I remember well the conventional wisdom among the riders: "If you want to win, you need a Honda."

And I remembered all those who insisted that leaving Honda for

Yamaha was crazy, a hopeless choice, an impossible challenge with no chance of success. And I also remember what the engineers told me. They insisted that a great racing department, like Honda's, could create and develop an exceptional bike even without input from the rider.

Well, from that moment on, this was no longer true.

To be honest, I don't think it was ever true, but in South Africa that day it became clear to everyone just how important human input and sensitivity are to the development of a racing bike, to its tuning, to its performance in a race.

By the end of 2003 I had taken on the responsibility of proving this and I had succeeded at the first attempt. That's why I can say with confidence that that day at Welkom will be remembered as the day everything changed in motorcycling.

The more I thought about it, the more I understood that, from that point on, no rider could trot out the usual excuses. And no engineer could be 100 per cent cocksure of himself and go about ignoring the rider's opinion on the bike. From that point on, we riders, and what we thought and felt about the bikes, the tracks, about everything, had to be respected. And I was very proud of this, not so much for myself, but for all the youngsters out there who would benefit from this in the future.

And yet, the night before that race at Welkom, just like the night before Philip Island six months later, was no different from every other pre-night race. I didn't think about the implications of what I was about to achieve. But for me this is normal, because I don't give too much weight to whether an important race or manoeuvre can change my life and my career.

The night before a race I'm so thoroughly immersed in the detail of what I need to think about – fine-tuning the bike, choosing the tyres or the set-up, working out how I'm going to tackle various points of the track and how the other riders might tackle them – that I don't really have time to worry about what's at stake in the race itself. I think about the revs to which I need to bring the engine so that I can start in the right way, or how I should pop the clutch, or that I need to take the first turn in a certain way, maybe half a metre back because otherwise I might lose half a tenth of a second. In other words, I think of how I'm going to ride.

When I put on my suit, get on my bike and make my way to the start line, my brain is free of every single thought apart from those directly linked to my riding of the bike. I can isolate everything else, nerves don't bother me, I don't even think, once that visor comes down, that my reputation, or my title, or even my career might be at stake.

Nobody made me like this, nobody taught me how to do this, racing just comes naturally. That's why it's not uncommon to see me joking and laughing minutes before the start of a crucial race. To me, this mental attitude is absolutely crucial. I couldn't conceive any other way of racing. Because once you put too many thoughts into your head, you end up making mistakes. I imagine that's how footballers must feel when they step up to take a penalty kick. When they start to think a little too much about what could happen if they make a mistake, they lose their concentration and they end up missing the kick. Those who are good penalty takers don't think to themselves, "This penalty can change my career." They just think about how they're going to score.

In any case, in motorbike racing, when you're about to start a race which will see you take on five to six hundred turns, over sometimes as many as thirty laps, each of them so taut that the slightest mistake will ruin everything, well, in those situations you have to try to deflate the pressure. Otherwise, if you get caught up in it, that pressure can become unsustainable.

That's why at Welkom, just before the start, I wasn't thinking thoughts like: "I'm at Yamaha, I'm in pole position, if I win this race I'll change my career and the history of this sport . . ."

I thought about that later, at entirely different moments. Sitting on the grass, next to my Yamaha. Returning to the pits to be with my new team. On my way to Johannesburg. Leaving Philip Island. Reclining on the plane as it flew me back home to London.

TWO

An adventure that begins with a secret meeting in Ibiza simply can't have an unhappy ending. Today I know this is true, but, back in February 2003, when Davide Brivio first came to talk to me about his project, the thought had not yet crossed my mind. I had just bought a house there and was utterly absorbed with the task of remodelling and renovating my new Ibizan hideaway. In winter, Ibiza is a virtual ghost island and there are never many people around, so Gibo and I figured it was the perfect place to meet Yamaha's team director.

"Let's hear what he has to say," I told Gibo. "After all, they're the second biggest motorcycle manufacturers in the world. If Yamaha are really interested in us, then we need to hear them out."

As I said this to him, however, the truth of the matter was I had no intention of leaving Honda at that time. To be fair, I wasn't entirely comfortable at Honda any more, but not being completely at ease is one thing; being prepared to leave is quite another. I had not even contemplated the possibility of a move.

I was still fast asleep when Brivio arrived, around noon. Gibo met him and they decided to wake me up. Once I was alert enough to realise what was going on, it was lunchtime, so, after a quick shower, I threw on some clothes and we were off. We picked a restaurant along the Las Salinas Beach. It's one of the most beautiful places in Ibiza, and, along the way, I pointed out the island's attractions to our visitor, like the perfect tour guide.

Although I already knew Davide well, I had never talked business with him. Or, at least, I had never spoken to him about the possibility of moving to Yamaha. And yet, this time, I knew this was the reason he had come to see me. I knew our relationship could potentially change. And that's the reason why I chose the neutral ground of Ibiza for our meeting. It was the kind of place where we could keep ourselves isolated – physically as well as mentally – from the world of MotoGP. Up until that point, it was Gibo who had done most of the talking with Brivio. The first time was back in September 2002, in Rio de Janeiro, a few hours after my victory there that clinched the world title. That race, run under a driving rain, was a historic moment, and not just for my career, but also for the sport of motorcycling: I had become the first rider to win a world title in each class: 125cc, 250cc, 500cc and MotoGP. Brivio had approached us and asked Gibo for a meeting, even though he knew all too well that my contract with Honda only expired in 2003.

Over lunch we spoke about many things: the island, my new house and, yes, even a bit about MotoGP, albeit always skirting around the issue, which was the real reason why Brivio had come all this way. We only really broached the subject after we finished lunch and began to part company.

"We want you," Brivio said, almost immediately.

I fell silent. I had been expecting this moment, yet his words sounded a little strange to my ear, somewhat unusual.

He went on: "You're the only reason we can't beat Honda," he said. "As long as you race for them, we're not going to beat them."

Then he explained himself further: "For now, this is just my own idea, it's not part of Yamaha's plan . . . I came here to sound you out, to see if you'd be interested. If you think it's something you might consider, I'm ready to go to Japan and present my project to them. If not, it all ends here."

Brivio was clear and honest with me. As I learned later, the whole idea was his and his alone. Yamaha hadn't even contemplated the possibility.

"Look, the Japanese know that I am here to speak to you, but for now they don't seem particularly interested," he added.

I continued to listen, although, to be honest, in that meeting nobody betrayed any real intent, one way or another. Neither us, nor him. Still, I was struck by the way Davide spoke of Yamaha, of his team, of his job. He was so passionate, so involved. And that really pricked my curiosity.

"It's interesting, it's something we can talk about further," I said. It may have sounded like I was being polite, but I wasn't. I was genuinely interested. I didn't want to give him any illusions, but I didn't want to discourage him either. And as it turned out, he was encouraged. When he returned home, he immediately started talking to his bosses, the Japanese. I, on the other hand, started taking a greater interest in Yamaha, albeit from afar. I started viewing them in a slightly different light.

Previously, as far as I was concerned, Yamaha was just another opponent: in fact, in 2001 and 2002, they were Biaggi's team. In 2002, the first season of MotoGP, Yamaha won two races with Biaggi. The first was in Brno, where I had problems with my rear tyre, though, to be fair, Biaggi was very fast. The other was in Malaysia, where I lost time battling with Alex Barros, while Biaggi raced ahead.

But in 2003, Yamaha seemed, in my opinion, most of all as a team without a rider capable of developing their bike. Towards the end of 2002, Yamaha's Iwata offices had decided not to renew Biaggi's contract. Relations between him and the team had been deteriorating for some time and were far from good. So they decided to start over, retaining Carlos Checa and hiring Barros to race alongside him. On paper, it wasn't a bad combination. Checca was fast and Barros had beaten me a few times in 2002, when he was riding the RCV. That season, however, demonstrated to everyone that the two riders could not develop the bike together, as a team. Some would say the problem was with the engine but that the chassis was fine; while others would come out and say the problem lay with the chassis, not the engine. And so the engineers and mechanics had no clue which way to go, which road to pursue. And thus, the bike made very little progress. That's why, at the start of the 2003 season, Yamaha looked to everyone – including, of course, yours truly – like a disaster zone. And, in fact, it was.

All of Yamaha's best and brightest had assembled at Suzuka, for the opening Grand Prix of the season. They were all there, board members, the president and his aides, mechanics, engineers. They were all present to see what was, for them, an absolute debacle. Checca, who had started in pole, finished tenth. The other Yamahas were even worse. And to add injury to insult (for once), Barros had suffered very serious knee ligament damage during the warm-up laps.

That day Yamaha took a massive blow. And not just from me, though I had beaten Biaggi and Loris Capirossi (who was making his debut for Ducati) to the finish. When the Yamaha executives returned to Iwata, they immediately held a general meeting, where they agreed that it was time to make massive changes.

"We can't be embarrassed like that ever again," they said. "We have to change."

That day, they decided to completely restructure the racing department, launching themselves on a new project to change the M1. The racing department seemed to me to be demotivated; they needed an injection of fresh ideas and energy. The engineers belonged to a different generation and they had little experience with the new technology related to the four-stroke engine. Also, I think, they were themselves were somewhat jaded and demotivated.

As for me, I had no bike problems with Honda. Nor did my opponents give me any real problems on the track. However, I began to feel the need to change things around. Let's just say I too was maybe becoming a little restless, I too needed some movement and change in my life. And, to some degree, this probably also had something to do with the fact that my rapport with Honda was no longer as wonderful as it had been. We began to view certain things differently. Thus, in some ways, it was the right time for me to weigh up other offers. On the other hand, when I looked around I didn't see any competitive bikes. And that's why I didn't want Brivio to harbour any illusions about my joining them. And the same went for Yamaha.

But Brivio had done his homework after our meeting in Ibiza. And so had the Japanese contingent in Iwata. In fact, just before the Italian Grand Prix, at the beginning of June, Masao Furusawa, head of technological development at Yamaha, as well as head of the motor-cycle department, met with Brivio and discussed his plan to bring me on board.

"Some of our top management have reservations about your plan," Furusawa warned him. Apparently, while everyone in Iwata seemed to agree that their MotoGP programme needed a shake-up, not everyone felt I was the right person for it. Even Furusawa didn't seem entirely convinced.

At Mugello the Yamahas were once again disappointing. Their best finish was a lowly eighth. Brivio saw it as an opportunity to press his case with Furusawa, who was back in Iwata.

"The rider is an important component in the renewal process that we are about to undertake," he wrote in an email to Furusawa. "That's why, in my opinion, if we want to win, we have to get Valentino Rossi."

He added that I had indicated that I was willing to meet him in Barcelona, a few days later. This was true, I had no problem talking to Furusawa, as long as he came to see me in Europe. Furusawa accepted the invitation. In fact, he left right away, getting a flight from Tokyo to Barcelona. We met in a hotel near the Montmelo track.

Furusawa simply could not believe that I was really considering leaving Honda. For him such a decision was simply incomprehensible, even illogical. But then again, it made no sense to the majority of Yamaha management, back in Iwata. Of course, I hadn't committed to leaving Honda, much less joining Yamaha, yet the idea stimulated me. And Furusawa was also curious, particularly about why I might consider such a thing.

"What are the reasons why you might be willing to come to Yamaha?" he asked point-blank.

"If I want, I can stay at Honda and, if all goes well, I can win another two world titles," I replied. "But that's something I've already achieved. And that's why, before I finish my career, I'd like to win on another bike."

I was being totally honest. There was no need to add much else. Furusawa and I had studied each other. For the time being, we had found the answers we were looking for. When he left, Furusawa seemed convinced that we were serious and he pledged to go back to Japan determined to bring the rest of the Yamaha management team on board.

The problem with Yamaha's top management was that, because they were so far removed from the MotoGP world, they plainly didn't think there was any chance that I would swap Honda for their team. This was why they had been lukewarm about the idea all along: they didn't think it could be done. And if I'm honest, I have to admit that even back then I was leaning towards staying at Honda. I liked the idea of speaking to Yamaha and exploring my options, but I wasn't going to make any decision at that point. Still, it was wise to take a look at what was out there, because Honda's behaviour towards me started to become a little strange.

Every time Gibo went to meet with the heads of the HRC (Honda Racing Corporation), he always returned with strange news. One, in particular, stood out: "They are offering you a contract similar to that of Ukawa."

I thought this was impossible. I thought I was the lead rider. And yet Gibo was sure and, since I was incredulous, he told me to come along at our next scheduled meeting with HRC, at the Dutch Grand Prix in Assen, at the end of June.

At our meeting HRC was represented not just by Koji Nakajima, HRC director and the man we had been dealing with over the years, but also by *his* boss, Suguru Kanazawa, president of HRC. The pair had clearly flown to Holland thinking the situation was entirely under control. I suppose the team had told them that everything was fine, which is why Kanazawa immediately said he was going to fly back to Japan with a signed contract in his pocket. Everything seemed rather surreal to me during our meetings. The HRC executives' positions on MotoGP were far away from my own stance. And this left me somewhat perplexed. I was left with a sense that exploring other opportunities, taking on new challenges, maybe even trying to win with a different bike was the right thing to do.

The HRC executives were steadfast, not budging an inch. I got the sense that they were not going to compromise, they certainly weren't going to meet me halfway. Maybe the time had really come to go elsewhere. That's why, a few days later, Gibo and I decided to take a serious look at next season and that meant having serious talks with other teams, not just Yamaha. Gibo was eager to get back in touch with Yamaha.

"Look, you've shown with Honda that you are so superior to everyone else that you'll beat them, even on another bike," he said.

I was far from convinced. Maybe I was influenced by all the talk in the press, which maintained that winning on any bike other than Honda was virtually impossible . . . for anyone. But Gibo had no such doubts.

"Look, on the Honda if you tried your hardest you would win with a huge margin, far greater than now," he said. "So it stands to reason that, on the Yamaha, if you try even a little bit harder, you might lose some of your advantage, but you'll still have an excellent chance of winning."

Most of my entourage shared his view. I remember one night, after the race in Barcelona, Flavio Fratesi (my "partner in crime" in many of my practical jokes as well as the driving force of the fan club, along with Rino Salucci, Uccio's dad) told me: "I saw it very clearly in that race, I was sure. You have such great potential that you can win on another bike! Even on a Yamaha!"

Indeed, the Catalan Grand Prix of 2003 was an exciting race. I was behind Capirossi, and I made a mistake, ended up off the track and as a result fell behind into a lowly position. When I came back on, I just started cruising, churning laps with leads of up to one second a lap over the rest of the field. I cruised past a number of riders in the space of a few laps. I finished behind Capirossi, but by that point I had narrowed the gap tremendously.

The funny thing was that when Flavio said I could win "even on a Yamaha", he had no idea that, in fact, we had begun speaking to none other than Yamaha. Still, it was comforting that he had unknowingly come to the same conclusion that I and especially Gibo had already reached: winning with Yamaha was a possibility.

Still, I let time pass, treating it all as idle springtime chatter. But then Lin Jarvis and Brivio asked to see me again. They needed to know that I was seriously considering their offer. And I did, in fact, owe them another meeting. The problem was that, around that time, I was simply never around. I was very busy, outside of race days I'd fly from London to Ibiza to goodness-knows-where. I just had a lot of things going on and, strangely enough, the best way to find me was to look me up on race weekends. And so that's what they did.

Of course, meeting in the paddock was, on the surface, not the most logical thing to do. There were risks, for all of us, and they were substantial. If someone figured out what we were talking about, all hell would have broken loose. And yet, precisely because it was such an open and risky setting, I think nobody would have imagined that we would be talking about such serious issues. Thus began our season of not-so-covert "secret" meetings, with the most significant being our talks in Donington and Brno.

It was at Donington in July that Honda started putting pressure on us. They had no hesitation about making their goals clear to us: they wanted to close the deal or, at the very least, obtain some kind of clarification on how to proceed. The truth was that Kanazawa was most definitely displeased that he had had to fly back to Tokyo from Barcelona without a signed contract in his pocket, as Nakajima clearly explained to us.

"You need to tell us what you want to do and you need to tell us by Sunday," Nakajima said. "Otherwise, come the very next race, you may not be working on the development of your bike."

As you can see he was blunt and direct. I did not expect such hard-ball pressure. After all, it was the time of year when riders look around and often change teams. It's normal for both teams and riders to re-evaluate things, maybe casting their net wide and talking to each other. As a result, I found his attitude rather oppressive. True, I was exploring new horizons, I had other things on my mind, new challenges, different projects. And it's true that I was listening to offers coming from elsewhere. But it's equally true that I had not made my mind up to leave Honda. I was a Honda rider and, as far as I was concerned, no decision had been made to change that.

In those moments, faced with having to make a concrete decision, I began to feel a strange sensation. Whenever my thoughts turned to renewing the contract with Honda, I was filled with unhappiness. It was a sensation I couldn't shake off and which I carried with me for a long time. And it only made me think even more.

That very same weekend something else had happened, something very important and very secret. I had gotten on the M1. Of course, it was a covert operation, in the middle of the night, in the Yamaha pits. As it turned out, I did exactly what I had done four years earlier, when Honda sneaked me into the HRC pit at Philip Island. It was also late at night. I had still been with Aprilia down in 250cc and I remember the sensation of climbing on to the NSR 500. Now I had a sense of déjà vu.

This time it happened in England, at Donington. We met up around the same time, midnight. I was wearing a hooded sweatshirt that concealed my face entirely as I slipped quietly and discreetly into the Yamaha pits, the door closing immediately behind me.

I pulled back the hood and my gaze met that of Ichiro Yoda, the M1's chief designer. I could tell he was tired and out of sorts: his eyes were red and, for him, it was late, very late. He had me climb on to Checa's M1 . . . one of the official race M1s.

My first impression was not good. I could tell immediately that the M1 2003 was far behind, at least compared to Honda. There was no comparison with my RC211V. The M1 was really quite an ugly, weak contraption . . . It was a very complicated bike, you could tell that too many people had been involved with it and, as they say, too many cooks spoil the broth. I noticed it wasn't put together with any kind of logic, too many wires that went all over the place, a lot of elements that seemed positioned incorrectly. The riding position seemed all wrong, as did the handlebars and the gas tank. I did not need to switch it on to realise that it was far less rational than the Honda. Because the Honda, like Mary Poppins, is practically perfect in every way. It looks and feels like a street bike, not a racing bike. Nothing is out of place. It's tidy, disciplined. It reflects the personality of its designers at Honda.

Still, the M1 did have a few elements that I found interesting and that I even actually liked. The problem was that they were lost in the jumbled mess that was the 2003 M1. At one point, I looked at the dashboard and noticed that Yamaha were already using a digital display. Honda, on the other hand, had a small, analogue dash which was very traditional. Yamaha's was not just electronic, but huge and full of information and data.

Yoda noticed that I was captivated by the dashboard. He came close to me and switched it on, showing me the various functions. To be fair, it had many things that the Honda RCV simply did not have.

"Very nice!" I said.

"We made it nice and big so that, if there's time during a race, you can sit back and watch a DVD on it," Yoda deadpanned, keeping a very straight face.

There was silence. Gibo, Uccio and I looked at each other for an instant or two, before bursting out laughing. And Yoda joined in heartily. I loved it. That episode showed me that Yamaha's engineers, indeed, the whole team at Yamaha, have a certain spirit, a certain joie de vivre. They'll laugh, they'll joke, they have a certain cheek about them. Such an attitude would have been unthinkable at Honda, where everyone is deadly serious and disciplined, constantly preoccupied with reaffirming the superiority of the Honda Empire.

That first encounter with the M1 and the shared joke that followed was prelude to what our team would become, a devoted and hard-working crew, but also working in an environment which was serene, relaxed and fun. I am not going to go so far as to say that it was then and there that the notion of joining Yamaha became real in my head. What I can say is that they made an excellent impression.

Having said that, even at the time, Yamaha's upper management approached our talks as if they had the handbrake on. They thought I was just trying to make Honda jealous, perhaps as a way of getting a better deal for myself. They didn't really believe I was serious about them, not at that point. Still, it was the beginning of July, and I was open to all options. In fact, there was now a new player on the scene – Ducati – and, all of a sudden, it was a three-way dance.

I was the one who had thought of sounding out Ducati. When things began to deteriorate with Honda, I figured it might be worth seeing what they could offer. Although I was already talking to Yamaha, hearing out Ducati as well wouldn't hurt. Especially since, at first, I loved the idea of racing with Ducati. Two of their chief mechanics, both of whom have Superbike backgrounds, Massimo Bracconi and Bruno Leoni, are friends of mine and we often joked around.

"Come on, join us, become one of us!" they would say.

It was all light-hearted of course, but we were sending each other clear signals. In a way, it was a kind of flirting and it wasn't too long before word got to the top of Ducati and their lead sponsor who, naturally, was delighted at the possibility of having me on board.

So one July evening Gibo and I took the motorway towards Bologna, to Borgo Panigale, the neighbourhood that is home to Ducati and their racing department. It was a very hot day and there were hardly any people around. We found Livio Suppo, the team director at the time, and Claudio Domenicali, the chief executive. Naturally, they had been waiting for us.

I was quite taken by the factory. Walking around, you could almost breathe in the history and tradition. The walls themselves are ancient, nothing looks new. Well, nothing except for what's inside, which is all about the future: technology, ideas, passion, you could feel the creativity surging through the place.

It was very late and, as I said, most people had gone home. We chatted for a while, mostly about racing and the possibility of having me come on board. They let me visit the factory, although I don't think I saw anything more than what a visitor might get to see on an official tour. After all, I was still a Honda man, which meant I was the competition.

I suppose it made sense from their perspective. They had only just entered MotoGP, they had lots of plans and they were developing an outstanding bike, the Desmosedici. Capirossi had just triumphed on it in Barcelona and he was never far off the podium. There is little question that, at the time, Ducati were streets ahead of Yamaha.

I was proud of them, not least because they're an Italian team and I was glad to be talking to them. It was just a meeting to get to know one another; nothing was going to be finalised then and there. Unlike my meetings with Honda and Yamaha, which were long and intense, this was far more straightforward. We compared plans and outlooks: the technical side of the bike and racing, the relations with sponsors, promotional duties. The more we talked, the more I began to feel that, while we were both up for a challenge, my outlook was somewhat different from theirs.

We both shared a passion for the sport, of course, and we both had the same will to win, but there were several issues where we were far apart. And that was what made me think that pursuing Ducati was not a good idea. Maybe it's a question of philosophy; whatever, I understood that their vision was different from mine, at least from what it was at the time. After all, it was 2003 and everything came easy on my Honda. We had a powerful company behind us, a winning tradition, maybe a bit of swagger as well. Honda had no trouble proving time and again that its technology was better than everyone else's. And that was the real reason Honda was involved in racing in the first place. They never made a secret of it. They raced to show their bike and their company was better. I felt somewhat trapped by this attitude, by this way of thinking and acting. As I say, I wanted to show that ultimately man was more important than machine, that the rider was crucial in developing the bike. That was my whole guiding principle.

And perhaps that's why relations with the Honda executives had become somewhat tense. The Japanese executives at Honda had a different way of viewing things which was out of line with what I wanted and, in particular, this new obsession I had: proving that the rider is more important than the bike.

You can call it ego if you like. And what became obvious to me at a certain point was that my ego was beginning to clash with the ego of the Honda executives.

Going back to Ducati, I saw a little too much of that Honda attitude in their plans. They were fighting to establish their bike and their technology and that was the absolute priority. Ducati are born fighters and I love that aggression they carry with them, the way they were unafraid to take on the big Japanese teams. The flipside of this ambition, however, is that it made them behave a certain way, a way which, as I said, was a little too similar to Honda. In other words, they were a team whose main goal was strengthening their own brand.

There's nothing wrong with that of course, though it did scare me. After all, this was the reason why Honda and I were growing apart.

I was on a mission. I wanted to wipe out all doubts about my own ability and, to do this, I needed a new challenge. I needed to test my beliefs, my way of doing things, my way of thinking about racing, bikes, even teams. Ducati and I had ambitions which overlapped, but we disagreed on the role a rider should have in developing the bike. For me, it's all about the rider, he has to guide the team, after all, he's the one who has to take the bike to victory. And therefore, the bike should be made to measure based on his needs and his characteristics.

To Ducati, however, the rider is not nearly as important in the development process. They are a company that believes strongly in technology. They are guided in many ways by data and information collected by computer. Their philosophy and methodology is very similar to that of a Formula One team. I can appreciate this from a technological aspect, of course, but it also set off alarm bells in my head. I feared the same type of oppression I was experiencing at Honda, a team that often thinks the same way. To Honda, you need someone to ride the bike, but it doesn't really matter who it is. After all, it was all about the bike. The bike won or lost, not the rider.

That night, in Bologna, at Ducati's headquarters, we all knew it was not going to be a decisive meeting, that it was just a preliminary talk. So neither side asked for specific commitments or promises. As the weeks went by, as I tried to make sense of all that I was feeling, I began to realise that Ducati was an entirely different proposition from Yamaha.

"This is not the challenge I'm looking for," I told myself at one point.

I felt that Ducati were not going to be willing to follow me and listen to me the way Yamaha were going to. I convinced myself that

Ducati's racing department would have tried to push their own ideas and solutions. I can understand this, from their point of view, but I also understood that I would not be able to build the kind of team and relationship I could hope for with Yamaha.

I'll give you an example. Months later, I was in the pits at the 2004 South African Grand Prix, watching Capirossi ride on the TV monitor. It looked to me as if he was trying to tame a wild horse, the bike was all over the place. And this was the famed Desmosedici. Jeremy Burgess came up to me, looked at the monitor and said: "And to think that, according to their computers, the Desmosedici is in great shape!"

He wasn't being mean. Maybe there was a bit of Anglo-Saxon humour in his words, but he wasn't trying to put down Ducati. But to me his comment underscored the fact that he understood what I wanted to do and shared my views on racing. I needed a team that would put the rider first, that would trust human experience and sensitivity as much as (or more than) computer readouts. A team that would be serene and relaxed. A team that would let me and my chief engineer Jeremy develop the bike.

It was not going to be easy, at this level, to find a team that would hand over so much responsibility to a rider and an engineer. Ducati, for one, had given me the distinct impression that they were going to be unwilling or unable to do this. And that's why I came to realise that Yamaha would come closest to meeting my own wishes.

And to be fair, there was a reason for this. At the time, Yamaha were in great difficulty, much more so than Ducati. They needed a shake-up, needed to try something different, just like me. And so it was obvious to me that Yamaha could give me what I most wanted: a lead role in developing the bike.

That's what it was all about. I wanted freedom. Ducati, in that sense, were like Honda – they were loath to grant me that freedom.

Yamaha, on the other hand, seemed more open. I had to weigh this versus the fact that, objectively, Ducati had a far better bike.

"If I'm going to leave Honda, I need to do it for a real challenge, an incredible, apparently impossible challenge," I thought to myself. "Otherwise, there's no point, I might as well stay."

And Yamaha were the biggest challenge.

I wanted to change their whole mentality, revolutionise their racing department. I wanted to improve a bike that, in technical terms, had been left far behind. I wanted to take a group of engineers, designers and developers who had experienced lots of disappointment and who nobody believed could ever succeed, and lead them to victory.

At the time, Ducati looked to be the surprise package of MotoGP and, to be fair, they had made quite an impression since bursting onto the scene in such an exciting and aggressive way. Yamaha on the other hand were down and out. They needed me more than Ducati did.

And so, towards the end of July I began to make my choice.

I was also attracted by Yamaha's recent history and by the legendary riders of the past such as Kenny Roberts, Snr, Wayne Rainey, Giacomo Agostini and Eddie Lawson. All of them had won on Yamaha. It was a good company yet they had not had that many world champions of late and so the challenge for me was to awaken this sleeping giant . . .

It was time for the racing department to catch up. After all, Yamaha did not just have a glorious past, they were also presently doing well in other departments, such as off-road and roadbikes. But in MotoGP they were a disaster. When I'd meet with Yamaha executives, I could tell they wanted me to understand the Yamaha spirit. At each meeting they would tell Gibo and me that a massive wide-ranging restructuring process had begun in Japan and that, by the start of 2004, everything would be different.

Their projects sounded interesting, but, to tell the truth, the situation seemed far from encouraging. The Yamaha bikes got murdered in every race, finishing miles behind everyone else. On average, they were twenty seconds behind in each Grand Prix. Sure, I was stimulated by all their talk, but I was hesitant when I actually sat down and analysed the facts. I need to do some thinking, which is why, at the end of July, when we got a week off, I "escaped" to Ibiza, far away from motorbikes and racing. I was under a lot of pressure, I sought refuge on the island to find a bit of relaxation, to find the time and environment where I could think peacefully. I was there with my friends and we were enjoying the summer: the sun, the sea, the sand. And it was there that I was able to take my decision: a choice that, at the time, seemed simply insane, but also enormously stimulating.

"I'm going to Yamaha, let's just see what happens!" I thought.

It was the summer of 2003. I was in Ibiza and I decided to cut my ties with Honda and move to Yamaha.

Strange coincidence, isn't it? Ibiza was the very same place where Brivio had first spoken to us about moving to Yamaha and I listened to his pitch politely, but with little conviction. And yet, five months later, I was ready to take up his challenge. After flirting with interest with Ducati and weighing up Honda once again, I was back on the road to Yamaha.

"I want a difficult challenge, a crazy challenge. The craziest and most difficult challenge I can possibly find. And that means YAMAHA!" I told myself.

And yet, I kept it relatively quiet. It was neither the time nor the place to make announcements. But I know myself well and I trust my instincts and the feeling that the future belonged to Yamaha was something that I could feel inside, welling up, stronger every day. Even if it was a crazy, crazy move. After the break, the MotoGP season continued and I was as determined as ever. I was also beginning to feel the stress. Not for the title itself. I was far ahead, my Honda was perfect, there was nobody who was going to stand in my way. No, that wasn't the problem. I had no fears about the present. The issue was the future. What would happen to me next year?

The next race was in the Czech Republic, in Brno. All the companies I had been dealing with – Honda, Ducati, Yamaha – they were all waiting for my answer. In particular, Yamaha were the most apprehensive, since they had had the most contact with me in the preceding weeks.

In Brno, Gibo and I arranged another meeting with Brivio. A secret meeting, obviously. This time, however, we had to be very careful. We had to find the right location, it had to be discreet and secure. We thought of the Mobile Clinic, which is located at the far end of the paddock, as far away from the pits as possible, towards the last turn.

The Mobile Clinic is where the riders go when they need help or medical attention. To us, it's our refuge, far away from our team, the press, the fans. I was pretty sure the doctors, in particular my friend Doctor Costa, would let us use the Mobile Clinic, if we only asked them politely. The problem was that, by the time we decided to arrange our meeting, it was very late and nobody was left in the paddock, especially not the doctors of the Mobile Clinic. And so we decided to engage in a little bit of B & E, Breaking and Entering . . . well, not really. I decided we would sneak our way into the hospitality area, not the clinic proper.

We arrived on our scooters. It was me, Gibo, Uccio and Nello, a close friend and member of my "Tribe". The gate was open. The tent was closed, but the big zippers were not locked in any way. So we unzipped them and slipped in. Just as we were doing this, the Yamaha guys, Jarvis and Brivio, arrived. They too emerged from the darkness on their scooters. They had cut through the woods. Just like us.

We looked like lovers on a midnight rendezvous.

"Who's this?" Jarvis immediately asked, pointing to Nello.

"He's a friend," I said. "Don't worry about him, he'll keep his mouth shut."

In fact, Nello came in handy. We told him to stay outside, as a lookout of sorts. His job was to warn us if anyone approached. To be fair, Nello, who is near-sighted, is not the ideal lookout, but we had little choice and had to make do. As always, Nello approached the task with diligence and dedication, hiding outside.

Inside, I wasted no time telling Brivio and Jarvis of my decision.

"I'm coming on board!" I said.

They just looked at each other, incredulous.

"Yes! I said I'm coming on board!" I repeated.

"Wait, are you telling us that next season you'll race for Yamaha?" Brivio said. The words came out slowly, deliberately, as if he wanted to make sure there were no misunderstandings.

"YES!" I said. Again.

"So what you're saying is, you want to race for Yamaha in 2004?" Brivio asked again, in the same slow disbelieving tone.

"Why else would I be here?" I said. I was beginning to enjoy the situation.

For a minute we were all silent. It was just a few seconds, but it felt like minutes. Everyone was lost in their own thoughts, reflecting on the importance of what had just been said. The silence was broken by Nello's high-pitched shout. Yes. Nello. The lookout.

"A scooter's coming!" he said. He had seen headlights approaching, gotten scared and sounded the alarm.

"Away! Away! Quick, let's hide!" we said, all at once. We all panicked, rushing around to look for a suitable hiding place. We couldn't run back outside, we would have looked like thieves, fleeing the scene of the crime. The only thing we could think of was hiding under a table. It was the table where the guys from Mobile Clinic kept the coffee, biscuits, sugar, stuff like that. We crawled under there, all of us. It was surreal, incredible. I don't know about the others, but I was loving it. The fun far outweighed the risk of getting caught.

Meanwhile, Nello had run off, a victim of his own panic.

We sat for a while and then I piped up.

"Excuse me, guys, but if someone comes in here and sees all of us hiding under this table, what the fuck are we going to tell him?"

Gibo and Uccio thought it was a legitimate question. Hiding under the table might have seemed like a good idea at the time, but, frankly we looked ridiculous: five grown men crammed under a tiny table.

So the three of us got up and planted ourselves in front of the table. We pretended to make small talk, while nibbling some of the biscuits. Jarvis and Brivio, however, remained safely squirrelled away under the table.

Just then, the nightwatchman, whose headlights had startled Nello, sounding the alarm, came in.

"Everything OK?" he asked, the slightest hint of suspicion in his voice.

"Sure, why, yes, everything's all right!" we reassured him.

He looked us up and down and then his gaze moved around the room.

"Well, goodnight then!" he said.

"Goodnight to you!" we all shouted back.

As soon as he was gone, the heads of Brivio and Jarvis popped up from behind the table. We looked at each other, knowing we had cut it close, very close.

We started to talk business. The fear was gone. But I really didn't have too much else to say. I had said my piece. And yet they still looked at me, full of incredulity. I don't think they were prepared for the possibility that I might say yes to them. And so, to prove I was serious, I decided to take matters into my own hands. Literally. I reached out and grabbed Brivio's hand, shaking it vigorously. Our handshake sealed the deal in my mind.

I didn't sign a contract, there was no need. My decision had been made. Immediately after that, we said goodnight and each of us went back the way we came. We slipped off into the night, into the silence of the paddock.

Oh, and, in case you're wondering, the guys from the Mobile Clinic never found out what happened . . . until now, that is.

My relief at having made my decision did not last too long. By the beginning of September, pressure started to mount again. Honda was demanding that I renew my contract. I had a verbal deal with Yamaha, but we still had to talk about all the details, the practical stuff, how I was going to assemble my new team. Because I strongly wanted Jeremy and the rest of the crew to join me at Yamaha.

The difficult bit was keeping everything under wraps. I didn't want anything to leak out and cause a storm of controversy. I felt like I needed to explain my decision to Ducati and I needed the time to do it. I also did not want to sour relations with Honda just as we were about to become world champions again. Why ruin the party?

As I think back to those moments, I have to smile. I smile because I now realise that I was exaggerating, I was too worried about things. But they were heady days. I know how important discretion is when you're involved in such important and delicate negotiations. Keeping quiet is part of the game. Looking back now, I'm sure that Honda would not have done much even if they had discovered my plans.

That's because the Honda ethos is to be tough, but honourable. In this regard, Honda is very serious. Even when they knew I was going to leave, they never messed with my bike. I always had the perfect bike and everything I needed, right down to the last lap of the last Grand Prix. To them, the fact that I was leaving did not mean they should treat me any differently.

Still, at the time, the tension was so high that I couldn't really be rational about things. There were too many unknowns, too much pressure. And I still had not signed anything, so, in theory, anything could yet happen.

In the middle of September I arrived in Rio de Janeiro and, straight away, Nakajima began putting pressure on me. From his perspective, it was the right thing to do. I was able to buy time, but I soon realised that the moment had come to speak to Jeremy and to my crew. And I chose to do it right then and there, in Rio. So I called them all together in a room. As soon as the thought of leaving Honda had begun to cross my mind, I realised how important it would be to take Jeremy with me.

"It's a huge step, but if I can take Jeremy along, everything changes," I thought to myself.

To be honest, I never considered the possibility that Jeremy might turn me down. Also because, when the first rumours of my departure started surfacing, he had always indicated that, if I left, he would leave as well.

"If you go, let me know, because I'm going with you," he'd say. "I don't care if they don't have a job for me, I'll do anything. I'll even clean the fairings."

I think that, like most other people, Jeremy never really believed that I could leave Honda. Still, he was very careful, monitoring the papers and rumour mill around the paddock. In fact, the more weeks passed, the more he joked about it. He was discreet about it and, usually, very funny. I remember, around the time when there were rumours that I was meeting with Ducati (which was true), he came up to me and said: "Remember that I love Italy, Italian women and tortellini!" Tortellini, of course, are the local speciality in Bologna.

I found comfort in his jokes because I saw them as confirmation that Jeremy was with me.

"I want to talk to you, but I want to do it in front of the whole team," I said. "Can we get everyone together?"

It was Friday afternoon, in the paddock in Rio. I wanted all the mechanics to be there because Jeremy had always told me that our team worked because we were a united crew, because there were people who had been working side by side for years and who fully understood each other. I knew he was right and that's why I wanted to see everyone together.

We met on the first floor of the long building that divides the two paddock areas at the Jacarepagua track in Rio. On one side, you've got the pit area of the bigger teams. On the other sit those of the private teams, the 125cc and the 250cc teams. In the middle lie the offices. To get there, you go up these steep metal staircases that take you to a wide balcony. The balcony is lined with the racing suits of the riders, which are left out to dry in the sun. The offices are small, but comfortable. When I walked in, they were all there, Jeremy and the boys. All of them.

I tried to read their expressions. I could tell they were wondering what it was I had to tell them. Everyone was curious and silent. So I just blurted it out.

"I'm evaluating the possibility of leaving," I said. "I would like to go to Yamaha and, for me, it would be important to have you all come with me."

The room was plunged into silence.

"It's not a joke, I think I really am leaving," I said, turning to Jeremy. I could see the shock and incredulity in everyone's face. It was the reaction typical of those who say, "We'll follow you always and everywhere," but, in reality, don't expect you to ever leave.

Jeremy had been through this once before, with Mick Doohan. On more than one occasion, Mick had the chance to move to Yamaha or to stay at Honda. In the end, he always decided to stay. In my opinion, Doohan could have won with a different bike, it's just that he never wanted to try. Jeremy thought it would be the same with me. He was sure that, in the end, I too would remain at Honda. There was no need for him to say anything, I could see it in his face. He did not say a word, but his expression said plenty.

"I'm sorry, I don't mean to put any of you under pressure, but I need an answer before the next race," I told everyone.

That did not leave them much time, ten days or so. Then again, I did not have much time myself.

Meanwhile, Gibo had begun talking to Yamaha, explaining that I needed Jeremy and the crew with me. This move was far more difficult than it first appeared. Not just because Jeremy seemed reluctant, but also because at Yamaha they wanted to keep most of the existing crew. After all, they were the ones who were most familiar with the M1.

I also knew time was running out. Honda wanted an answer from me. So did Ducati. That's why I myself needed an answer from Jeremy and the crew. And I needed it quickly.

By the time we returned to Japan to race at Motegi, the tension was obvious. For the whole summer, Gibo and I had regularly held meetings with the higher echelons at HRC. They were constantly changing and amending the contract on the table and we were never really on the same page on the things that really mattered. Yet as soon as I arrived in Japan, I was given an ultimatum.

"This is the final version of the contract," Nakajima told me as soon as I arrived at Motegi, the Thursday before the race. "If you don't sign it by Sunday morning, to us it will mean that you do not want to ride for Honda next season."

I understood that, one way or another, it was time to resolve the issue.

"Thank you," I said. "I'll read it in my room."

I went off to find Jeremy. It was time for some answers.

I had noticed that, from the moment I arrived at the track, none of the boys really felt like talking about this subject. As for Jeremy, I felt like he was trying to avoid me. So I waited another day. And he still tried to avoid the issue. I had no choice. Saturday afternoon I went right up to him and asked him point-blank.

"Well?" I asked.

Jeremy knew what I was talking about. There was no need to explain myself.

"I'm sorry, we're all sorry," he said. "But we've decided not to come with you."

It was a terrible blow. A huge disappointment. And I felt really bad. It seemed incredible to me that my team would not follow me. And I was especially disappointed by Jeremy.

For him, I had gone way out on a limb with Yamaha. In fact, their initial refusal to hire Jeremy and the crew had made me very angry and I fought for his case. At Yamaha, they had been sceptical when we told them just how important my team was to me. And, at one point, I was fighting on two fronts. I had to convince Yamaha to take them on board, rather than saddling me with their old team, and I had to convince Jeremy and the others to follow me to Yamaha.

Instead, at Motegi, Jeremy led me to understand what his plan really was: he and the crew wanted me to change my mind. That way they would have avoided having to choose. The easiest thing for them was for me to remain at Honda.

"Where do you think you're going?" Jeremy pleaded. "Honda has more experience, particularly when it comes to engines. Yamaha will never catch up, they simply don't have all the means and the engineers that Honda has."

I started to see things more clearly. Jeremy and the crew were faced with a dilemma. They did not have the courage to go, but then, neither did they want to stay at Honda without me. I knew, in fact, that the Honda management team had told Jeremy that, if I left, they wanted him to work with Nicky Hayden, my teammate that season, who was making his debut after winning the Superbike AMA in the United States. The idea was to pair up a promising young rider like Nicky with a veteran like Jeremy. So, from his perspective, this meant that, whatever happened, Jeremy had excellent prospects at Honda.

This did not make me feel any better. In fact, hearing Jeremy, who, in technical terms was my guide, say all those things about Yamaha made me sick to my stomach. I left Jeremy and started thinking about returning to the hotel. The Honda contract was still sitting there, unsigned.

I grabbed the scooter and quickly left the track, climbing up the hill to the team hotel. Inside the "Twin Ring" of Motegi you only get around on foot or on the scooter. Each team provides a scooter to each rider. And, at the hotel, they are all parked outside. The Motegi track hotel is high up on a hill, totally isolated. It's a faintly disturbing place that reminds me of the Overlook Hotel in Stanley Kubrick's classic film *The Shining*. In fact, it's nearly identical. Every time I stay there, I think of Jack Nicholson going insane in that hotel. And I can see why. In Motegi, for four days you do the exact same things at the exact same time, all based on fixed and immutable rules. Each morning you leave your room, you see the guys from the paddock, you go to your table. Yes, "your" table, because each table is assigned to you, you have to book it for your entire stay, it's not like a normal restaurant where you can show up and ask for a table. If the Japanese waiters don't see your name on the bookings list, you go hungry, even if the restaurant is totally empty.

So anyway, you go out, you see the same people, you eat at the same table, you eat the same things, you grab your scooter, you follow the same route to the track, you go into the same office, you do your tests and, at the end of the day, you hop on the same scooter, go back to the hotel, go to your room and then go back down for dinner at the exact same table (provided they have your booking, of course!). Motegi means four days just like that.

So that night I felt terrible. Honda had left me just a few more hours to decide and, on top of that, my chief engineer was not coming with me. I was all alone. This time I had to test my own mettle. I felt trapped and I did not know how to get out. The fact that I was racing the very next day and that a world title was at stake seemed very far removed. I decided to call another meeting with Yamaha and, naturally, it was another top-secret affair. I arranged a room in the hotel and made my way over with Gibo.

This time it really was a tense, high-stakes summit. As if to show how serious they were, they brought along the deputy head of sport at Yamaha, a man called Kitagawa. I immediately told them about my meeting with Jeremy and explained that neither he nor the crew would be joining us. Then I asked Furusawa for more technical assurances: I wanted him to clear up some questions I had about their project and whether or not they would be able to deliver as promised. After all, Jeremy's words had left me shaken: Yamaha did have a long way to go. Could they really bridge the gap between them and Honda?

Furusawa asked me to have faith in his programme. He had big plans for Yamaha, he said. They were beautiful words, but, ultimately, they were just that: words. I listened to him, I looked at his face to try and figure out what we was really thinking and, in the meantime, I kept my thoughts to myself.

All of a sudden, in the middle of our discussion, Kitagawa fell asleep.

Just like that. HE SIMPLY FELL ASLEEP.

"What the hell?" I thought to myself. "We're talking about the future, very important things, both for me and for them and this guy just falls asleep?"

I could see him on the bed, fast asleep, and I began to panic. We were deciding my future, Furusawa was trying to convince me to accept their offer, everything was tense and decisive, it was make-or-break time and this man was FAST ASLEEP! Only later did I find out that many Japanese simply do not stay up late. They go to bed very early because, in turn, they get up very early in the morning. And, to be fair, it was very late. But I did not know this at the time. And seeing this guy sleeping while my future was being decided made me uneasy and even a bit nauseous. Still, I didn't say anything. I had far more important things on my mind.

When I returned to my room, I had trouble falling asleep. That night, the eve of the race on Sunday, I stared out my hotel-room window, high up on the hill. And slowly I came to the decision that I'd be joining Yamaha even if Jeremy wasn't coming with me.

"The story ends here!" I thought to myself. "This is where we draw the line. I'm dropping everything and going to Yamaha. Even if Jeremy doesn't come with me. I'll just have to make do without him. I'll figure something out." I had finally made my decision. This time for real. There was no turning back.

In August, Brivio and I had shaken hands. Still, before me nobody had ever decided to leave the most important and successful team in the world in its moment of greatest technological splendour to move to a team in the absolute doldrums, living through its worst ever period. So, even though I had made my decision, I continued to agonise over it. And that night I hardly slept.

By dawn, I had slept a couple hours at best. And yet, I was ready. For the first time in my career, the race itself was not the most important item on the agenda on a race day. I was about to leave the room when the phone rang. It was Carlo Fiorani, he asked me if everything was OK.

"Just remember to drop in on the big bosses, just to assure them that everything is OK with your contract," he said.

"Sure, I'll remember to do that," I replied, reassuring him.

I jumped on the scooter and from the hotel made my way to the paddock in a few minutes. Fiorani was waiting for me. The Honda executives were also waiting, along with their lawyers. Everything was ready. But then they realised I hadn't signed. And I wasn't going to sign. And their expressions darkened. Their disappointment was obvious.

The amazing thing about it was that, despite the fact that it was such a significant and important moment, we exchanged only very few words. There was no real meeting. They looked down at the blank contract and understood straight away. I remained silent and so did they. There was no discussion, no request for an explanation, no attempt to reopen talks. They understood there was nothing to add.

Besides, there was no time for that. I had a world title to win. And the warm-up sessions were about to begin. So we said our farewells and I went to the team office to change. A few minutes later Fiorani came up to me, visibly shaken.

"Look, they don't get it!" he said. "They don't understand what you're trying to do . . . they don't understand that this is just a negotiating tactic . . . they're not like that, you have to make it clear to them!"

I looked him in the eye.

"I think that, in fact, they understand perfectly well," I said. "They understand me more than you do. They understand that I want to make a change, I want to try something new, experience a new challenge."

He didn't react. So I put on my suit and my boots, grabbed my helmet and slipped on my gloves. And off I went to the warm-up session. I ran a decent race and finished second, with a few regrets, because had I been more relaxed, I probably would have won. Still, I knew that seven days later, in Malaysia, I could win the title. And, at that point, all the pressure would be gone.

After the race was finished, I still felt like I had some unfinished business for the day. I need to clear things up with Jeremy. I found him and took him to one side.

"I'm going to Yamaha," I said. "I'm going on my own if I have to. And I'm very sorry for you."

I think my words left no room for interpretation. Maybe I was a little harsh, but I couldn't find any other words. So I put in all the emotions I was feeling inside: a cocktail of disappointment, hurt and anger. Because the whole affair had change our relationship as well: there was embarrassment, we had trouble speaking freely and openly. Jeremy must have felt miffed, because he had tried to convince me to stay but had failed. In addition, he felt disappointed because he realised that I had found the courage to leave Honda, something he felt unable to do.

But at least I had planted the seed of doubt in his mind.

From Japan we flew straight to Malaysia. We won both the race and the title in Sepang. It was my third consecutive world title with Honda: one in 500cc, the other two in MotoGP. And it was the fifth world championship of my career.

After the race Jeremy took me aside and, with his usual calm, said to me: "I'd like to speak to Yamaha."

"Great!" I said, smiling and with an enormous sense of relief washing over me. "I'll arrange a meeting for you."

Immediately after the race Jeremy and the boys went to Australia to enjoy a few days off before the next race at Philip Island. Still, when I heard Jeremy's words, I knew that something in him had changed. He had clearly spent those few days between the races in Japan and Malaysia in deep reflection. He had gone back on his decision: he had decided to follow me.

I was not flying to Sydney until the following day, in the afternoon. That's because I was going to sign the pre-contract with Yamaha. True, they had trusted me that night in Brno in the Mobile Clinic, when we shook on it and I told them I'd be joining them. But this time they needed to be sure. I can understand that. Because if I, at some point, had decided to behave dishonestly or even if I had just had a change of heart, maybe an anxiety attack or goodness knows what else, they would have faced serious problems. When I make up my mind about something, it's unusual for me to go back on it, but they could not have known that, they did not know me that well. So, from their perspective, I can't fault their attitude.

We had our own fears, although they were very different. We were a little worried that if we had signed the contact, someone – either through incompetence or malice – might have leaked the news. Because it's one thing to know that there are negotiations going on, quite another to confirm that there is a signed contract. We did not know the Yamaha organisation that well. We were rightly concerned that there might be a leak to the press.

That's why I had always said: "I'm not signing anything until I win the title."

And since on Sunday afternoon in Sepang I had become world champion, Yamaha asked me to put pen to paper. Besides, by this point, Honda knew for sure that I was not going to re-sign with them. And, equally, we had informed Ducati that I would not be taking up their offer. Thus, we were ready to formalise everything with Yamaha. You may be thinking that, given the stakes and the situation, such an important contract would be signed in the Presidential Suite of a five-star hotel, in front of a team of lawyers and notaries, perhaps with a golden, diamond-encrusted pen. You may expect me to show up with an elegant leather briefcase, decked out in a Savile Row suit, looking all serious and professional.

Well, you might as well forget all that.

You see, on Sunday night we went out to celebrate with the boys from the Honda team, in a bar high up on a skyscraper in Kuala Lumpur. As we were returning to the hotel, we ran into Angel Nieto who started regaling us with stories of his triumphs, his adventures, his legendary duels with his rivals. We were having so much fun that, before we knew it, it was five o'clock in the morning. Which meant that we all overslept the next morning. It was one of those days. I knew I should be getting up, but I just couldn't do it. I tried, I really did, but then I'd fall asleep again, unable to move, only to wake up a few minutes later, when the whole thing would repeat itself.

Naturally, I was late, very late for my meeting with the Yamaha executives. They were waiting for me in a hotel room, and the more time passed, the more worried they became. They knew I had to catch the flight to Sydney and as the minutes ticked by, they started to think that maybe, just maybe, I wouldn't show. That I would stand them up. I appeared suddenly, all out of breath and dishevelled. I had my rucksack on and I was dragging my luggage behind me.

"Here I am!" I shouted, bursting into the room and tossing my bags to one side. "I only have fifteen minutes to spare, so let's make this quick, shall we? I have a flight to catch!"

They looked at me with disbelief. I was just trying to lighten the mood, to break the tension. And it worked. After all, when you know you're wrong, dead wrong, you might as well go on the offensive straight away, before they have a go at you.

"Come on, we're late, we'll miss the flight, let's see this contract . . . Great, looks great to me! Fine!" I said, barely skimming it. "Let's get this thing signed."

Thus, I showed up to sign one of the most important contracts of my life in exactly the same way I do most things: at the last minute. For, you see, I am always, absolutely and constantly, late. It's one of my greatest flaws. I can only concentrate and be at my best if time is tight, if everything is on the edge and we all have to rush. If there's time, if we can do things calmly and quietly, I just can't perform.

Before I left, I announced to the Yamaha executives that Jeremy was still thinking about it, that perhaps he was about to make a U-turn.

"Jeremy wants to meet you," I said. "Please, it's not over yet. Please do everything in your power to make sure he joins us."

We agreed to meet again in Philip Island, a few days later. I grabbed the opportunity to take a day and a half off in Sydney, before heading over to Philip Island, via Melbourne. I had won the title, it was complete, and mentally the big chapter of my life on a Honda bike was over. I just wanted to relax and think calmly about my future.

I arrived in Philip Island on Wednesday afternoon. Jeremy and I were due to meet Yamaha that very evening, so I rushed over to collect him. Alas, as always, I was late. Because 11 p.m. had come and gone and I had not shown up yet, Jeremy had simply assumed he would see me the following day. So he met up with some of his mates. And he hadn't held back when it came to ordering pints of beer.

When I did find Jeremy, well, let's just say he was rather . . . happy (in a tipsy sort of way). I loaded him up into the car and told him that I was taking him to see Furusawa and the rest of the Yamaha executives. That's when he realised this was serious and he did something truly amazing. In the five minutes it took us to arrive at the meeting spot, he totally sobered up. It was incredible. It was as if he was a computer and someone had just rebooted the hard drive. He was his usual charming self and, when he began speaking to Furusawa, won him over very quickly.

I think Jeremy did so well because Furusawa had totally misjudged the type of person he was. I think Furusawa figured that Jeremy would be somewhat stuck up, a little bit arrogant given his incredible career and triumphs (he won nine world titles in ten years at Honda). Furusawa expected Jeremy to talk down to him, to treat him as if he were incompetent. Instead, he quickly understood the kind of man Jeremy Burgess is and he was won over by his personality, intelligence and demeanour.

"I never thought he was so humble, so laid back, so willing to take on a challenge," Furusawa told me after our meeting.

Jeremy was very clear.

"Honda is a good team, but what they do isn't witchcraft," he said. "If you do what Valentino says you'll see that everything will work itself out."

I could see that the assembled Yamaha people, in addition to

Furusawa, Jarvis and Brivio who were also present, were transfixed by Jeremy's calm, knowledgeable ways.

"To avoid misunderstandings, it's best if the engineers speak directly to Valentino, because if I have to translate and get involved something might be missed," he added. "And the engineers need to speak a lot, they need to make their voices heard. They actually build the bike and Valentino drives it, so they need to have good communication. Look, if you do this there won't be any problems."

Accurate, concise and comforting: that was Jeremy. As always.

He signed the contract the following night, Saturday, on the eve of the race. Sunday night we called in all the mechanics, who spoke to Yamaha one by one. Most of them signed the contract a week later, in Valencia. Among those who joined us were Alex Briggs, Bernard Ansieau and Gary Coleman, plus Bren, a mechanic from New Zealand who lived in Australia and had already been working for Yamaha. He knew the bikes well, plus he was a natural in fitting in with the Australians. Matteo Flamigni stayed on as telemetrist, as he already knew the software and electronic systems of the M1 down to the very last detail.

Thus the only ones who were left out were Dickie and Peter. They had to stay with Honda because there simply wasn't room for them at Yamaha. Curious how quickly things had changed. Two weeks before, nobody wanted to follow me to Yamaha and now there were so many people wanting to come on board that there wasn't any space left.

Honda's press conference in Valencia was intense. There was a weird vibe in the air. We had decided to organise a joint conference after the race, but in reality everything was tentative until the last minute. Nakajima wanted to make the announcement right away, to let everybody know that I was leaving. Then, at one point, he changed his mind because it seemed that back in Japan they didn't want it made public even after the last race. As far as we were concerned, we wanted everyone to know the truth.

Saturday afternoon I ran into Gibernau in the paddock.

"I heard that tomorrow HRC are having a press conference," he said.

"That's right, just after the race," I replied.

"You'll say you're staying at Honda, won't you?" he asked.

"No, actually. I'll announce I'm moving to Yamaha," I answered.

I saw a flash in his eyes. First astonishment, then happiness. I could tell he had done some quick thinking and figured that it would only be good for him. He reckoned that I wouldn't do much on a Yamaha. I could read it in his face, just as I later could read it in the faces of so many other people who doubted me and my choice.

The press conference was my farewell from Honda. Afterwards, I went over to hug all those with whom I had gotten along well in my years at the team: Fiorani, Florenzano, Peter, Dickie, Roger. All weekend long, as I wandered around the pits or as I cleared out my personal belongings from the Honda motorhome, I faced moments of sadness. These were strong emotions, because I knew that an important period of my career was coming to an end. I was leaving behind a lot of certainty to take a road that was uncertain and unfamiliar. Exciting, yes. Stimulating, yes. But definitely uncertain.

What I did not notice among the team was any sense of desperation at my departure. The whole Honda team were so sure that in 2004 they were going to beat me that they were not worried at all. They were convinced that they would win the title without me. To them, I was just another rider. A cog in a machine that could be easily replaced. All it meant was that they would give the "official" bike to Barros, Biaggi or Gibernau. They had nothing to worry about.

I was the one who worried. Saturday night I took pictures of myself hugging and embracing the RC211V. I wanted to say goodbye to my bike because I knew that tomorrow we would race our last race together. Leaving the RC211V was what hurt most. In fact, I now believe the reason it took me so long to say yes to Yamaha was because I was so attached to that bike.

As I looked at the RC211V and thought that we would soon be separated, I genuinely feared that it would take very long time before I once again tasted victory. That's why I decided I had to win that last race of the 2003 season. It would be a great way of saying goodbye of course, but also I wanted to stock up on victories, I wanted to have the taste of triumph fresh in mind because who knew when I would ever win again with Yamaha?

As it turned out, I was wrong. I didn't have to wait long at all, just until the first race of the next season. Of course, at the time, I could never have imagined that.

THREE

The year 2003 was a long and taxing experience that led me to leave Honda for Yamaha. But it was also a very intense mental journey for me personally. It was a voyage of self-discovery, a process of exploration and internal reflection. I put myself through heartfelt self-analysis. And it's thanks to this process that I can now freely admit that, had it not been for the exceptional group we put together at Yamaha between the end of 2003 and the beginning of 2004, I might have given up racing before my twenty-fifth birthday.

I'll never forget that incredible six-month period during which I discovered what I was truly looking for: serenity and happiness. I needed a fun group of friends to be with, both in the pits and outside. I needed them so that I could experience to the full life beyond the bike. Besides that, I think I was also searching for something else: motivation. And I think that's a problem for those who, like me, achieved so much so quickly and at such a young age. Yes, because everything happened at breakneck speed with me. I turned twenty-four in February 2003 and already I had to take stock of my life. And I discovered that there were many things I no longer enjoyed, many situations that I could no longer tolerate.

Of course, I knew I was no longer happy at Honda. I had known this for a while. But I had not yet realised, in the initial months of 2003, that I could just as easily do without Honda. When Davide Brivio came to Ibiza to talk to me about Yamaha I had not yet understood that his offer was really a metaphorical permission slip to set off for faraway places where no man has been before – in modern motor-cycling, at least. I hadn't truly understood that only by accepting another challenge, one which was even tougher, could I take my career to another level, finding within me the strength and will to continue to improve, to become even better. Better as a rider, certainly, but probably also better as a person. It took time to understand this and many other things. But eventually I got there.

Leaving Honda to join Yamaha at a time when the latter was going through the darkest period in its history seemed crazy to me. Even though I wasn't too happy about being with HRC – even while every rider, especially my direct opponents, dreamed of being a Honda man – it was difficult mentally to picture a competitive future without Honda. I had lived and breathed Honda since 1999, when I joined them with dreams of glory, especially since I got to ride what I thought – indeed, what was – the most beautiful bike in the world, the official NSR 500.

And yet, after three seasons of triumphs attained at a record-breaking pace, as I began to prepare for 2003 and my fifth world title, my third with Honda, I could feel the embryo of something forming inside me. All it would take for that embryo to grow and come out would be that single event that would change everything.

At the start of 2003 there was only one thing that was clear to me: I was not happy at Honda. I say again, I was simply not happy. The main reason for my discontent was their philosophy, which was so different from mine. I no longer wanted to live in that environment and I was no longer going to put up with a situation where my merits were not recognised, where I lived in a tense bubble, under constant pressure. Particularly for me, a person who loves to feel his team and his teammates embracing him, who wants to see them suffer with me and rejoice with me, it was hard to accept that the idea of "team spirit" was totally alien to Honda.

I need to feel part of a group and, at Honda, there no longer was a group to be part of. The situation was so bad that the unthinkable was happening: I was no longer enjoying racing. It seemed impossible to me. Impossible and unthinkable. And yet that's exactly what was happening. I remember sitting there and looking over the pre-contract which Honda had offered me. I immediately felt a bad taste in my mouth. I thought back to those people who have to get up and go to work every day, punch a time card, oppressed by working hours, their boss, their colleagues, trapped in a senseless job they don't like and a life they don't love. You can't live like that, not if you're a MotoGP rider.

My priority was always the group. By this, I mean the people with whom I have interacted – including work – since the days back in 125cc. In my racing pits I want people who I can love, people with whom I can talk about things other than bikes, people who smile. One of the reasons I became disenchanted with HRC was the way you had to live within that team. There was a rigour, a discipline, which stifled the will to laugh and joke. And I'm just not comfortable in such an environment, one where people are unable to even smile.

I need around me a group where everyone expresses basic human emotions like gratitude and participation. Joy, enthusiasm, shared experience. Otherwise, I can't claim to be in a truly united team. We were winners, sure, and this might have been enough for the Japanese managers, but it was not enough for me. I want to do things and enjoy myself while I do them. And that means I want to win while having fun. If I can combine the two, winning and fun, I can achieve anything.

At Honda I was number one, true. Except Honda management and I had a very different definition of what being "number one" meant. To them, all it meant was that I got to try out the technical upgrades a few weeks before the others: new material would come in,

I'd test it, develop it and then, once it was ready, everybody else got it. What they were never able to understand – especially my rival Honda riders, who made such a big issue out of it – was that my bike was never that much better than any other Honda. By the end of 2003 my RCV, compared to Gibernau and Biaggi, had an additional 250 laps on it. That's it. Nothing more.

I know all too well just why this was: at Honda, what was important was proving that the in-house technology was better, so that they could then transfer it from racing bikes to roadbikes. At Honda, it was all about proving that winning was all about the bike. That's why it was so important to finish first, second and third. And that's why the other Honda bikes were virtually just as good as mine. It always was that way and it remained that way even after I left.

By 2003 Honda had entered into a spiralling cycle: when you keep winning year after year, winning by itself isn't enough: you have to dominate. Being used to winning, having that culture of victory, does have many positives of course, but I found it almost depressing. In 2003, at the peak of our success, when we were virtually unbeatable, I started to get the sense that by winning I was only doing my job. And that was it. Nobody would celebrate, nobody would go wild. It was just another win.

And it did not matter if I won or if Biaggi or Gibernau won, because we were all Honda guys. In fact, if they won it was even better, because that way they could prove that their "unofficial" bikes were just as good. I realised this on my own, but I wanted to be sure, so I asked them straight out. And I heard it direct from Honda management.

"Well, yes, our objective is to always win first, second and third place in every race," I was told. "We want three Hondas on the podium, always!"

And they said this without batting an eyelid, as if it was the most natural thing. And, in terms of results, it was, it happened quite often at Honda. Perhaps the other Honda riders were never too interested in this attitude. Biaggi and Gibernau seemed obsessed with proving that my bike was better than theirs and that was the only reason I won. They must have known as well as anyone that the only difference were those 250 laps and they could not explain the gap between myself and them, yet, naturally, they would never admit it.

Another thing that annoyed me at Honda was the tendency to never recognise openly the validity of a choice, a suggestion, a bit of feedback that our engineers offered the racing department. They were always very cold. Efficient, yes. In fact, they were very efficient. But on a human level, they were cold, ice-cold.

When I joined HRC at the beginning of 2002 I started to truly get into the Honda world. Before, in the previous two years, in the Nastro Azzurro team, everything was different. We had a Japanese guy on the team, a fellow named Sato, who was in charge of telemetry. Apart from that, we had no direct contact with the guys from HRC. We decided everything. Jeremy and I were happy, we had the official bike, but we ran things on our own, helped by my group of Italians and by Jeremy's boys.

But at the end of 2001, with the beginning of the MotoGP, circumstances took me direct to the Honda team. Their in-house crew, Team HRC. That's because, obviously, only the official team could develop the first four-stroke RCV. In 2002 it was truly a prototype in the very first phase of development, none of the satellite teams had the technical know-how and the ability to handle it. I tried the first RC211V, the very first version, at Suzuka, after the "Eight Hour Race" in August 2001. It felt really weird. It was very small, with no protection from the fairings. It was tiny; the whole bike felt like a toy. When it came off the support, the set-up seemed very unusual. It was very high in the back and sloped down towards the front, making it very low compared to the rear. When I actually climbed on, it felt even smaller.

At the time, the priorities were the engine and the chassis. But as soon as I tried it, I could tell they had big problems. When the rear tyre began to heat up, the RCV would start sliding all over the place: the lack of traction was so great that the rear tyre would slip and slide even on the pit lanes.

It did have a great engine, you could tell that straight away. It was immensely powerful and the margins of development were huge, there was so much potential there, although that first version couldn't fully harness all that power. That's why I had said that I wanted to race 500cc even in 2002, the first year of MotoGP. I was a bit worried, I really felt that, at that stage, the four-stroke Honda was less competitive than the 500cc two stroke. Then again, we're talking about Honda here. And, already, in the second test, in Jerez in November, they had overhauled the bike entirely and it was going strong. Evidence that, whatever Honda's other shortcomings might be, they knew how to develop a bike. When I joined Team HRC, there was a new management team in place. And, with it, an environment and company culture which was very different from that of the previous years. They were far more formal, colder, more distant. I realised this straight away, when we were putting the finishing touches on the 2002–03 contract.

I was in the mountains, skiing, when my mobile rang. It was Gibo, wanting to update me on negotiations.

"We're on our own," he said.

"What do you mean?" I said. "I thought everything was in place ..."

"Yes, everything *was* in place ... it's not any more ..." he said, leaving me shocked. "I think it's best if we see each other soon."

As it turned out, Honda had decided they were in no hurry to sort out the new contracts. This left us in a delicate position. We had to decide if we wanted to stay with them or if we wanted to look elsewhere.

Thus, on the eve of the test period, I found myself without a contract and without a team. I reluctantly left my friends and skis behind and hurried to Rome, to the headquarters of Honda Europe, where Gibo had arranged a high-level meeting.

It was far from pleasant.

We tried to reason with them, to walk them through every scenario, every possibility, just so we could reach an agreement. And, at the very end, after a lot of difficulty, we did reach a deal. And so I renewed my contract with Honda for another two seasons. But I was very far from pleased with this turn of events. When I walked out, I was somewhat shaken up. It had been a surreal experience.

"OK, now a camera crew is going to pop out of nowhere and tell us we are all on *Scherzi a parte!*" I joked, trying to lighten the mood. '*Scherzi a parte*' is an Italian television programme where people are subjected to practical jokes, while a hidden camera films everything. It's a bit like *Beadle's About* in England or *Candid Camera.*

Unfortunately, it was all true. Still, I had to stay positive and look ahead. The 2002 season was coming up, there was a lot of work to be done. For several months now I had been developing the RC211V, together with the Japanese engineers. It was brand new and already after two tests it had made very good progress, though there was still plenty of work to be done. And the clock was ticking. Even though I was working hard, I hadn't forgotten the drawn-out contract talks. That was when my relationship with Honda really began to deteriorate. And that wasn't the only unpleasant incident.

One thing for which I have never forgiven Honda is that they reneged on a promise to let me keep the NSR 500 bike, on which I won the title in 2001. That, in particular, was a huge disappointment, because I was very attached to that bike. And it wasn't just the bike, it was the way they handled the whole matter. I had started asking for it well before the end of the 2001 season and, within the team, they kept assuring me that I would get it. And yet, it never seemed to show up.

"It's coming," they kept repeating.

And I would get suspicious.

"Don't worry," they insisted.

And I would worry even more.

The strange thing is that they never said "no". They always said it wouldn't be a problem, but then they would never name a date for the handover. Then they said they would do it in some kind of public ceremony, but then they could not find the right sponsor or event to do it.

"It's in customs, it's on its way," they once said.

"Great, I'll wait," I said. What else could I do?

"We're missing an exhaust pipe and a few bits and pieces, then we'll be ready," they said another time.

"OK, I'll be here, waiting,' I said.

Between imaginary customs officers who weren't doing their imaginary jobs and missing bits and pieces of the bike, they managed to draw the whole affair out. And so 2001 turned into 2002 and then 2002 slipped into 2003. In the winter of 2003, I had had enough of this whole affair and I became more aggressive. I started with Fiorani, but he had coolly removed himself from the equation.

"Well, what happened to my 500cc?" I asked him one day.

"I don't know what else I can do. At this point you need to speak to the Japanese guys," he said, deflecting me towards the HRC executives.

"Fine!" I said. At that point, I was so exasperated I would have talked to anyone. I just wanted the bike!

But then things slowly became clear to me. I began to realise that I would never get to see my beloved NSR ever again. And that's what happened. Oh yes, I did go to see the Japanese guys. And they fobbed me off with the most varied and creative excuses one could imagine. They never actually said no point-blank, they just didn't give me the bike. This went on until, eventually, I felt so offended that I stopped asking for the bike. And this decision cost me a fair bit.

Once again, I asked myself just why they had such an attitude. I really felt I deserved that bike. After all, I had won the world title with it. I thought I deserved a little bit of gratitude, given the results I was collecting. I had won the Eight Hour Race, the 500cc world title (and, along the way, notched Honda's 500th victory in 500cc) and the first ever MotoGP title in 2002 (with eleven wins). I think those results warrant the right to at least ask for a small favour. I guess I was wrong. I was denied. And, to this day, I don't understand it.

Another unpleasant episode came at the end of the 2001 season, when Honda scheduled a test with the NSR 500. For some time now I had asked them if Graziano, my father, and some of my friends could try the bike. So I asked if we could do it during the test days that Honda had arranged in Jerez at the end of the season. Naturally, they said it wouldn't be a problem. But then, the day before the test, they said, "We can't do it, because tomorrow the journalists will be testing the bikes."

"What do you mean, the journalists are testing the bikes?!" I said. "You're letting journalists ride around on my bike and then you tell me that, in two days of testing, there is no chance for my own father, who is a former world championship rider, to do a single test?"

Yes, that's what they were saying. And they had their way. Just as they always did.

Still, during my year of self-discovery, I reflected upon other things as well. Things that, looking back, were far more profound. At a certain point I asked myself what I expected from my future. Setting aside the troubled human relationships, I had the chance to stay with Honda for another two years. And, in the best-case scenario, I would repeat exactly what I had done in the two previous years: I would have won the title.

It may seem rather banal, but to me this was an important point. In fact, it was the tipping point. It really bothered me that people kept saying that I had only ever had the best in life, especially the bike, and that's why I had won. They always said that. In my first year in MotoGP, only Ukawa and I had the RC211V and everybody said that the bike was so far ahead that anybody could have won on it.

The following year, 2003, the Honda RC211V was given to a whole bunch of riders. Among them Biaggi, who the previous year complained that his Yamaha was underperforming. When he got the RC211V, he started complaining that it wasn't as good as my version. And Gibernau did the same. One might have gotten the impression that my bike was twice as fast as theirs! So, if I ever finished second, I'd find myself on trial for not winning. Nobody ever considered the fact that I might have still run a good race and that maybe one of my opponents had basically performed better than me on the day. No, I had lost. And I ought to be ashamed of myself. If I won, it was normal, no big deal. If I lost, I had failed.

I knew our bike was good, to be sure. But I also knew that I was the one who developed it, together with the Honda engineers. And, in fact, it was exactly because I had developed it, that I knew perfectly well that the other RC211Vs were not as bad as the others were making out. As a case in point, in the races in which there was something wrong with me or the bike, I was beaten by the other RC211V riders, not other guys on other bikes.

This magic aura around my bike and the certainty that it was so good that it basically raced itself, that I was just an appendage, created a situation which really annoyed me. Not to mention the fact that it put a lot of pressure on me.

I found myself in a situation similar to that which I had witnessed, indirectly, following the case of Mick Doohan via the newspapers and the gossip in the paddock. It seemed that, at one point in his career, he had the greatest bike in the world, one which his opponents could never dream of having. They talked about this all the time, and, along the way, influenced the press and public opinion. Even I, who should have known better, started to wonder just how good his bike was and whether he did indeed have some kind of superbike.

That's why, as soon as I joined Honda, I went straight to Jeremy, who had been Doohan's chief engineer, and asked him about it.

"What did his bike have that the other bikes did not?" I enquired.

"Nothing," he said. "It didn't have a thing. Maybe he had a part or two before the others, but that was it. The simple reality is that he was faster than they were."

Funny how history repeats itself. I found myself in Doohan's own position, facing the exact same problems.

I realised I could have won with Biaggi's bike or Gibernau's bike. Yet I didn't have the necessary peace of mind when I raced: I would stress myself out all weekend, giving everything I had, only to hear my opponents say, "Well, it's easy for him, he's got the best bike!" When you arrive at a track knowing that your only option is to win and, on top of that, when you do win, your victory will be viewed as totally normal, par for the course, because you had the better bike . . . well, this simply disgusted me.

I myself had started becoming slightly paranoid. In fact, one day, I even thought of swapping bikes. Yes, I decided I was going to approach Biaggi and Gibernau and we would exchange bikes for a few races. I'd try their bikes, they could try mine. I asked Gibo to enquire with Honda whether they would let us do this.

"Look, it's simple," I said. "On Thursday, I get to the track, I give them my bike and take one of theirs. Of course, we both accept the risk related to the set-up. But then we see what happens."

I thought it was a brilliant idea. In fact, I thought we could even swap the bikes on race day, I'd just walk up to Gibernau or Biaggi and say, "Hey, get off the bike and take mine . . . you'll get it back after the race!" Of course, it was all in vain. Honda would never permit such a thing and neither would the sponsors.

In the summer of 2003, HRC sent over new exhaust pipes. I chose not to use it, precisely because I was sick and tired of hearing that I had an edge over everybody else. But, partly because of the stress, partly because I was also in negotiations with Yamaha, Honda and Ducati, I was in far from perfect form. Sometimes I would lose concentration and make mistakes. When I famously missed that turn in Barcelona and ended up in the run-off area, it was a result of the fact that I was napping behind Capirossi. This incident, and others, caused people to say that my bike was so much better that I could afford the luxury of sitting back and simply turning on the juice late in the race, beating everyone in the final lap.

Obviously this was not the case. If I have the chance to pull away, I pull away. Always. Because if you hold out for the last lap you're taking a huge risk: you might finish second! Whereas if you can pull away at an earlier point in the race, you can avoid trouble later on.

I only ever sit and wait when there is no alternative. That's when, for me, lying in wait is a good tactic and the best way to win. In Germany, for example, I made a mistake in the last lap and Gibernau made me pay for it. But it's not as if I was planning to wait for the end, as a way of humiliating my opponents. I simply made the mistake of not passing him earlier, so that I could then build a gap. It was a tactical error. After losing that race in that way, because of a distraction, I got so angry that on my way home I told myself, "Enough! From now on, I'm taking no prisoners!" So from that moment on I raced with the aim of dominating every lap and I won five of the last six races of the season. The only one where I finished second was the Grand Prix of the Pacific, in Motegi. But as you know, that day I raced after getting virtually no sleep the night before, because that was the night I had decided to leave Honda. As you can imagine, I wasn't totally focused, to say the least.

All these incidents with Honda sprang to mind in 2003 as I reflected on my future choices. At one point, I found myself in a curious situation. The more I thought about the reasons to stay at Honda, the fewer reasons I actually found. And one day I realised that it was Honda who were holding me back.

It may seem strange and I myself took some time to figure this out, but Honda really did represent the wall that prevented me from getting out and exploring new horizons. Contrary to what others have said, it wasn't money which fuelled my choice. It was a question of motivation. Besides, after our long negotiations, Honda had given us practically everything we asked for financially. When I received the final draft of the contract, in Japan, there were no more problems: Honda had accepted each of our conditions, they really did want to keep me. But I had already made up my mind in October 2003: I was not staying. It was a decision I took with great calm and peace of mind after a long period of reflection. It was the product of a profound analysis.

Of course, Brivio and the other Yamaha executives, all of whom were very nice, made my decision easier. I had known Brivio for some time. He was one of those guys I always enjoyed talking to. We first met back in 1995, when we were both in the Italian championships. I was a rider in the 125cc category; he was a manager at Yamaha, working on the Superbikes. I loved the livery of their bikes, and the laid-back environment in their team. That's why I spent a lot of time hanging out with them.

Ultimately, I chose Yamaha because I relished their challenge and appreciated the people who worked there. I understood that I would have the chance to recreate a unified team, a group of Italians and foreigners who I knew well, most of whom had worked with me at Honda. What I was looking for was a relaxed environment, a solid group who could rally around me, people with whom I could relax and feel at home around, without feeling blackmailed or threatened, without having to put up with that air of superiority which was endemic at Honda. I was tired of the authoritarianism and the pressures. And when I finally understood it would be a little more difficult to find a relaxed environment at Ducati, it was at that moment I also realised that the Yamaha executives had understood exactly what I was looking for. In addition, the men from Yamaha had approached me politely, without putting on any airs. Yamaha at one point seemed to me clearly capable of delivering the atmosphere I wanted. With the added bonus of being the second biggest team in the world: it's not as if I was moving to a mom-and-pop hillbilly operation.

Yamaha management, from the top bosses to the racing department, had told me explicitly that Yamaha needed me. They had asked for my help, they made me feel special and integral to the development of their bike and to their results on the track. In addition, the experience I gained negotiating with Ducati, even though it was brief, proved to be very useful. It allowed me to break the psychological dependence I felt towards Honda.

It was while thinking of Ducati that I first began to consider a competitive future away from Honda. After all, as I mentioned, at first I was more drawn towards Ducati than Yamaha. When I accepted that the mentality at Ducati was not quite right for me, I had already begun detaching myself psychologically from Honda.

"If you're willing to go to Ducati, you're willing to go to Yamaha," I told myself. "And that means you can do without Honda."

Step by step I realised there was more to racing than Honda. This was an important point in my thought process. I could never have truly evaluated the possibility of moving to Ducati, much less to Yamaha, if at first I had not made the decision to leave Honda. At one point, during the summer, when I decided that I was going to Yamaha, I finally figured it all out. I simply used a logical argument, one which was not so clear to me earlier.

"Honda does not treat me the way I feel I deserve to be treated," I thought. "Yamaha, who are number two in the world, came to me and said I could have whatever I wanted, I just needed to ask. That's a huge difference!"

With Yamaha, we had reciprocal respect from the beginning, and even a bit of tension, which is normal in a long negotiating process. At every step, however, I was struck by the passion of those who worked there. Yes, it's true, they too have that Japanese mentality, but, importantly, they are far more open than the guys at Honda. There are people at Yamaha who gave everything they had, who put everything on the line to reach their objective: signing me. That shows passion.

Sure, there were moments of tension, like I said. The worst part was when Jeremy and the boys told me they were not following me to Yamaha. I was so highly-strung around that time. I was working on several fronts, I was tense for many different reasons, so when Jeremy said "no" I thought to myself: "Great, I'm working so hard to take you with me, to convince Yamaha that they need to take you on board, and this is how you repay me!" This caused days of tension and embarrassment between myself and Jeremy. Still, the Yamaha guys had also ruffled my feathers at one point. I was sure that Jeremy would be a crucial element of our success at Yamaha, so I could not understand the scepticism Yamaha was showing, both towards him as well as towards the other boys.

If anything I could see how the guys might have reservations about Yamaha, not the other way around. Especially Jeremy. I tried to put myself in his situation. He's nearing the end of his career, he's well past fifty and he has to leave the best company in the world after over twenty years of service, at a time when everything is totally comfortable and familiar. I mean, I was asking him to put himself on the line once again, to take risks and to complicate his life. At twenty-four, my age at the time, it's much easier to take decisions like that, but when you're over fifty, it's much tougher.

But even though I could understand Jeremy's position, I still felt disappointed. Because, at the same time, I thought that Jeremy and my team shared my determination to prove certain things to certain people. After all, the same people who said the Honda was so great also said that the team was nothing special, particularly since they thought all the material came shipped from Japan, ready to use, all they had to do was assemble it and install it, nothing more.

I knew this kind of talk bothered them. I knew it. And yet even this wasn't enough to motivate them to change, to take a chance. Without ever losing our cool, talking and analysing the situation, we were able to reach an agreement on everything. Make no mistake, that whole period of time – the end of the summer – certainly was uncomfortable. In fact, the whole summer was tough for me. The tension built itself up week after week. It was all a crescendo.

That summer I never raced with the necessary serenity, but nobody noticed, because in 2003 we were really, really fast. In fact, it was my fastest year on the Honda. It's true, the bike never went better. It took a big, big mistake for me to not win. For the others it was all very difficult.

When I think about it, that's what enabled me to race at the highest level while spending the whole season planning such an ambitious project as my move from Honda to Yamaha. And as if all this wasn't enough, in the summer of 2003, the old theory that my success was only a result of the bike and nothing else, made a sudden return. So many people were saying it that I simply could not handle it any more.

"You know the only way to get these people to shut up would be to move to Yamaha," I thought to myself, time and again. "But do I have the balls to go out and do it?"

I could only come up with partial answers.

"I know I can win without the Honda," I thought. "Which means I can with the Yamaha, but maybe I don't have the balls to leave."

"Balls, balls, do I have the balls?" I kept asking myself. "Do I really have the balls to do this?"

Only when I was able to tell myself, "Yes! Yes, I do," was I able to break out of my situation. Only then did I free myself from this tension.

One morning, waking up, I said: "I'm going to do it!"

And I was free.

I'll never forget the Saturday night and following Sunday morning at Motegi: they were some of the most intense, but also the toughest, moments of my career. That was the most difficult point of the whole negotiation. In fact, I hardly slept at all in those days. Thursday, Friday and Saturday marked the moment when I started working towards the realisation that I needed to attain. I freed myself only once I began to free myself from the mental brakes and shackles that restricted my thoughts. The trick was to imagine myself spending another two seasons at Honda. That was enough to make me understand I had to make a choice.

All my thoughts, both negative and positive, began mixing and mingling in my head. And at one point I told myself, "Staying at Honda means spending another two years with people who don't treat me well, who believe the bike is more important than me . . . do I really have to do that? Do I really have to spend another two years in a situation where others can keep saying that the only reason I win is because of my bike? No, I don't think so!"

And so I freed myself once and for all. But I also got rid of another gremlin, one that I had harboured from the very beginning. There was a part of me that was very disturbed at the prospect of giving up the Honda, which I had worked so hard to develop into a great bike, and handing it to my rivals. Especially since, at the same time, I'd be moving to the Yamaha, a bike which it seemed likely would not be able to compete for a while. It looked to me like I was giving away a lot to my opponents. But all of a sudden that thought was gone and I had no uncertainty any more. And I really did not care what happened to Honda. In fact, leaving my best bike to my rivals and taking them on with a seemingly inferior bike was the best way to put an end to all that talk about the so-called advantages I had supposedly enjoyed over the years. It was a huge incentive.

"Let's go with Yamaha and see what happens," I told Gibo. And with that, I'd only have to worry about myself and the task in front of me.

And Jeremy was in the same situation. As soon as he signed with Yamaha, he underwent an instant change. I saw in him the same mental journey, the same reasoning, the same thought process that I underwent. I saw his initial curiosity, but also his initial reluctance. I then saw the intermediate phase, filled with uncertainty, fear, indecision. And then the final phase, when he told himself, "If I don't do this, I'll never forgive myself for the rest of my life."

That's the stage where I was.

In the most delicate stage, the final one, I always told myself, "If you don't hang your balls out there and just do it, you'll never know what might have happened, you'll never know if you're capable of winning with another bike." I saw the same gremlin gnawing away at Jeremy. I saw him change suddenly, just as I had. In the following few days I felt the tension ease and I felt not only relief, I also felt real enthusiasm. It wasn't a coincidence that in the three races after Honda announced that I would be leaving – the Grands Prix of Malaysia, Australia and Valencia – I won effortlessly. For Jeremy it was pretty much the same. He threw himself with enthusiasm into a new challenge. And so we found that unity, that determination to go forward, side by side. As for me, finding myself face to face with such an important decision, only made me stronger. Mentally stronger, that is.

Because Honda did not allow me to test the Yamaha before the end of 2003, in the winter of 2003–04 I had the longest holiday of my life. I had nearly three months off. Three months to enjoy some wonderful time off. The kind of days when you get up at three o'clock in the afternoon, because you went to bed after daybreak. I did a lot of skiing and spent a lot of time with my friends. I relaxed and had a lot of fun. This helped me unwind and allowed me to locate a level of serenity I hadn't experienced in a long time.

If finally making a decision was very liberating mentally, the long rest was very important physically. By the time I did my first test on the M1 I was very happy. I was pleased to start a new adventure alongside Jeremy and the rest of my team, glad that I was working with Brivio and with the Japanese guys at Yamaha, and above all, Furusawa, head of the research and development department, a very open and communicative man, who was ready for new ideas and to think outside the box, one of those guys with whom you could discuss just about anything. To me he embodies the Yamaha spirit. He leads a team of people who put their souls into the bikes they build. And this is part of the reason so many people are fascinated by Yamaha. It was the first time that I felt so in tune with my employers. I felt very proud to be involved with them. Because everything about Yamaha is beautiful: its logo, its history, its spirit, the bikes they make, the pilots who race them. Who, by the way, include the likes of Agostini, Roberts, Lawson, Rainey and yours truly. Not too bad, I'd say . . .

FOUR

CAPITOLO QUATTRO

I have always been a motorcyclist, even when I was racing go-karts. Even when I was two and a half years old and I had yet to learn how to ride a bicycle, I already wanted to ride a motorbike.

It was a small minicross which my father, Graziano, had bought me. It was 1982 and I was two and a half years old. Graziano raced cars; he gave up motorbikes following a very serious accident at Imola. My minicross was the only kind of mini-motorbike available at the time and I used the house and the garden as my racing tracks. It all started with that little minicross. That's where my hunger for racing, for competing, for testing myself against others came from, even though I was still very little.

At Christmas 1989, when I was ten, the first real mini-motorbikes, proper miniature versions of Grand Prix bikes, made it to Italy. It was love at first sight. I made my parents buy one for me straight away and with it I began to race on a track. In fact, I began to race with some regularity. The minibike era was a very happy chapter in my life. It wasn't my first experience with motoring, but the minibikes were, for me, the moment where my education as a future MotoGP rider really began. True, my first races were on karts. But that was because back then, at my age, you were only allowed to race karts, at least on a track. I suppose I could have raced minicross bikes, but I was attracted to the asphalt of the track. That's why I raced karts and, later, minibikes.

For two years I raced both. Karting is more serious, at least at first, because it's more professional even at lower levels. Racing on four wheels, rather than two, makes you seem more important when you are little. I don't know why exactly, but I took karting very seriously, whereas minibikes for me were like a game. The way I see it, I raced karts and played with minibikes. As I grew up, however, I slowly grew disenchanted with karts and fell in love with motorbikes. In fact, when it came time to choose, I chose the bike. It was the winter of 1992 and I was thirteen years old. I was driving along with Graziano and we were passing through San Giovanni in Marignano, a town of about 8,000 people, situated halfway between Tavullia and Cattolica, in the Valle della Conca.

"Why don't we race motorbikes?" I asked him, all of a sudden.

He replied with an expression I'll never forget. It was a mixture of joy, because motorbikes were his great passion, and fear, because motorbikes seemed far more dangerous than karts. And I knew that Stefania, my mother, felt the same way.

Still, we had to make a decision, we had to figure out which direction we were going to take. Karts or motorbikes?

To me it wasn't hard to decide. My ideas were clear. Inside me, I could feel the passion for motorbikes growing. Besides, as far as karting was concerned, there was a financial problem as well. We needed a budget of 100 million lire (today, around 50,000 euros). Because of my age, I had to leave the 60 minikart category and, if I continued, enter the 100 class, and that meant coughing up 100 million lire. We had no sponsor of course, because nobody is going to invest such amounts in the 100 class, a division nobody follows, apart from the drivers, their families and friends.

And thus my parents would have had to come up with the money. Graziano and Stefania mulled it over for a long time, trying to figure out if spending such a sum really was a wise investment.

I could see that they were torn, they could not decide, so I made the decision for them!

"Let's try the bikes," I told Graziano and then repeated myself to my mother. It just felt right. It came naturally. As soon as I found myself at a crossroads, it was easy to take the direction which would lead me to race motorcycles, it was far closer to my character. I guess the fact that the 100 kart class required such a hefty investment is what pushed me towards motorbikes and my dream of becoming a MotoGP rider.

When I was very young, I would tell everyone that I wanted to race in Formula One, but that was just because karts were the first motorised vehicle I ever raced. They're what made me want to get out on the track and race. I enjoyed kart, I loved guiding machines, controlling them, though I always enjoyed it more when they had two wheels rather than four. Still, if I'm honest, I have to admit that had budgets and money not been an issue I would have gladly continued racing both, alternating between car and bike and bike and car. But it simply wasn't possible.

So I'd say that the financial aspect was important, but not crucial. I'm sure that if I had loved the four wheels as much as the two wheels, we would have found a solution. But I love motorbikes. And that's why I can say that it was my decision and mine alone.

"We can go to a real track, Misano, and try the Aprilia 125 of a friend of mine," I told Graziano, just as we passed through San Giovanni in Marignano, just a few kilometres from Misano. "Please, let me do a real test on a real track and then we'll see."

I had already thought of everything and was enacting my plan.

"Look, my friend will loan me his Aprilia 125," I insisted. "His name is Maurizio Pagano, I'm sure he'll lend me the bike."

I spent a lot of time with Maurizio and his brother Marco, two kids from Gatteo a Mare, who, like me, raced minibikes. They were just getting into real motorbikes, Sport Production bikes, and they had an Aprilia 125.

"All right, let's give it a go," Graziano said.

And I felt happy. Very happy.

Thus, in November 1992, on a rather cold day, in the middle of the week, on a public track (though it was virtually empty), I did my first lap on a proper track. And I did it with an Aprilia Futura 125. It certainly wasn't motorcycling weather, but, that day, the weather really did not matter to me. I was wearing one of Graziano's suits, a Dainese. It was yellow and red and he had received it when he went to do some tests a few years before. My helmet was an Arai Schwantz Replica, which I had used on minibikes. I have always used Schwantz replica helmets because, as a child, I was a huge fan of Schwantz.

I did not get much of a thrill from my first lap. I was excited, sure, but I was mainly just soaking everything up. Everything changes once you're on the track. I was particularly struck by how the perspective changed, how you follow that asphalt ribbon with your eyes, how the scenery around you races past. I saw the gravel, the hills behind, the grandstand . . . everything seems so far away, even though it's close, very close. I did not try and pretend it was a race, imagining tens of thousands of spectators watching my every move. That's because it was difficult enough to get a handle on the Aprilia 125. At thirteen, I was still rather thin and lightweight. The bike just seemed so big and heavy. And I suppose it was. Those "sport production" bikes were, in fact, streetbikes. They certainly weren't Grand Prix bikes. The 125 weighed 150 kilograms, as much as a MotoGP!

I cruised along slowly, I looked around. I was very safe. Approaching the Tramonto turn, I eased off the gas at 250 metres, when, in fact, you normally do it at 150. I was surprised to see that the years on the minibike had taught me many things that now were coming in handy. True, it was not easy given the size and weight of the bike. And, besides, it was the first time I was driving a bike with gears, which meant I also had to learn how to use the clutch. None of these problems, however, were insurmountable.

I soon forgot all about karting and concentrated on motorbikes. I could not have known it at the time, of course, but it was the start of an adventure that would profoundly change my life. But I want to make clear that motorbikes were not my second choice. The doubts over money only contributed to my choice, but they were not the decisive factor. It's true that Graziano was always reluctant to throw money away and thus he was a little bit alarmed about the investment necessary to race karts. I think the financial benefits of motorbikes over karts balanced out the fear he felt for me on two wheels. For both Graziano and my mother were afraid of motorbikes. And, at the time, that was a real problem.

Graziano had endured a difficult career. He had suffered frequent injuries. And, at times, he got hurt, badly hurt. In 1982, when I was just three years old, he suffered a terrible accident at Imola, seriously injuring his head. He was very lucky to survive, and doubly fortunate that the paramedics who were first to the scene did such a good job as did, later, the Mobile Clinic and Doctor Costa. He got away with it that day, even though the knock he took was so strong that Graziano lost his memory. Nothing too dramatic, it's just that sometimes he needs to be reminded of things . . .

After the accident, Graziano had to retire from motorbikes, so he began racing cars instead. My mother had been by his side through it all, experiencing the highs and lows, and she did not like the idea of seeing me race motorbikes as well. This is also why, as soon as I expressed the wish to race, my parents put me on "four wheels", because they were convinced that cars are safer than motorbikes.

Graziano knew exactly what somebody wanting to race motor-bikes would have to face. And I can understand his fears as a father, just as I can understand my mother's fears. Motorcycles are dangerous, maybe not as perilous as some people imagine them to be, but they are nonetheless dangerous.

And yet Graziano loved motorbikes. After all, he was a rider. My mother, because they were married very young, grew up in the paddock. I think they felt the motorcycle world was quite familiar to them.

And then there was another factor. It was going to be impossible to make me forget about motorbikes. Yes, I've always had a love affair for the motorcycle. A love which dates back to when I was two and a half, when Graziano took me along to ride that little minicross bike, even before I got my first bicycle. When I finally convinced my parents to let me race motorcycles, Graziano and I immediately focused on the benefits. And it was true, when it came to motorbikes, I did have it easy. Graziano had plenty of friends out there who were ready to help. Doors were very quick to open. After convincing Graziano to take me to Misano to test my friend's Aprilia 125, I decided that it was time to race. A few months later, in February 1993, I would turn fourteen – the minimum age to race competitively on a 125.

Graziano got to work. He called Virginio Ferrari and, from there, a friend spoke to a friend who spoke to a friend, and I ended on a Cagiva.

"We need to find a ride for Valentino, can you help us?" Graziano asked Virginio.

"Sure, I'll help you," said Virginio who immediately spoke to Claudio Castiglioni, the owner of Cagiva.

"We need to help Graziano's kid," Virginio told him.

"OK, let me see what I can do," Castiglioni said.

He put me in Claudio Lusuardi's team, which was the official team of Cagiva's Sport Production bikes. Lusuardi allowed kids to race with his team, provided they paid a share of the expenses. So, thanks to Graziano, Ferrari, Castiglioni and Lusuardi, we hammered out a good deal. We paid the mechanics and the travel expenses, while Cagiva would provide us the bikes and the spares.

For me it was an excellent solution, because the Sport Production championship was an important competition, at least back then. And I felt very important. Back then the 125 roadbike looked just like a racing bike and it really was the best a boy could hope for. It was very hip, and the streets and the school car parks were full of them. And so were the tracks, because the Italian Sport Production championship was immensely popular.

For my first test with the Cagiva 125 we all met up at Magione. Because I was born in Urbino, I was placed in Zone C. At the time, there were so many different riders that the pilots were divided up by zone. There were four: D was for the islands, C for the south, B for Misano and Mugello, while A included Monza and Varano. I didn't mind being in Zone C because the level was not as high as Zone B, which included all the riders from Emilia Romagna, and Zone A, which included the north.

The day of the on-track debut is something that you'll always remember in vivid detail. I'm no different, because, honestly, there was no way I could forget my debut. No, I wasn't fast. And I can't tell you too much about competing with the other kids, because in fact I spent the whole time fighting against my bike.

The Cagiva in Magione was just like the Aprilia in Misano. It was big and heavy. I put on the suit, slipped on the boots, the helmet and my gloves. I hopped on the Cagiva, left the garage, took the pit lane and entered the track. So far, so good. Except, almost as soon as I had left the pits, I fell. There was a small left turn and I fell. On my real debut, I fell on the first turn of my first lap (the laps I took with my friend's Aprilia don't really count). I had new tyres, it was cold and I hit the ground right away.

"Well, this is harder than it looks," I told myself as I returned to the pits.

I was a little scared and, most of all, I was demoralised. So as my teammates saw me returning to the pit lane, head down, shoulders slumped, the fairings all badly scuffed, it's easy for me to imagine what they were thinking. As they were sorting out the bike, they were saying the usual things, but, mostly, "Be careful!"

Graziano was worried too, like the rest of the team. I got back on the track, overcame the hurdle of that first turn, started shifting through the gears and giving some gas. And then six laps later I fell again. Yes, once more. And for the same reason as before: the steering locked up.

And so I had embarrassed myself all over again.

"Two falls in six laps!" that was all I could think about as we returned home.

I had seen quite clearly how the rest of the team was beginning to harbour serious reservations over my ability (or lack thereof). And, to be honest, so did I. There's not much you can say about it, other than it was a very poor debut.

The thing is – as I discovered many, many years later – on all my debuts I've pushed myself and the bike to the limits very quickly, but also rashly, in other words before I have secured total control of the bike. And so I quickly fall or end up off the track. This happened to me both on a bike, in my 250cc and 500cc debuts, but also in the rally, in England, in my first rally world cup race, where I crashed out almost immediately. And, of course, when I did a test with the Ferrari F1, we spun out at the very first turn. So I suppose it was a typical debut by my standards – though I obviously did not know this at the time!

We even asked ourselves if it was even worth continuing. But everything was arranged for the season, we had a schedule and a programme to follow, so we just pressed ahead.

But if you think I turned things around quickly, you're wrong. Almost the whole first season went by before I started to loosen up a little. I finished ninth in my first race, at Magione. And as the season went on, I was usually in or around the top ten. I only started going faster towards the end of the season, in the race to qualify for the final phase of the Italian Sport Production championship.

It was held at Binetto. I fell in qualifying, so I was somewhat more cautious in the race itself. Still, I finished sixth, which was enough to qualify for the final. It was held in Misano, which was great for me: maybe I could exploit my home turf advantage . . .

My teammate, Andrea Ballerini, had the official Cagiva bike, while Roberto Locatelli, who was going head-to-head with him for the title, had the official Aprilia bike. For them it would all come down to this race. Ballerini had two bikes actually: one was prepared by Lusuardi, the other had been set up by Cagiva up in Varese. Both were considered "official" bikes. I had only one bike and, incidentally, it was totally different, and not just in terms of the colour.

Anyway, I suspect Lusuardi liked me by this point because he told Ballerini to choose which bike he wanted out of the two "official" ones. He chose the one tuned in Varese, and so Lusuardi turned to me and said I could have the other one. Naturally I jumped at the chance. I would get to race an "official" bike. With it, I won pole position. I could not believe it because in the previous races I was actually slower in qualifying than in the race itself. And yet, here I was, in pole position, ahead of Locatelli, who was second, and Ballerini, third, the two title contenders. And I would start ahead of them!

Except that's not what happened. I was so excited, that I

completely screwed up the start and was demoted to twentieth place. Still, I pulled off a very good race and finished third. I couldn't catch Locatelli and Ballerini, but I still joined them on the podium. I was ecstatic. To me, that race was the first time I really raised the bar. Thanks to my performance that day, Misano will always be a magical place to me. The next season, owing to the experience gained at Misano, I won the title. It always took me a bit of time to figure out how to be fast. But, once I learned, I knew how to be fast. Very fast. It was like that throughout the early stages of my career.

Back then I didn't really think that this could lead to a real career, but after that performance at Misano in 1993, I became the official Cagiva rider for the 1994 season. And the prospects were very good, since the three guys who had finished ahead of me had all moved up to the GP championship. And even though I raced for fun, Graziano put together a real professional programme for me. And it's a good thing he did that, because it helped me tremendously. In some way, Graziano has always been ahead of the pack. He had a brilliant idea: he signed me up for the Italian GP championship and the Sport Production championship. I would be competing in two different championships at the same time.

Because Sport Production is, after all, a roadbike, which is very different from a racing bike for GP, Graziano thought I'd be wasting time if I spent another year racing Sport Production alone. He wanted me to start gaining experience on GP bikes, the kind of bikes which, in a few years' time, I'd be riding anyway. Or so we hoped.

Graziano had raced in the world championship and thus had his sights set quite far into the future. He had thought of everything. I would be racing with a Sandroni 125. It was an almost a home-made bike, the dream of some local bike enthusiasts from Pesaro and Tavullia, led by Peppino Sandroni, who was able to arrange some local sponsorship deals.

The Sandroni had a Rotax-Aprilia engine and the frame was designed by Guido Mancini, a mechanic from Pesaro who had worked with Graziano. He and Graziano were good friends and together they planned my season. It was pretty time-consuming as I had to race four regional races plus four finals in Sport Production, plus another five for the GP championship. The GP races were all at the beginning of the year and this certainly helped us, because it allowed us to focus on one thing at a time.

Still, the bikes were very different, and I found that as soon as I got used to one, I lost the sensitivity on the other. Lusuardi was by no means happy. He thought I was going to run into serious problems this way. But we stuck to our guns and it paid off.

I reached all my objectives, which were to win the Sport Production title while learning the ropes in GP. Graziano's idea turned out to have been a stroke of genius. I was able to compete with Locatelli, Ballerini, Omarini, Cremonini and all the other top Sport Production guys who had moved to GP. So in 1995, when I moved up to the European championship, I was already familiar with these kinds of bikes. I was making my debut, but I was already an expert.

Sure, I had problems at times with the Sandroni. At Monza I finished fourteenth; at Vallelunga, I fell; but then in the final races we started getting better engines from Aprilia and my performances improved. At Misano, for the fourth race, the Team Italia was the benchmark. Locatelli, Ballerini and Cremonini were all very fast and all had excellent bikes. They were the favourites, but I stayed with them, just behind, in fourth place, at least until my engine failed. Later, at Mugello, we raced with guys from the world championship, including Gabriele Debbia. I spent the whole race next to him and finished fifth. For me, at the time, the prospect of racing with a world championship rider was a dream.

Sport Production that year was tough on the track and lots of fun outside it. At the end, I won the Italian title, but I had to fight until the finish. My great rival that year was Paolo Tessari, both in the regionals and in the finals.

In the first regional race, Tessari and I duelled in a way I will always remember as one of the most fun races of my career, even though I lost. He and I were well ahead of everyone and, in the last two laps, we overtook each other at every turn. Literally. He had the Aprilia, I was on the Cagiva. At the very end, I passed him on the final turn, but then the steering locked up again and I fell! I knew I wasn't going to make it. I realised it while I was overtaking. I had pushed so hard I could not stay on the track. But I tried anyway, because this was the culmination of a healthy rivalry and we were both giving our all.

Then I got the new Cagiva (in the first race we were still using the previous year's version) and in the second regional, at Misano, I won. And that was my first victory ever on a bike. I was wearing number 26. Tessari won the last two regionals and we both advanced to the finals. But, at the end, I won the title, following a last race and an argument with Cruciani, which went on for months.

The small world of Sport Production was wonderful. I remember it fondly. It was an aggressive environment – we were all hyperactive – but it was also very "real". The finals were very intense because you had to give everything on the track and then, after the race, the appeals ritual would begin. Everything mattered. Each race was a battle.

But we had friendly fun in the paddock. And that's really what we were: friends. Maybe not all of us in the same way, but what we shared was pretty close to true friendship. It's not a coincidence that even today I remember with so much affection and nostalgia many of those races and the adventures I shared with kids who were my rivals on the track and my friends off it.

Needless to say the world championship is not like that. I don't know if it ever was any different in the past, but these days the relationship among the riders is different. The paddock is deserted by 11 p.m. There is nobody around, we're all shut up in our motorhomes, nobody goes out, not even to talk. It's impossible to build relationships among us, as riders, even just to be able to joke or talk a little bit. There is only isolation; at best we'll nod or say hello. Our relationships don't go beyond that, even though we live so close together, even though we've known each other for years, even though we've shared so many amazing moments.

Sport Production was totally different. And much better. I remember the finals very well, because they were truly special. You would see all sorts of different kids and you could tell immediately the ones who were from outside our zone. The kids from Zone A, Lombardia, felt more important and were all more fashion conscious.

At the final I met Marco Dellino, from Bari, and we became very close, just as I was with Diego Giugovaz from Milan. He too is a good friend. And then, of course, there was Paolo Tessari: we had some great battles and we've remained friends. Everywhere we went, we caused havoc. I was the youngest, but that was never a problem. At night, in the summer, we'd have massive battles with water bombs. Then, after midnight, we'd all get on the scooters (all of which, needless to say, had modified engines) and we'd ride out to the track, to organise a night-time race.

We raced with our headlights off, so that we wouldn't be caught. The moon was our only source of light. And if it was a cloudy night, it didn't really matter, because we all knew the track so well. We had a great group of guys and we all graduated to the European championship, taking our mischievous ways abroad. We would leave restaurants without paying and trash rental cars.

Anyway, when dawn broke and it was time to get ready, everything changed. We all became mean and single-minded. Nobody got any discounts, nobody was granted any favours. You had to fight for everything. In the first final, at Vallelunga, my engine seized up and Tessari won hands down. The Cagiva was having problems with a piston, which we then solved. But that time I was lucky because, apart from Tessari, the other fast riders all fell.

At Mugello, it was an epic race. There were fifteen of us, all bunched up, leading from start to finish, among us Tessari, Cruciani, Dellino, Borsoi, Goi, Giugovaz. At the finish, after several falls and collisions, Borsoi won and I finished second. The next race was at Monza, where I won, which meant that going into the final race at Misano there were four of us in the running: Tessari, Cruciani, Borsoi and me. And I had home-court advantage. On the last lap, I came into the Brutapela turn in second place. I had virtually won it all. But Cruciani, who was riding very close to me, came into the turn behind me practically without braking at all! Our bikes nudged each other, we wobbled in our trajectories, but he came out of the turn ahead of me and ended up finishing second, with me third. Which meant that he won the title.

A Sport Production championship could not end like that. And so almost as soon as the race was over the fighting broke out between us: pushes, insults, followed by appeals and counter-appeals. In the end, Cruciani was disqualified.

And so I became Italian Sport Production champion.

FIVE

At school, teachers often like to make outrageous statements, the kind that bounce off the walls and then roll down the hallway. They love to pass judgement on you, especially when you're very young and aren't quite as confident or sure about yourself. To be fair, while I was young, confidence wasn't a problem for me, but school and I simply were not on the same wavelength. I had no passion for it.

My teachers realised this early on, which is why they've left me a whole legacy of outrageous judgements and catastrophic predictions, which then proved to be completely and absolutely wrong. Thank goodness.

The most incredible one, the one most wide of the mark, came from my Art History teacher, who one day said: "Do you really think that if you keep going around with your silly motorcycles one day you're going to make a living off them?"

That question, that remark, which at the time seemed so cutting, today is something I can only smile about. I have thought about it several times during my career. Because, I suppose, the one thing even my critics could agree on is that I have managed to eke out a living racing motorbikes, no?

I thought about what my Art History teacher said again in May 2005, when I received my honorary degree in Communications from the University of Urbino.

I think my teacher's words represented rock-bottom for me. Art was perhaps my least favourite subject, along with mathematics. It wasn't the teacher's fault, but I really could not stand studying the history of art. And so, as a result, I wasn't the best student – and I certainly wasn't the best in terms of paying attention in class. Naturally the Art History teacher would get very angry with me since I really wasn't interested. She was exasperated and that's why she launched herself into one of the least accurate predictions in history.

But that was my style. It was the way I defended myself from my teachers, who did not exactly throw me "Welcome back!" parties when I returned from racing abroad, usually after missing a few days of class.

"Where were you all last week?" one teacher asked me once, after I returned from a long trip in Spain.

"I was racing in Spain!" I replied, sounding as enthusiastic as possible. "And I did well. I finished third. Third at Jarama!"

Actually that was a great race. It was part of the Open Ducados championship, a series that was primarily based in Spain. Racing there was an excellent idea because it included all the best Spaniards, including those in the world championship. I learned so much about racing from the Open Ducados and I was very proud of my podium finish, because I had been racing really fast. Alzamora had won, Martinez was second, and I, despite my youth and inexperience, was third, behind two world-class riders.

Still, my teacher was not impressed. I could tell this by the way she went on, the sarcasm dripping from her voice.

"Bravo then!" she cackled. "Keep going on your little holidays, keep racing your little motorcycles . . . Keep having fun, instead of studying!"

Fortunately none of my high school teachers' prophecies became true. I did manage to achieve one or two good things. But I have to recognise the fact that, when I was in school, I wasn't exactly a model student.

Blame my love of motorbikes, of course. That's what kept me far from the classroom. In those years I was racing both for the Italian title and the European title. We're talking about the 1994 and 1995 seasons. I raced motorbikes and amused myself on a scooter. It was 1995 that I really started competing abroad and I began collecting long absences from school. I'd be away from home and thus from classes for long periods at a time, as much as a whole week towards the end.

I also fell a lot, all the time, and often returned beat up and full of bruises. Around that time, at European level, I had a great rivalry with Lucio Cecchinello. He had a Honda with the HRC kit: he was fast, but I have to admit, he also knew how to ride, which is a very different skill. To keep up with him, I took some huge risks and some big spills. He won many races. In contrast, I reached the podium a few times but I never actually finished first that season.

I'll never forget one particular fall as I vainly tried to keep up with him. It was at Assen, in Holland, and that day I hurt the little finger on my left hand, an injury that never actually healed. That day, I was faster than him, at one point I attacked him, he cut me off, we touched bikes and I fell. Every time I look at my mangled finger I think of Cecchinello. And I also think of all my teachers who said the same things every time they saw me return banged up from a race abroad.

"Can't you see that all you do is hurt yourself with those silly motorbikes?" they would say, in unison. "Quit the bikes, and focus on studying, it will be much better for you."

I certainly wasn't famous at the time. I was the son of Graziano Rossi, who happened to enjoy motorbikes. That was it. It's funny, because in my very same class there was a boy who played lots of football. He too was very busy and missed lessons, but nobody seemed to have a go at him . . . nobody ever told him that he should give up football and only think of studying. I guess motorbikes are a less "noble" sport . . .

I attended – well, when I was around, that is – the Liceo Mamiani in Pesaro, a high school specialising in foreign languages. Every week the students had an hour or two of assembly, when we could speak of the problems or issues we were facing in school. To be honest, I wasn't very interested in the problems I was facing at school. I really didn't care. But I worked hard to convince them all that we should have our weekly assembly on Wednesdays. Why Wednesday, you ask? Because that was the day that *MotoSprint*, my favourite motorcycle magazine, hit the newsstands. Thus, while they talked about things such as school lunches, the state of the showers or the curriculum, I could curl up quietly and read *MotoSprint* cover to cover.

By this point it was very obvious to me that I was not going to have a long and successful academic career. It was a slow, pointless slog. And so, when I started racing in the world championship and the demands on my time started to grow even further, becoming increasingly incompatible with schoolwork, I knew it was time to choose. And, unsurprisingly, I chose the bikes. I chose sport. I chose to give it a go.

Besides, the first three races that season were all in the Far East: Malaysia, Indonesia and Japan. They were all on consecutive weekends and I realised that I would lose more or less a whole month of school. My teachers had made it quite obvious that they would not tolerate such a long absence, particularly not in the spring. And so at that point I called a meeting with my parents. We decided together that I would simply collect too many absences and, at the end of the year, I'd be held back anyway. And so I decided to quit school.

Still, it's a shame that I never got my high school degree. On the other hand, there was not much love lost between me and schooling. It's funny though; even after leaving school, for the next three or four years I would often wake up suddenly in the morning, thinking that I had missed the alarm and that I had to hurry off to school.

When I decided to concentrate fully on racing, I also decided to dedicate myself totally, at least in terms of effort. My first exposure to the world championship came at the beginning of 1996, in the tests at Jerez. I was impressed by the other riders. They were all so fast. Kazuto Sakata was terrifying, but the others weren't far behind.

It was very tough for me. During those tests that winter I discovered just how much better the world championship riders were. It was a different world.

Still, competing in the 1995 European championship helped me tremendously. That was the last time that races were held concurrently with the European Grands Prix of the world championship and this gave me two big advantages. First of all, I was able to get to know the tracks and that's nothing to be sniffed at. Second, I got to see the world championship riders up close, studying their style, their decisions on the track and the way they took turns. In short, I tried to figure out just why they were faster than those of us on the European circuit. It was quite depressing because I'd look at their times and then I'd consider my own and see just how far behind I was. There were times when I was as much as four seconds a lap slower. But at least now I had a reference point, something to aim for.

That season, 1995, I had been very fast in the Italian championship, which I easily won with races to spare. The European circuit, however, was much tougher. I fell a bunch of times, and I was slowed by a wrist injury I sustained in training with a motocross bike. Eventually I did manage to grab third place. And that was a virtual passport to the world championship.

That autumn, Gian Piero Sacchi, then sporting director at Aprilia, contacted me via Carlo Pernat. They had some sponsors and were putting together a team for 1996. He wanted two bikes in two different classes: Luca Boscoscuro was all set for 250cc, while the 125cc was destined for me. Sacchi was very good at organising things and he built a solid group. We were known as Team AGV, because that was the main sponsor. Aldo Drudi, who is very talented, did the livery, which was gorgeous: yellow, blue and black. Aprilia had given me the "official" bike from the previous year, the one which Perugini had used. Mauro Noccioli, my engineer, was sure he could make it fly. We were a good team. And we had a lot of fun in that 1996 season. Or rather, I had a lot of fun. That was me at my craziest. I really was an absolute pest. I had no respect for anyone on the track. To me they were all the same, it made no difference if it was a veteran vying for the title, or a debutant like me. I just wanted to go fast, very fast, and if I saw an opening, I went for it. I wanted to overtake everyone, come what may. In other words, I made people uncomfortable.

I was fast, but I made mistakes. Too many times I threw away decent positions. I think I must have fallen fifteen or so times that season. In the very first race, I got into an argument with Jorge Martinez. We were at Shah Alam in Malaysia. I was making my debut and had secured a spot in the third row. I started very well and I'm not sure how, but I somehow found myself alongside the leaders early on. I was cruising along somewhere between seventh and eighth position. At one point, Dirk Raudies was in front of me and Martinez was just behind me. Raudies' engine seized up, and, to avoid him, I instinctively braked, changing trajectory. Martinez was unable to avoid me, hit me, and fell.

That was the year in which Martinez, riding the "official" Aprilia, was heavily favoured in the race for the title. I had just upset one of the darlings, one of the "untouchables" of the world championship. I finished the race in sixth place and was quite pleased. In fact, everyone around me was pleased, we were all celebrating.

Then, suddenly, I came face to face with Martinez and Angel Nieto.

My helmet . . . as you can see I chose the sun and the moon. They represent the two sides of my character. Off the bike, I'm bright and light-hearted. On the bike I'm more dark and aggressive.

Maybe I was dreaming about becoming champion of the world . . .

Top left: My mum always followed me, ever since the earliest races. Even today, we talk all the time when I'm at a race. On the phone, she always tells me to "be good".

One of my favorite races, the British Grand Prix. This was my second "home" race and it was back in 1997, when I was racing 125cc. I was inspired by the legend of Robin Hood.

Minicross was my first passion. But when I started racing mini-motorbikes, which looked like miniature GP bikes, well, that's when I realized I had a passion for speed.

Mugello, Grand Prix of Italy, 2002. One of my best gags ever. That season, they said I only won because I had the fastest bike. After winning in Italy, they gave me a speeding ticket.

Mick Doohan, one of the all-time greats in the 500cc. In 2001, it was my turn to reign at the highest level.

Sea or mountains, for me it
makes little difference, as
long as you have the right
friends and enjoy yourself.
I love being in the water,
under the sun, in summer.
But I also love skiing in winter.

This gag was supposed to be ironic, underscoring my situation with Honda. Everybody expected victory from me. Sol was a condemned man, condemened to win . . .

Malaysian Grand Prix, 2004. After winning the race, "La Rapida", the quick, came onto the scene. "La Rapida" was my maid service. It was a way of poking fun at what happened in Qatar, when my team cleaned my start area.

Opposite: Maranello, April 2004, Fiorano track. That's where I tried the Ferrari F1 for the first time. Schumacher came by in the afternoon, perhaps to check that I hadn't damaged anything . . .

Notice the tattoo of the turtle!

I love football, my favorite club is Inter Milan. When Inter signed Ronaldo, one of my heroes, I just had to go and meet him.

I love going into the pits at night and spending time on my own with my bike. Sometimes I like to check that everything is right where it should be. Including the stickers . . .

Jeremy Burgess and I have a special relationship. We met at the end of 1999. At Honda, we were part of a winning team, most of which we transferred to Yamaha.

"Son of a bitch!" they shouted. "We're going to tear you a new arsehole!"

That's when I realised they probably did not like me very much. So I slipped behind the mechanic, who was a big guy, using him as a shield. The two Spaniards were rabid, they looked as if they wanted to beat me up, so the big mechanic did come in very handy, as a deterrent. But I soon started enjoying the scene, rather than being frightened. The pair of them were absolutely furious, but they also looked so funny, in the way that only short people can look funny when they get really angry. And both of them were tiny, unintimidating in every way. I was not really worried at all.

I was still making many mistakes and not finishing nearly as well as I should have been. But that season I won my first world championship race, at Brno in the Czech Republic. It was a turning point, because from then on, my riding became somewhat more controlled.

Of course, it wasn't an immediate switch. There were still times when I clashed with the rest of the team, precisely because of my riding style. I remember one race at Assen, the Dutch Grand Prix, where I started with intermediate tyres and was twentieth, just after the start. Yet I was driving like a madman, overtaking someone at every single turn and, by the end of the second lap, I was third. I was still not satisfied, though; I really wanted first place. So I kept pushing the bike as hard as I could. At one point, on the final "S-curve", my tyre slipped on to the white line and I fell.

Sacchi and Noccioli had seen enough. They called me into Sacchi's office.

"Look, we simply can't go on like this," Sacchi began, as I listened quietly. "If you learn some discipline, you'll run good races, because you know how to be fast, but you must calm down!"

I thought he was finished. But he wasn't.

"You need to choose who you want to be like," Sacchi added. "If you keep riding like this, at the very best, you might become like [Kevin] Schwantz one day . . . but if you calm down and learn discipline, well, you might even become like Biaggi!"

I felt bad, but I did not answer back. I just thought to myself: "Like Biaggi? Forget that! I'd much rather be like Schwantz . . ."

But, of course, I never told him.

At the time, diplomacy was pretty much an alien concept to me. I usually said what came into my head. I spoke my mind, particularly on certain subjects. And I was incapable of making distinctions. For example, at the time I had not fully understood how to behave with the media, so I regularly got myself into embarrassing situations. I judged others, without really thinking about it. Sometimes journalists came up to me and said, "Hey, did you know that such-and-such rider said these horrible things about you?"

And I wasn't exactly restrained. I always answered back. They all laughed and loved it, because I was always good for a line. I laughed too. The difference is that, once they finished laughing, the journalists went away and wrote my words in their computers and, soon thereafter, they ended up in the newspapers.

I was too outspoken. Too direct. And that's how my long-running feud with Biaggi began.

SIX

CAPITOLO SEI

My feud with Max Biaggi began in 2000, as soon as I made the step up to 500cc. Or, rather, my *on-track* feud with Biaggi began in 2000. My first actual run-in with him dates back to 1996, in the paddock. But from 2000 onwards, we would be competing elbow-to-elbow, at every single race.

Biaggi and I never really talk to each other. I mean, we've never had a real conversation, anything that's lasted more than the requisite time to insult each other or put each other down, in the nastiest way possible. In any case, I don't hate him. It's true, we've never been friends, but hatred is something different, and that's too serious a word to describe our relationship. Far too serious. No, we have a reciprocal antipathy. No doubt this is a result of what we do for a living and the fact that we both want to win every single time. And perhaps it's also a function of the fact that we have very different personalities and very different ways of seeing things. Still, I don't think this means we hate each other, as some journalists have written. I think I could feel hatred for someone, but only for something far worse than anything Biaggi has done. For example, if I were betrayed by a friend, then, yes, I could hate him.

But Biaggi will never betray my friendship for the simple reason that we are not, and never have been, friends. Our relationship is very clear: we compete on the track – outside the track, each goes his own way. You could say we detest each other cordially. Well, not always cordially: once we even got into a fistfight.

It happened in Barcelona, in 2001. It was the year that our relations sunk to a new low. Over time, the cutting remarks and little jibes had grown into major insults and, when I moved to 500cc, the competition between us moved on to the track. We went head-to-head amid a spiralling crescendo of tension.

If you want to know where it all started, I must admit that I started it all, I cast the first stone. But then he's the one who continued the feud and took it to a new level. I have a reputation as someone who is a troublemaker, someone who picks fights and arguments. This reputation is largely due to the fact that, when I made my debut in the world championships I regularly provoked Biaggi. And, at the time, Biaggi was untouchable, the golden boy of motorbike racing. But not to me.

The funny thing is that a few years earlier, when I was fourteen, I had had a poster of Biaggi in my room. It was one of many posters on my bedroom wall and it showed Biaggi on the Honda 250. Nothing strange in that: he was Italian and I supported all the Italian riders. Besides, he was an aggressive rider and I always had a lot of respect for those riders who went on the attack. But, back then, I did not know him personally. It was only when I started to listen to his interviews and read what he said in the papers that my opinion changed. With Biaggi, no matter what happened, it never seemed to be his fault, there was always something wrong with the bike or the tyres. I thought he said a lot of things that I believed simply couldn't be true. As soon as I got to the world championships, I said what I thought of him. I gave an interview where I said I did not like Biaggi, that I had a certain antipathy for him. I did not see anything wrong with this, not at the time. But my words were cleverly used by the press to create a rivalry that allowed them to publish all sorts of headlines and, consequently, sell more papers. These rivalries are constructed ad hoc, by newspapers hungry for stories from the circuits. The truth is, our rivalry was fuelled by such reports. Because it was in everyone's interest to have this massive rivalry. It served the interests of the fans, the press, the whole racing world. Because, frankly, it generated headlines, column inches and interest from the fans.

I may not have been diplomatic in expressing my impressions of Biaggi's attitude, but things rapidly escalated. In 1999, in Malaysia, at Sepang, I suffered a very bad fall on the 250cc. The bike was trashed and I would have to walk back to the pits. Biaggi was passing by and stopped a few metres away.

"Hop on!" he said, gesturing with his head.

I accepted the lift and he took me to back to the pits. At the time I was a little naive. I thought it was a nice gesture, an altruistic gesture. But then this episode was reported so as to make me appear ungrateful. It was as if they were saying: see, he helped Rossi out and gave him a lift back and now Rossi treats him like crap . . .

As I see it, the spark that lit the blue touchpaper was a little too much sincerity. All I did was speak the truth, at least as it was in my mind. And that was a mistake. Over time I understood that it doesn't pay to be truthful, not in our world. But I was – and still am – like that. I tend to say what I think. I still believe this is a positive trait, but, as I discovered, in certain circles it's also a bad trait. In any case, Biaggi was idolised in the mid-1990s. He was number one, in every sense, for the Italian press. I can imagine then how unpleasant it must have been, for someone in his position, to hear a debutant put him down. But at the time I was just seventeen and didn't worry about this sort of thing.

According to the "official" version, the genesis of our conflict dates back to the Malaysian Grand Prix in 1997. It was my second year in the world championship. We were racing at the Shah Alam track, just outside the capital, Kuala Lumpur. On Saturday I won the pole; on Sunday I won the 125cc, while Biaggi won the 250cc. He was making his debut on the Honda, after winning three world titles with Aprilia and going through a rough separation from the Noale plant team, and thus his win was huge news in Italy. And yet, the press decided to devote some attention to me as well.

"Do you want to become the Biaggi of 125?" they asked me, knowing full well that it was one of those questions that was bound to cause controversy, no matter what the answer.

"I'm sorry but I think that, at best, it's going to be him who dreams of being the Rossi of 250!" I replied, throwing petrol on the open fire.

The press loved it and went to town with it. This only fuelled the rivalry. Biaggi was offended. After the race, we moved on to Japan. The day before testing I was sitting at the track restaurant in Suzuka, together with some Italian journalists. Biaggi showed up and, as soon as he saw me, he walked towards me, as if he was trying to intimidate me.

"Before talking about me, you should wash out your mouth!" he said. Those were his exact words.

For once, I was the one who stayed calm, who played the good boy and bit his tongue. He was the one who added to the controversy. I did not expect that reaction from him. I looked him in the eye but did not say a thing. After all I was eighteen, he was twenty-six. But from there things got steadily worse between us. At the start of the 2000 season, in winter, I had moved up to 500cc and Biaggi, in a magazine interview had said: "Rossi is with the big boys now, he's up in 500cc, he'll have to taken on real riders now."

Yes, I suppose he had evidently forgotten about all Rossi's time in 250cc, when he was racing against "imaginary" opponents!

In any case, he added: "Now he's going to have to take all his masks and put them back in to his closet, he can no longer play the clown."

It felt as if everything between us had become this endless back and forth. And by 2001, things had gotten really ugly. Part of it was that everybody expected the two of us to compete for the title. Just the two of us, Biaggi and Rossi. And then, at Suzuka, Biaggi elbowed me on the straightaway, at 220 kilometres per hour. This was an incredibly severe action, one that I consider unforgivable.

Suzuka is not the place to do certain things. It's one of those tracks where you run massive risks even if you're very careful, let alone if you start throwing your elbows around at 220kph. Suzuka is a very fast track the whole way round. In addition, at the time, the chicane prior to the arrival straightaway was designed in such a way that you were going downhill . . . in other words, it wasn't one of those chicanes that forces you to slow down; quite the contrary.

Biaggi was just in front of me when we arrived at the chicane. He didn't want me to pass him as we came out of the "S", so he delayed his braking, as he figured I would try to sneak by on the inside. By braking late, he was hoping to close the door on me. Instead, I crossed his line and was able to open the throttle sooner and accelerate away. I could do this because he waited too long to brake and thus was in serious difficulty coming out of the "S". So by the time we hit the straightaway, I was just about to pass him.

He heard the sound of my motorcycle arriving from the outside. When I pulled alongside him, he looked at me and then he elbowed me. I will always believe that he elbowed me to shove me off the track. I kept control, but raced a long stretch of the straightaway on grass, at 220kph, and I can tell you it was quite a feat just avoiding a fall.

I lost several positions, obviously, but all I could think about was how angry I was at what he had done to me, at such high speeds. In a race you can be aggressive, but there have to be limits.

Still, I managed to calm myself down. After the initial adrenalin spike, not to mention the rush of blood to my brain, I moved back up the track, passing several riders and, before I knew it, I was right behind Biaggi. I passed him on a big, fast right-hand turn and, as I came out of it, I lifted my left hand from the handlebar and gave him the middle finger. It was my way of letting him know how I felt about what he had done.

I won the race, because, after passing him, I was determined not to concede an inch. But the controversy continued at the finish line.

"I didn't do anything," he shouted as soon as I confronted him verbally.

"Oh, no? All you did was toss me against a wall at two hundred kilometres per hour!" I shouted.

"What the hell are you saying?" he snapped.

"Look, next time you feel like doing something like that, just grab a gun and shoot me," I replied. "It will be a lot quicker."

This back-and-forth continued right up into the press conference room as the tension between us escalated. Then we each went off separately.

Today, just like the moment I did it, I see nothing wrong with what I did. Sure, that raised middle finger was a far from elegant gesture, but in my view Biaggi had put my life at risk. So I was understandably both tense and angry. And yet, when I look back, I still think it was one of the most beautiful moments of my career.

The Italian press, however, felt the need to put my "vulgar gesture" and his attempt at intimidating me on the same level. Several journalists wrote that I had behaved like a madman, like a hooligan.

This moralism, in my opinion, was uncalled for. The two things simply could not be compared. One may have been vulgar, but it certainly wasn't dangerous. And yet, instead of asking themselves if Biaggi's move was legitimate, if his elbow should be censured, all that some papers could focus on was my middle finger. Still others bought Biaggi's argument lock, stock and barrel, arguing that it was all actually my fault. They insisted that Biaggi had lashed out with his elbow for safety reasons. My attempt at overtaking was dangerous and he had to intervene so that the handlebars would not get tangled up. Incredible!

And this was at Suzuka, the beginning of the season. You can imagine how tense things had got by the time we made it to Barcelona. We were peppering each other, on and off the track. We were quite close in the table as we arrived in Barcelona, though I was ahead of him. I had won the first three races: in Japan, South Africa (Welkom) and Spain (Jerez). He had won in France. And at Mugello, I had fallen on the wet track, in the very last lap. He had finished third, gaining some valuable points. There was no question, then, that Barcelona was going to be a tricky race. I simply could not afford to make a mistake.

I won pole position. Because I was so fast, I thought I wouldn't have any problems during the race. Boy, was I wrong. I created my own problems. My start was terrible and, at the first turn, I found myself stuck in tenth place, amid a whole group of nervous riders. Gibernau attacked Alex Crivillé, who had to straighten up to avoid falling. Alas, as Crivillé straightened, he "straightened" me as well, as I was right next to him. Thus, the two of us went through the first turn straddling the white line, and suddenly our only concern was trying not to fall. To give you an idea of how bad it was, when we came out of the turn, the Sabre was ahead of me!

"What the hell kind of way is this to start a race?!" I thought to myself, basically insulting myself, for there was nobody else to blame.

But I set off in hot pursuit. I wanted to win and could not accept that I was going to lose because of such a poor start. Brake after brake, turn after turn, I passed all of them, every single one, until I came to Biaggi. I overtook him too, without too many problems, but then I made a mistake on a crucial turn. I was a little wide, I left the door open, and he raced past me. After two more laps, however, I caught him and passed him once again. This time, I made no mistakes. I left him behind and won the race.

It had been a fantastic Grand Prix for me. And a terrible one for him. Boy, did he pay for his mistakes. After the race, we found our-selves near the finish line, in the sectioned-off area where riders leave their bikes. He was absolutely furious, whereas I was happy, very happy. So happy that I immediately started celebrating with my friends and everyone around me.

These days it would not have happened that way. Today, the top three finishers are immediately sequestered by the race officials and kept away until the awards ceremony. But, back then, we were all together in a room, surrounded by tons of people, far more than are allowed in now. And, in fact, the protocol was changed as a direct result of what happened that day at Montmelo. There was a huge crush of people surrounding me: mechanics, managers, friends, cameramen. Lots and lots of people making lots and lots of noise. When I saw Gibo, we celebrated together. At one point, the Dorna officials told us it was time to go up to the podium. To get there, you had to go up this rather narrow staircase. Biaggi wanted to get up there as quickly as possible, but with the huge crowd of people there, it was far from easy. His path was partly blocked by a cameraman, Biaggi barged past him, only to find Gibo in front of him, with his back turned. So Biaggi elbowed him squarely in the back and slipped past. Gibo shouted at him, at which point Biaggi turned and shoved him again.

"What the fuck are you doing?" I shouted, as he went up the stairs.

"You want some?" he said, turning towards me. "Come right up, there's plenty for you as well!"

"Great, I'll be right there!" I said, accepting his challenge.

And that was the point of no return. I rushed up the stairs. Biaggi was waiting for me at the top. His eyes were red, he was furious. I'd never seen him like this. There were slaps and punches. People screaming. Carlo Fiorani, who at the time was my team manager, burst onto the scene and divided us.

That's where it ended, because the Dorna guys pushed us straight out on to the podium. We were a little late and, when we stepped out in front of the crowd, we were both shaken up and out of breath, our faces all red and our hair dishevelled. Still, we had a role to play. After the awards ceremony, we faced the press. We both tried very hard to appear calm, as if nothing had happened. As we leaned towards our microphones, however, people could tell that our faces were all red.

"Tough race, eh?" said one journalist, his gaze penetrating both of us.

"Oh yes, very tough!" I said, nodding along. As my head bobbed up and down I was thinking, "Forget the race, what was tough was the fact that we had just been in a fistfight!"

Nobody in the room seemed to be aware of what had just happened. Looking back, I suspect some of them must have sensed something was wrong, because we had made lots of noise. Still, the journalists didn't seem to have a clear picture of what had gone on.

"What's that?" another journalist asked Biaggi, pointing to a mark on his cheekbone.

"Mosquito bite," he snapped, not elaborating.

The press conference went by without any more hiccups, nobody asked any more questions about our condition and we avoided bringing up anything controversial. Immediately afterwards, however, Biaggi and I, together with our respective managers, were summoned by the race stewards. I was with Fiorani, while Biaggi was accompanied by Lin Jarvis.

"OK, now you're going to tell us exactly what happened," the stewards said to us.

They wanted our version of events. And both of us did just that, each giving his side of the story. Then they told us they would be meeting to decide if we should be punished and, if so, what sanctions we would face. And they left us there, in that room, the four of us. We faced each other and were totally mute, nobody felt like saying anything. It was a surreal situation.

The silence was embarrassing and the tension just mounted. Fiorani, wanting to lighten the mood, turned to Biaggi and tried to talk football.

"So," he asked. "How did Roma do today?"

"I don't know!" Biaggi growled, without even looking up.

"Oh, great, wonderful!" Fiorani said, as silence descended once again.

I felt like bursting out laughing, but I knew that would have been a very bad idea. And yet, it was hilarious. To avoid cracking up, I shoved my hand in my mouth and clenched my jaw.

What the hell was Biaggi doing? As if he didn't know about AS Roma! That day Roma had won the *scudetto*. Even I knew that. And Biaggi came up on the podium with a red-and-yellow bandanna, Roma's colours, in honour of the new Serie A champions. In fact, he was still wearing it! It was clear that Biaggi had absolutely no intention of talking to Fiorani, but, fortunately, the uneasy silence was quickly broken by the stewards, returning to the room with news of our reprimand.

"All right, neither of you will be punished this time," they said. "But you must not tell the press about this. We have to keep it quiet. If anybody asks you, play it down. And please, next time, behave!"

"Certainly, thank you, sir," we both said. And we agreed, we would not tell the press.

Except they were just outside, waiting for us. They were all bunched together like a pack, hungry for news and anecdotes. They wanted the big story and the big quotes. It was easy to see that by that point, word had gotten out. They knew what had happened, they just did not know the details. The RAI crew, who were next to us when it all kicked off, had not seen anything, but they had heard us *and* they had the audio on tape.

"Well, we exchanged viewpoints and opinions and we were a little bit passionate, but that's it, nothing serious," I said to the press. In other words, I did what I had been told to do, I played it down, I glossed over it.

Biaggi, on the other hand, told them everything in great detail. He told them that I had pushed him and then attacked him. So, once again, for the umpteenth time, I was the bad guy, it was all my fault. In the Italian press I was once again depicted as the spoiled little kid who couldn't help but pick a fight.

Still, the altercation in Barcelona was not what definitively killed any remaining rapport with Biaggi. What really caused us to hit rock-bottom occurred in Holland, in the very next race. When we arrived in Assen, Honda basically forced us to kiss and make up. They wanted to put the events of Barcelona behind us, once and for all. And so they organised a meeting where Biaggi and I would shake hands in front of everyone. Which meant we would seal our peace in front of journalists and photographers.

Neither one of us wanted to do it. But the Dorna guys were very insistent, to the point that I told myself, "Well, if they're going to keep busting my balls like this, I'll shake his hand so that these guys can be happy and they'll leave us alone. Besides, we can continue to detest each other privately."

Still, when I shook his hand I was relatively sincere. He, on the other hand, was very sweet and friendly and said very nice things when the press was around, but when it came time to shake on it, he didn't even look me in the eye.

"Whatever, it's not a big deal," I thought to myself.

The following day, we bumped into each other at the track. We were both on our own and both on foot.

"Hello!" I said.

He ignored me.

"All right, that's fine," I told myself. "If that's how you want it to be, I guess we're done. We're finished, you and me."

And that was it.

At the time, I did not think it was such a big deal. After all, we had never gotten along, never been close, so not much was going to change. I don't think there's anything wrong with that. Who says you have to get along with everyone? Antipathy is normal, it's a human emotion and not just on the track.

Even over time, we've done very little to make up. Both on the track and off it. Still, after my initial verbal salvos, he's the one who has been doing most of the talking, attacking me much more than I've attacked him.

Of course, on the track we continued to annoy each other. And our rivalry climaxed in 2000 and 2001. True, we tangled after that as well, but it was never as nasty or as intense in those two seasons we spent racing 500cc.

Sometimes it was minor stuff, sometimes it was quite serious. Very often we each did things to intimidate and irritate the other. He has always been one of those riders who'll suddenly come very close, at high speeds, when you least expect it. You're cruising along slowly, maybe because you're on your way back to the pits and, all of a sudden, he'll be all over you, at 200kph. He has always done that. And he's done it with everyone, not just with me. And it's really annoying. He enjoys doing it while going very fast, especially when you're heading back after the test lap and you're unprepared. At Donington, in 2002, he even did it during my lap of honour. I had won the race and was celebrating, sitting sideways on the bike and he zipped right up to me. He loves this kind of bullshit, and he's not the only rider who thinks these shenanigans are useful. The problem is that this type of skullduggery really does not affect me either way. Maybe it bothers other riders, but not me. And yet, I would have thought that I had proved to him, at Suzuka in 2001, that nobody can intimidate me.

At times, I proved it to him during the tests. Often I just ignored him, other times I accepted his challenge. And, once, during the 2000 season, I really had a lot of fun doing it. We were in Japan, at Motegi. After the day's tests, he did his usual routine as I returned to the pits, brushing up against me all of a sudden.

Instead of letting him go, this time I hit the gas and raced after him. I saw him a little further up the track. He had stopped, because he wanted to test his starting mechanism. I slowed down, went into neutral, so that I'd be totally quiet, and bumped him from behind. My front tyre hit his rear tyre. It was a good, solid hit and it was also unexpected. He spun around and looked at me. I was motionless, my arm raised, the palm of my hand open, and I waved to him, as if to say "Bye-bye."

He took off and I followed him. I caught up with him on the straightaway, just before the tunnel. Once again, he wanted to test something to do with the starting mechanism, without anyone disturbing him.

I slowed down and – bam! – I hit his rear tyre once again, just like before. He whirled around and, again, I waved to him. He did not react, we simply went back to the pits and that was the end of it. If somebody wants to joke around, I'm happy to react. I'll quickly sink to their level, because I never hold back, on the track or off it. So if Biaggi enjoyed playing these games, well, I would play them too.

What's more, it's not as if he limited his tricks and games to the track. Oh, no! He loved to do these things in the paddock as well, using his scooter. I'll never forget the time in Jerez, in 2000, when I was on a scooter with Alby, a friend of mine, Alberto Tebaldi, and we were taking a box filled with fairings that had been coloured at home. That season, the fairings were painted by Aldo Drudi and Roby. I took them to the track in the motorhome and gave them to Jeremy, who had the mechanics fit them. That time, on the scooter, we were in a somewhat precarious situation, because there were two of us. I was in front and I held in my hands the bubble and other accessories. Biaggi saw us and went for us, at full throttle. He was so close, we shook for many metres – though we did not fall, I'm proud to say, and neither did we drop the material we were carrying. We avoided a potential disaster.

As I said, many riders engage in these games. I learned some of them from Jorge Martinez. He and I had a great rivalry back in 125cc. Martinez was great at breaking and he was also very clever. He had a whole bag of tricks. At first, we really did not like each other. I only began to appreciate his company after he retired. Martinez is much older than me, so at first I was the inexperienced kid and he was the grizzled veteran.

One of the things I most hated among his little games was his habit of blocking off my trajectory on the fast laps. He did whatever he could to hinder me. At the Open Ducados in 1995 we were in Cartagena, a few days after an epic race at Jerez, in which I had grabbed the lead but was then forced to relinquish it when my tyre fell apart. It was Martinez who rescued me by the side of the track, before going on to win the race.

This time, in Cartagena, we were side by side in the third row of the grid. He said, "OK, kid, slow down, make sure you don't fall over . . ."

I could have impaled him on his bike.

"I'll show you," I said, almost in a whisper.

We both started badly. We fell behind, but began to make up ground. I overtook three riders and was in the lead after three laps. Shortly thereafter, however, I fell and – surprise, surprise – Martinez won.

The next race was at Misano, my home turf. I did exactly what he had done in Cartagena.

"Good luck, son!" I said. "Just don't get too carried away."

I said this on the starting grid, after giving him a big pat on the back. He gave me a rotten look. And I won the race. Nothing new there, then.

During the 1996 World Championship, I learned a lot of things. In particular, I learned that I did, in fact, have the ability to eventually triumph and win the championship. And I knew it was what I wanted to do, above all else. I loved 125cc and I wanted to come full circle, completing the journey which had begun in Sport Production. After 1996, Carlo Pernat decided to back me once again. He wanted me to have the best possible bike, so we stayed with Team AGV, with Sacchi and Noccioli, although as a sweetener Pernat was able to get me the "official" Aprilia bike.

I could feel that it was going to be my year. That was why I didn't really consider jumping to 250cc straight away (that was another option I had: Aprilia had offered me a spot in 250cc and on the "official" bike no less).

"You're tall, you're strong enough, you're much more suited to 250cc," Pernat said. "Why don't you leave 125cc and step up right away, racing 250cc next year?"

Graziano agreed with him, but I felt differently. And I explained just why I had no intention of moving up.

"Look, I had the world title within my grasp last season and now you want me to leave?" I said, wanting to make a point, but also looking to provoke them a little.

"You're right, but if you get a year of experience under your belt in the 250cc, you may get the official 250 bike in '98 and, at that point, you could win the world title in 250cc," Pernat replied, illustrating Aprilia's plans.

"Yes, but why would I do that?" I said. "I want to win 125cc first. I'm not going to 250cc, unless I become world champion at 125cc first."

I made it very clear there was no room for negotiation on this point; my mind was made up. I didn't budge on that issue back then, and I wouldn't budge on it now. I think a rider needs to take one step at a time. If you have the chance to win a title, you need to try, really strive to achieve that aim, before moving up to the next level. At least, that's how I wanted to do things. And I remained consistent, because years later, when Honda wanted me to move to 500cc when I still had not won the 250cc title, I was just as stubborn: I would only move to the next level once I had conquered the level I was at.

So I stayed at 125cc. And it was the right choice. The following campaign I was absolutely dominant. I won on dry tracks, wet tracks, every kind of track. One of the best races that year – come to think of it, one of the best races ever in 125cc – was at the Dutch Grand Prix at Assen. It was quite chilly before the race, so I started with carbon brake-covers. Then the temperature changed, it became warmer, causing the brake to "swell" to the point that the lever was actually touching the handle.

Back then, the brake balance was not directly on the handle, it was positioned in the dashboard area. I did not want to step off the gas, because I did not want to lose touch with my opponents, so I tried to fix the register with my left hand. I did this for three or four laps, but to no avail. In fact, during one of my attempts, my glove got stuck on the dashboard and, on the next turn, I was in danger of losing control of the bike. That's when I got fed up. I eased off the gas, slowing down suddenly, took my hand off the gas entirely and fixed the brake lever. I had obviously lost a lot of time, because I had nearly slowed down to a halt, but when I started up again, I was like a wild man. Halfway through the last lap I caught up with the group, grabbing fourth place and, eventually, passing everybody, crossing the finish line before everyone else. I had won!

Everything came so easy to me, back in 1997. I had learned my lessons, I handled the bike well and, most of all, I handled myself well during the race. That season I started to become very popular in Italy. You could call it Rossi-mania. I think it was partly due to my victories, partly due to the way I celebrated them. Either way I had become . . . Valentino Rossi, the star. That's when my gags, my little flourishes which allowed me to lighten the mood in a world which often took itself much too seriously, really started to take hold. I should point out that, while they may seem spontaneous, each of my gags is meticulously planned and prepared beforehand, so that I can execute them quickly, precisely and flawlessly. I think up many of them myself, others are the fruits of my friends' labour. When we plan out our little skits, we think of everything: if I win, we meet in such-and-such place at such-and-such time, if I finish second, we don't do anything.

Things have changed somewhat over the years. At the beginning, the gags originated at the sports bar in Tavullia, which belonged to my friend Pedro, who now owns a restaurant, also in Tavullia. At the time we were kids, and the village bar was like our second home. We always met there and that's where the gags were born. Every night, when the bar emptied, we stayed for hours talking about everything and nothing. The seed of each idea was planted there. That's when the idea of the inflatable doll originated, for example. But as we got older, the conception and planning became the domain of myself and Flavio Fratesi, my trusty partner in crime when it comes to celebratory gags and T-shirts. Any one of my friends might come up with the concept, but it's the two of us who actually go and execute it.

In the first few years on the world circuit we did them all the time, and then later on, little by little, they became less frequent. I suppose it's partly because, as you get older, you begin to change. And, partly, as the years go by, it's tougher to come up with the kind of brilliant, hilarious ideas that make people laugh. And it all starts with an idea, an intuition, which is something you can't go and buy in a store or from a catalogue. It has to come to you. And it doesn't come at every race. That's why it was decided that I would only do things that had a certain symbolism. And, most of all, I would only do it if I actually won the race. That was something I decided after the Italian Grand Prix in 1998. At Mugello, I was in the 250cc category; the race was won by Marcellino Lucchi. Prior to the race, I had planned to go to the podium as if I were going to the beach: bathing suit, sunglasses, beach towel around my neck. Doing it even though I had not won was a big mistake.

At the time I did not realise it, because I was very happy, since I had beaten Capirossi and Tetsuya Harada, my true rivals. And so I thought it would be fun to celebrate anyway, and I performed my little routine, stepping up to the podium as if I were strolling down to the beach.

The next day, when I read the newspapers, I saw that everyone was disappointed in me. They said that I had been unfair to Lucchi. He was forty-three and did not win many races. This was his moment in the sun, his big day. And I had unwittingly upstaged him. I did not mean to do this, of course. In my mind, I just wanted to celebrate and make people laugh. And yet the newspapers claimed that, because I had to always be the centre of attention, I had robbed Lucchi of his big moment.

"Enough, I should only do these things if I win," I told myself. I was very upset by the whole thing and the fact that the press went on and on about it.

Before the 2004 world championship I started planning some kind of celebration, or a new gag, just in case I won straight away, at the very first race. But then, I decided not to plan anything. So what I did at Welkom was entirely spontaneous. If you're reading this book, you've probably seen or read about what I did. I got off the bike, leaned her against a wall and sat down on the grass. I then got up and kissed her – my bike, I mean – on the "bubble". It was completely unplanned.

In fact, I shouldn't even be talking about it in this section of the book, amid the stories of my gags and celebrations. It was really a very intense and personal moment. So much tension and pressure had built up that when it was over, I felt like I had to release all the emotions that had amassed inside my psyche. So it was instinct that made me stop and kiss my bike. And it was an extraordinary scene, to mark an extraordinary occasion. Gags and skits, that's something entirely different. They're planned and programmed to the slightest detail; there is no improvisation. We arrive at the track knowing full well exactly what we're going to do. That's why Welkom was nothing like Sepang or Philip Island. Those were places where I knew exactly what I wanted to do, where I wanted to make a certain point. "La Rapida", in Malaysia, was a way of commenting with irony on something which was . . . not quite clean. And the shirt that read "Che spettacolo!" ("What a spectacle!") was to celebrate a feat which was . . . spectacular.

You see, these shirts are not easy to make. They can't be banal, I don't do banal, ever. At the same time, it's not easy to be original every time. But the "Che spettacolo!" T-shirt was the result of a dream, believe it or not. It wasn't something I had thought of. It had literally come to me while I was asleep. It was in 2004, towards the end of the summer, when I could really start thinking of winning the world title. One night, I was asleep at home in bed, when the podium of the Australian Grand Prix appeared to me in my dream. I was there,

celebrating, and I was wearing a shirt which read "Che spettacolo!" That dream had a big impact on me, because I hardly ever dream of motorbikes or races. I did not tell anyone about the dream. But, after the Malaysian Grand Prix, I was with Gibo and Uccio and I said: "I've thought of what T-shirt I want when I become world champion."

My words were met with silence. Because when you get to the point that you can start planning what you'll do if you win the title, you're already in an incredibly clear and unbelievably strong position. I had won in Sepang, we were on our way to Australia and spirits were high. Gibo and Uccio knew what my words meant. Indeed, we did win the crown at Philip Island.

Flavio had left straight away, back to Italy. He only had a few days to make the shirt, before having to set off immediately, all the way back to Melbourne. It was going to be a gruelling trip, but one which was worthwhile. And anyway the boys in my Fan Club are willing to go through anything and everything, when it comes to organising such important events.

The Fan Club started up before my first race in the Italian 125 championship, back in 1995, at Misano. That was the first time that a group of people left Tavullia and came to the track to see me race. Granted, it wasn't much of an away trip. Misano is about a ten-minute drive from Tavullia, but, for me, it was still special. Besides, that race is one which I will never forget. I made a mistake at the start and found myself in last place on the very first lap. Undeterred, I pressed on and passed every single rider until I was behind Lucio Cecchinello, who was leading the race. He fell and I went on to win. It was a great victory for me and for those who travelled from Tavullia to see me. They had so much fun celebrating that my Fan Club was born then and there.

Anyway, it was in Sepang, after the race, that I began to explain to

Uccio and Gibo just how I wanted the T-shirt which I would wear at Philip Island.

"It needs to be white, with just two words, 'Che spettacolo'," I said. "Nothing else, no logos, no design, no mention of the fact that I am world champion once again. Just those two words."

They looked me with a bit of amazement and didn't say anything.

"Nobody expects me to come out with a shirt like that!" I said, by way of explanation. They knew me well enough that this was reason enough to do it. And even though they were surprised (and maybe even a little disappointed at first), they soon understood what I was trying to do. To be honest, I didn't even want my number, 46, to be printed on the shirt, but in the end it was there. After all, it's my number, I couldn't just leave it out.

The "La Rapida" gag, when we pretended we were part of a cleaning crew, came to me just a few hours after the Qatar Grand Prix. I was still in the hotel with Uccio. We were watching Italian television via satellite, waiting to make our way to the airport to fly home. When I left for Doha I had no idea that I would be returning so soon. But I was angry and disappointed over what had happened, Honda having lodged an appeal because Jeremy had dusted off my start area, and I felt the need to pick myself up. I had two big races ahead of me – the Grands Prix of Malaysia and Australia – so I decided to go home, back to Italy, to rest and prepare. But as I sat there in the hotel, watching the flickering TV to pass the time, the whole concept of "La Rapida" came to me.

"That's it, if I win in Sepang next week, I'm going to start cleaning the track!" I thought to myself.

I had injured my hand during a fall in Qatar, and I had to get it treated. It was after getting my hand seen to, back in Italy, when I grabbed the phone and called Drudi.

"I need to see you," I said.

I could tell he suspected something was up. Because, without me mentioning anything, he immediately said: "I too have an idea. Let's compare notes and see whose is better."

And so we went to dinner, feasting on fish in a restaurant on the coast of Romagna. Amazingly, we were on the exact same wavelength. In fact, we'd pretty much had the same idea. And that's how "La Rapida" was born. As always, I summoned Flavio Fratesi, my partner in crime and chief choreographer. We always rehearse the skits ahead of time, just the two of us. He's the only one who can correctly realise the shirt, both graphically and in terms of content. Of course, it's convenient that he has a company which does just that – making T-shirts. With the "La Rapida" shirts, it was my friend Aldo who designed it, but Flavio who actually produced it. Only two copies were ever made, one for me, one for Jeremy. Oh, and, according to our superstition, nobody was allowed to see it ahead of time, except for Flavio and me. Otherwise, we believe it's jinxed and, not only will the gag fall flat, I might not even win the race.

I have a personal mental podium of my best gags. Without question, Pollo Osvaldo (Osvaldo the Chicken) has got to be up there. In fact, the Jerez Toilet Pit Stop is probably number one, but I put Osvaldo the Chicken and the Tavullia traffic cops right up there alongside it. And, naturally, I also enjoyed the first true gag, the inflatable doll. The whole concept of the inflatable doll began – where else? – at the sports bar in Tavullia. We needed to think about celebrations for my possible victory in the upcoming Imola 125cc Grand Prix (this was back in 1996). And, to be fair, I did have a very good chance to win at Imola. But as I didn't win, we kept the doll concept hidden away. The year 1996 was my debut year in the world championship and my friends and I kept track of everything that occurred on the world circuit. We studied the other pilots, the way they raced and the way they interacted with others, whether riders, the press or fans. The more we thought about it, the more we realised that too many of them were boring, unremarkable, conformist.

"How boring, they win and then all they do is wander around with their country's flag!" we said. "Why don't we do something nobody has ever seen in motorcycling?"

And so we started to think of strange things, things you don't get to see too often. And then somebody blurted it out and we were all in agreement.

"Yes! Let's get an inflatable doll!" we all shouted in unison. We were all very enthusiastic at the idea.

And so we sprang into action. A delegation of us set off for Misano's one and only sex shop. We were a little shy as we entered, even though we were all more or less of age (well, some of us less so: I was still only seventeen years old). And, once we arrived, we realised we were all somewhat embarrassed.

"Excuse me, sir, we would like to purchase an inflatable sex doll," one of us said, trying to sound as polite, adult and formal as possible.

"You see, we're playing a practical joke and . . . " I piped up, trying to be helpful.

"Oh, yes, of course," the owner said, giving us a look of pity. "Funny how they all say that. OK, guys, whatever you say . . . you need it for a joke . . . "

It was obvious he did not believe us, and he thought we were a bunch of pathetic teenage losers who needed the doll for rather different purposes.

"Look, sir, we really do need the doll for a joke," we replied, all of us rather annoyed. "You're badly mistaken, we're planning a practical joke and —"

"Sure, a joke, never heard that one before," he repeated. "But whatever! Who am I to judge. Here's your doll . . . enjoy!"

I supposed he didn't really care what we did with the doll. We left the sex shop with our new inflatable friend. She would make her debut at Mugello in 1997 and create quite a stir, not least because the media speculated that we were having a dig at Biaggi, who had recently been seen with Naomi Campbell.

What caused some confusion was the name we chose for the doll: Claudia Schiffer. Except that in this case, you were supposed to pronounce it "Skiffer". In Italian, "skiffer" sounds like "schifo" which means "gross' or "disgusting". This was a mistake, because some people misinterpreted our pun. Without any intention on our part the media instantly associated Schiffer with Biaggi, especially because he had announced that Naomi Campbell would be among his guests at Mugello. When the press asked me what I thought about it, I said: "Well, Claudia Schiffer will be among my guests!" This certainly did not do much for my relationship with Biaggi.

Which brings me to my all-time greatest gag. For me, it sits at the top of the podium, possibly because it's also the only one that wasn't planned and organised very far in advance. Everything to do with this gag happened there and then, at Jerez, at the 250cc Spanish Grand Prix in 1999.

To go into the portable toilet was my idea. It came to me while playing football. That's right, football. At the time, I was in the habit of taking a leisurely lap around the track on the Thursday before the race, usually on a bicycle or on roller skates. On that occasion, together with Michele, Uccio and Albi, I decided to go around the track playing football. We passed, crossed and dribbled our way around until we arrived at the point where the track becomes a sort of football stadium, with the stands enveloping the track. Right in the middle of it, by the track,

117

there was a Portaloo, or portable toilet, the kind you might see on a building site. I thought it was weird, because it seemed totally out of place. There was the hill on top and the two ridges on either side and the portable toilet did not seem to have any business being there. But then I imagined the crowd, huddled on the three sides, looking down at it and I thought to myself: "That's it, on Sunday I'm stopping here and going inside."

I didn't tell anyone, I only focused on preparing for the race.

And, on Sunday, I won. On my victory lap I stopped right near the portable loo and leaned the bike against the wall. The crowd was clapping and shouting, they were really loud, I think they thought I was going to climb the hill towards them, the way a footballer might run towards the fans to celebrate a goal. Instead, I turned and walked towards the loo. The crowd was going wild, they had no idea what I was doing. And then I stepped inside. For an instant, silence descended on the track, as if God had pressed the cosmic mute button. In the toilet, I couldn't hear a thing. And it was wonderful. It only lasted a second or two, but it was incredible. I stepped out and the crowd, once again, went nuts, louder than before.

It was beautiful. Unforgettable. It was the greatest idea I have ever had. So many people around the world who perhaps were not really motorbike fans nevertheless talked about what happened that day. And they still talk about it now, years later.

You know, that's the whole spirit of my gags: to make people laugh, to help them have fun. That's why I always chose to do simple things, which were easy to understand and which could get an immediate reaction. As a rule, the gag or skit has to last no more than a few seconds and it should get laughs straight away. Equally, it should have some basic significance; it should be linked in some way to an event that everyone can relate to. For example, at Mugello in 2004, I showed up with a helmet decorated like a wooden medal. It did not quite work out the way we planned it, but it was cool regardless. I had finished fourth two races in a row, which, for me, is unusual. Many started saying that I was a "racer in crisis" and that all the problems which the experts had predicted as a result of my move to Yamaha were now catching up with me. Nothing new there, the usual gossip, hasty judgements, empty talk of the critics. And so that's why I painted my helmet the colour of wood. Because I remembered an old saying, which stated that, at the Olympics, fourth place received a wooden medal, after the first three got gold, silver and bronze.

By the same token, in 2003, I chose to wear a ball and chain. After all, I was "condemned to win". If ever I finished second, people would say I was finished. I was a prisoner of my own success and my ball and chain represented that.

Osvaldo the Chicken, on the other hand, has been a recurring gag. It too started with a football match and thus had nothing to do with motorbikes. Every year, in Tavullia, there is a "bachelors v married men" match. We play every year among our Fan Club. My Tribe, which was pretty much the bachelor team, since we were a bit younger, would take on those who were a little older and already married. Kids versus adults, that was essentially the idea. We took the game quite seriously. We even had a manager. One day Flavio Fratesi came to us and said: "Guys, this year we even have a sponsor! The only thing is he demands that he be allowed to choose the kit . . ."

"OK, after all if he is good enough to sponsor us, it doesn't seem like too much to ask," we replied.

When we arrived at the pitch for the match, Fratesi pulled out our jerseys. They read "Polleria Osvaldo", which means "Osvaldo's Chicken Shop".

"We're not playing in that!" many of us protested. We were actually a little bit offended. It looked ridiculous. In fact, some of us rebelled and played with the top inside out.

That year I had made my debut in 250cc. It was 1998 and it had been a very tough season. That year, in fact, I had been a "chicken" – but only in the Italian sense of the world, which is very different from what the word signifies in English. In Italy, the term "pollo" (chicken) means someone who is gullible or naive. And, to be fair, that season I had been a "pollo" on more than one occasion. I was fast, but Capirossi and Harada often got the best of me late in the races, when I thought I had victory in my grasp. In that sense, I was a "pollo" – especially with regards to Harada. And that's why Fratesi began to think that the Polleria Osvaldo shirt might come in handy down at the track.

And so it did. At Imola, in September, my Aprilia's livery was changed to Italian colours. Red, white and green. And I had even dyed my hair to reflect the Italian tricolour. I felt great, regenerated, concentrated and serene after our summer break. And I won. When I stopped under the stand where my Fan Club was assembled, just before the lower chicane, Flavio ran up next to me.

"Take this," he said, tossing me the shirt. "It's the jersey from the game."

"What the fuck am I supposed to do with this?" I asked.

"I don't know, just keep it, now go!" he said.

I took off down the track with the shirt inside my suit. As I was finishing the lap of honour, I was asking myself: "What am I going to do up on the podium with that dumb Polleria Osvaldo shirt? I need an idea, and I need it quick!"

When I saw the journalists and the TV cameras arrive on the scene, I still had no idea what I was going to say. But suddenly, just as I was about to open my mouth, it all came to me.

"Now, I'd like to thank my sponsor, Osvaldo, because he has been with me from the very beginning of my career, from the time I raced minibikes," I said with the straightest of straight faces. "He always believed in me, he always supported me, even in a season like this, when I haven't won much. And that's how you tell who your real friends are. Thus, in this happy moment, I hereby give him my long overdue thanks!"

"Who is this Osvaldo?" I heard people say. Some looked perplexed, others confused, still others bought the gag hook, line and sinker. They were the ones who immediately applauded me.

"Well done, Valentino!" they said. "It's so nice to see superstars show gratitude towards the little people!"

Of course, you have to wonder about those who were congratulating me. Had it not occurred to them that it was a little strange that nobody had ever seen a single advertisement from my supposed sponsor, Osvaldo?

We even had a slogan for the shirt. On one side it said "Polleria Osvaldo". On the other, "every chicken knows Osvaldo." After that performance, as far as we were concerned the gag was over. We had no idea of what was going to happen next. A few days later, the Fan Club got a phone call from a guy who designed mascots for basketball teams.

"I heard that Valentino is sponsored by a chicken shop," he said. "Well, I designed a chicken mascot suit for a basketball team, but they never used it. I was wondering if you might be interested in having it?"

"Are we interested? What are you waiting for? Bring it over right now!"

And he did. And his giant chicken was so beautiful that we decided he would come with us to Barcelona for the next Grand Prix. He featured in our lap of honour, which meant that one of my friends had to crawl inside the chicken costume. And that's when the Pollo Osvaldo story spun out of control.

Few journalists actually believed that Polleria Osvaldo was my sponsor. In fact, almost everyone actually saw through it after the first few minutes. But there are always exceptions.

One day I was approached by a journalist from RAI, the Italian state broadcaster.

"Come on, Valentino, let's do a story on Osvaldo for the evening news," he said. "It will make a nice feature, he's a positive character."

Of course, this was rather problematic, since Osvaldo did not actually exist. He was just a giant chicken costume.

"What are we going to do?" I asked myself. I was amused that somebody had been fooled so easily by the gag, indeed had read it in totally the wrong way, but now we were about to be found out.

We tried to discourage the TV journalist.

"Look, Osvaldo is a bit of a strange character," we said. "He's prickly, he's a little shy and irritable. He doesn't want to speak to the press, he just can't do it. It's not worth your time, just let it go."

But it was all to no avail. The TV people wanted to meet Osvaldo. They brought it up every time they saw us.

"OK, fine, let's have the journalist and the camera crew along and we'll get somebody to pretend they're Osvaldo," we decided. It was the only way to solve the problem.

And, once again, our great organisational machine sprang into action. We needed to find somebody who could play Osvaldo. We imagined Osvaldo to be a little overweight, perhaps with a nice beard. So we picked a friend of ours from Rimini, Stefano Bordoni, who worked as a toll collector at the motorway toll booths. He was a big guy and he did have a beard, so he seemed perfect to us.Having created our fake Osvaldo, we needed to create a fake chicken coop, where Osvaldo would keep his chickens. Palazzi, a guy from the Fan Club, remembered that his father owned some land out in the countryside, including an old farmhouse which had fallen into disrepair. We went out there one day, cleaned it up, and filled it with chickens. Lots of chickens. We also made a big sign, featuring the same logo that was on the shirts, and painted the slogan – "Every chicken knows Osvaldo" – on the side of the house.

We then realised that Osvaldo needed a suitable method of transportation. So we took an Apecar and . . . OK, time out, you probably don't know what an Apecar is, I had better explain it to you. Apecar comes from "*ape*" which means a bee. And car comes from – well, you know what that means. And so an Apecar is basically what the offspring of a motorcycle and a truck would look like. The back is a flatbed, the front features a small cab but, instead of a steering wheel and a car-style dashboard, it has a handlebar like a motorbike. It's quite popular in farms out in the country, because the flatbed in the back is quite spacious. I guess it's the Italian version of those American pick-up trucks they have out in Texas and places like that. Anyway, we transformed the Apecar into a mobile chicken coop. It was perfect. Osvaldo had quite an impressive set-up.

"Look, if you really want to come and see Osvaldo, we'll see what we can do for you," I told the journalist the next time I saw him.

Of course, he jumped at the chance and we arranged a visit.

When he arrived at the fake chicken coop at the pre-arranged time, we were waiting for him. The play-acting began immediately.

"Look, we're very sorry you came all the way out here, but Osvaldo changed his mind," we said. "He would really rather not to do anything with the media, he's a very private man."

Suddenly, over to our left, the Apecar/mobile chicken coop came into view, trundling along a country lane.

"There he is!" we shouted. "That's him! That's Osvaldo!"

The cameraman immediately switched on his camera and began filming.

"Let's go! Follow him!" the journalist ordered the crew.

"No, look . . . please, don't do that!" we pleaded. "Osvaldo is very private, he'll get very cross with us!"

"What are you talking about? Let's go! After him!" the TV crew insisted.

"OK, fine!" we said, looking as serious as we could. "But if he gets mad, don't say we didn't warn you."

"Whatever, let's go!"

"All right, suit yourself, but don't blame us . . . "

So off we want, running through the fields, chasing Osvaldo on his mobile chicken coop.

When we caught up with him, the fake Osvaldo gave a perfect performance.

"Who are you?" he started shouting at the top of his lungs. "What do you want? Go away! Away! How did you find me?"

"No, please, Osvaldo, calm down!" we pleaded.

"Go away! Awaaaaaaaaaaayyyyyy!" he kept shouting.

It took all our professionalism as practical jokers to suppress our laughter.

"I'll have a word with him, perhaps I can calm him down," I said. I made my way over to him and pretended to be deeply involved in conversation while the others looked on with bated breath.

I jogged back to where the camera crew had been waiting and announced: "OK! He'll do it. He'll grant you an interview."

They were delighted! The interview lasted about fifteen minutes and Osvaldo actually said some intelligent things. Or, rather, my mate Stefano, playing Osvaldo, said some intelligent things.

It worked perfectly. The feature duly went out on RAI's evening news and they never suspected a thing.

My other famous gag involved the traffic cops. In 2002, my first season in MotoGP, like I said, everyone became convinced that I was dominating just because I had an exceptional bike. My Honda, everyone was claiming, was simply too fast.

And thus I hatched another plan. At the Italian Grand Prix, after the Mugello straightaway, where you hit speeds of 340 kilometres per hour, I would stop just past the finish line, during my lap of honour (assuming I won, of course, but the odds of that seemed pretty good). And that's where I'd be approached by traffic police, armed with a handheld speed detector like the ones they use in speed traps. And they would give me a ticket for speeding!

The idea came from one of the guys in the Fan Club, Stefano Franca. He played the part of one of the cops, although in real life he's a violin teacher. My friends and I knew a thing or two about traffic cops, since we had spent much of our youth trying to avoid them. And yet, we would always run into them, usually when they stopped us for messing around on our scooters. And, I remember, they always came in pairs. Like the *carabinieri*, the Italian military police who are the frequent butt of jokes. There was usually a thin one and a fatter one. And the thin one – goodness knows why – was usually the mean one, the one who would never give us a break, the bad cop. The chubby one, on the other hand, usually said something along the lines of "Come on guys, slow down, it's dangerous out there". And the thin one would be the one who wrote us the ticket. Like I said, it's the classic good cop/bad cop scenario. At least, that's what it was like when we were growing up.

So we needed a slim cop and chunky cop. Stefano was already in line to play the thin one. And then Uccio's dad, Rino, agreed to be the fat one. The uniforms were real – we had borrowed them from the Tavullia Police Department. We even had to sign a document certifying that we would not use them for "improper purposes".

We asked Dorna, the company that organises the world championship, for permission to position our fake patrol after the finish line. They were glad to oblige. And so, as I finished my lap of honour, I received yet another ticket for speeding.

Though, thankfully, this one was fake. Unlike all the others!

EIGHT

As I've explained, Jeremy only decided to leave Honda after I'd made the decision to leave myself, but when it came to believing in the possibility that we could actually win on the Yamaha in our very first season, Jeremy was the first to believe it could actually happen. I first understood this in November of 2003, during a test that Yamaha ran in Malaysia. I wasn't allowed to be there in person, since Honda had not granted permission for me to test with another team until my contract officially expired on 31 December 2003. We decided that I would stay home, but Jeremy flew out there to get better acquainted with the bike. Jeremy's opinion was crucial to me. And I thought his trip was invaluable in understanding exactly what the situation was.

"He has had twenty years of continuous success with Honda. He'll be able to figure out right away what Yamaha need to win," I thought.

He too had realised that there were serious difficulties to overcome. Despite his outward enthusiasm, Jeremy could not hide the fact that there was still a lot of work to be done on the bike. They had huge problems, and that's why he needed to be there. He wanted to know just what I would be getting myself into come January.

At the time, Yamaha were not winners, we both knew that. But the motivation for us was to find out exactly why that was the case. We wanted to figure out what was missing. That was our priority during that November, before I even climbed on to my very first M1. That's why Jeremy's trip was so important to me.

"All he needs to do is tell me that the basic building blocks are there to win," I told myself as I said goodbye to him, on the eve of his departure for Sepang.

"Don't worry about it," he reassured me. "I'll go see how they work and report back."

But I did worry. Every day, I would eagerly await his updates from Malaysia. We spoke on the phone twice daily.

"Don't worry, we're fine," he said on his last day. "I can tell that Yamaha has what you need."

Those were the words I was waiting for. When he called, I was driving around London. I was very excited.

"Great! Fantastic!" I said, bursting with curiosity and a dash of anxiety. "Tell me what you know about the bike!"

"Well, from what I can tell, and I do have to do some more research, the gas is on the right, the clutch is on the left, the front brake lever is on the right . . ." he deadpanned in his usual way. Typical Jeremy, always the most dry sense of humour in the room. We both burst out laughing, me in London and him in Sepang. I understood exactly what he meant and Jeremy was pleased because he had gotten his point across.

"The Yamaha, ultimately, is just a bike, everything depends on who develops it and who rides it," was his message. And, a few months later, I finally discovered first-hand what I already knew: Jeremy was right. Again.

Still, in that last phone call, the one in which he reassured me, Jeremy probably wasn't being entirely straightforward with me about the bike. Nothing major, just a slight hint of apprehension. Having said that, his attitude didn't bother me, because I knew it was all geared towards our ultimate objective: success. Jeremy was trying to be positive, he realised that there were problems, but at the same time he understood that together we could solve them. There was no reason to despair. I understood this and appreciated it. Because I know Jeremy well, I knew this was his tactic: he wanted, above all, optimism and a positive vibe throughout the new team. This was because he knew that, at that time, in the initial period of our adventure, serenity, confidence and enthusiasm were absolutely crucial. They were the launch pad from which we were ready to take off and they were the things we needed most. And I was in complete agreement with him. Besides, this was Jeremy Burgess. That's how he is. That's who he is. And that's how he approaches racing as well as his work in the pits. His weapons are calm, reflection, positivity and intuition. I like his attitude a lot, because if there is one thing I can't stand it's pessimists. Especially when they're nervous. People who analyse a situation by pointing out the negatives first really make me angry. They truly annoy me.

Jeremy is the opposite. When something goes wrong in a race, his analysis is always based on optimism. Jeremy is not a dreamer or a romantic. He doesn't see things that aren't there. Yet he truly does go and look for the positives, so that he can use them to find the strength to overcome the negatives. I fully share his way of seeing things. That's why Jeremy and I work so well together.

When I think of Jeremy's mentality, I always remember the German Grand Prix in 2001. I still use it as an example to follow for myself, but it's also instructive for everyone else.

It was a very tense moment. I finished seventh at the Sachsenring. Biaggi had won the race and, while I was still in first place in the overall ratings, my lead had shrunk to just ten points. I had run a bad race, and I knew it. Afterwards I was sitting on the crates that contain the spare parts. My morale was really low. All around me, people were despondent, and I could already see the buzzards circling around us, waiting to prey on the carcass: me. I could see the Italian journalists and I knew they could smell the wounded prey, ready to be finished off in the public eye. They wanted to speak to me, but I had no interest in speaking to them. I had my own thoughts, of course, but I wanted to keep them to myself. I was talking to Jeremy about things that I felt were very important, so we told the press that we would speak to them later. And that's when all hell broke loose.

It wasn't the first time that we had postponed the post-race interviews for similar reasons, but this time the journalists lost their cool and started saying the most absurd things.

"Oh, great, now that you've had a bad race, Valentino doesn't feel like talking! Well done, you're a great example of sportsmanship!"

I was in the pits when they were saying these things, but I could hear them because there was only a thin wall separating us. I just sat there, my legs hanging over the edge of the crates, hunched over, holding my head in my hands, with my elbows digging into my knees. I was very disappointed, but also angry and irritable. I was twenty-two years old, this was my second season in 500cc, and it's true, I was still gaining experience – but I was also in first place. Jeremy came over to me and we began to talk.

He began analysing the race, trying to find the reasons behind our problems and then drawing conclusions about our situation. And he seemed to be in very good spirits. I realised that his whole analysis was based upon optimism.

"I don't think this is the time to look on the bright side," I said.

Jeremy smiled. He looked as if he was enjoying himself. I don't know, maybe he thought it was funny and to an outsider it might have seemed funny. But the fact is that I don't accept losing at all. I can't stand defeat. I've always gotten very angry when I lost. Many times I was furious even when I just finished second, so just imagine how I felt after finishing seventh!

"Look, you've never liked this track," Jeremy said. "We just returned from Japan, after testing for the Suzuka Eight Hour Race, a test you never wanted to do, but Honda forced you, so you came here in a rotten mood. In addition, by the time you got here, you were absolutely exhausted, not to mention the jet lag. All this undermined your psychological condition. You didn't come here filled with peace and happiness, which meant that you were in no condition to race in this Grand Prix."

His words made me think.

"Besides, in this race you finished behind five Yamahas and that hardly ever happens," he added. "That means these were unusual conditions. This race wasn't normal. It was the opposite of normal. It's upside down. And, in the real world, normality is rather different. In the real world, we're the fastest."

By this point he had won me over.

"Besides, we're still in first place," he said. "And we have a ten-point lead. Ten points, that's quite a lot. So, when you stop and think about it . . . what's the problem?"

I looked at him a little bit differently.

"Well, yes, when you put it that way, I suppose you're right . . . *what* is the problem?" I said, eyes twinkling. I had rediscovered my good humour, and all because I had begun to see things from his point of view, using his positive outlook, and I had found that there was another way of seeing the world. And that's when I learned that, when examining a situation, you can look at things positively or negatively, and it's always better to choose the former.

And that's what I did. I started working for the future, thinking about what we had yet to do, the races that had yet to be run. The next one was the Czech Grand Prix at Brno. There was a whole month's break between the Grands Prix of Sachsenring and Brno but I already knew I would not get much time off from practising. Immediately after the race I set off for Suzuka, even though I didn't want to at all, so that I could race in the Eight Hours of Suzuka (which, by the way, I won).

When I returned from Japan, I tried to get some rest, but it did not last long, because I had to put up with a whole month of articles and columns in which everybody said that Biaggi had virtually caught up with me, that ten points were nothing, and that this time he was going to teach me a lesson. This was the opinion of a large slice of the press and also of a good number of fans.

Besides, Brno was Biaggi's favourite track, he had won there many times and had always raced well. That's why it made sense to presume that Biaggi would race aggressively whereas I would remain on the defensive. And, like most of our epic duels, the build-up only contributed to the drama.

A previously unknown group in a town near Tavullia started a Max Biaggi fan club to rival my Fan Club. These things are all part of the game, of course, but, in this case, they only made relations that much more strained.

I tried to be low-key at Brno; at least at first. In the Thursday press conference, I remained cool. I let others do the talking. I kept my sunglasses on and I sat quietly to the side, although I was right next to Biaggi!

"We've never seen you so unhappy," I was asked. "You seem cross. Is the tension getting to you?"

"No, I'm like this because I don't enjoy the company," I replied. Everyone knew who I was talking about.

During the Friday tests Biaggi was exceptional. He was the fastest and I was only seventh, a full second and a half behind him. On Saturday, he won the pole, but I was second and I was now just one-tenth of a second behind him. I was improving very quickly.

Biaggi started very well, trying to impose a very fast pace, but I managed to stay right behind him. Strangely, around that time, I was starting very well, which is very unusual for me, since I tend to start badly. The first part of the race followed the same pattern. Biaggi would take off and I would catch him. Then he would take off again and I would catch him again. Time and again, the same thing. It was a bit like the race at Welkom. He had to win the world title that season and, at that point, given the standings, he had to go on the attack. He had to beat me. I struggled to keep up, because he was really fast. It took every ounce of my physical and mental energies to hang in there. We were taking big chances, both of us. And yet, I had to keep up.

There was one point of the track, at the exit of the left–right chicane, where he would always turn round to see where I was. Thus, I tried to be as close to him as possible every time we went past there. And, each time he turned round, I'd take my left hand off the bike and wave to him. It was my way of telling him that, far from being stretched to the limit, I was there with him, every inch of the way.

We were both pushing our bikes very hard, stretching their qualities as far as they would go. And, because he pushed so hard, Biaggi eventually fell. We came into a left turn, he was bent over so far that his Yamaha lost contact with the asphalt and slipped away. It was a slow fall – it looked like it happened in slow motion, nothing like the mega-spills you would see with the 500cc. It was as if his bike had simply decided to lie down on the asphalt.

I was in a strange emotional state at the time. I did not realise – or, perhaps, I did not want to realise – that Biaggi had fallen. I was so focused on my only objective, of not allowing him to take off and build an insurmountable gap between the two of us – that when he fell I almost felt bad for him.

"Maybe it didn't really happen, let's wait a while longer," I told myself.

Then, on the next lap, I saw his skid marks on the asphalt.

"Unbelievable, he really did take a spill!" I told myself.

And yet I kept pushing the bike to its limit, even though I had built up a big lead and there were still ten laps to go. At one point, I heard a sound come from my NSR. I could here a vibrating noise, which made it sound as if something was coming loose. I had never experienced anything like that, not on a Honda. In fact, nothing had happened. I was so wound up that I had imagined it. There was no noise coming from the bike.

Brno was the final showdown between us. We both knew that that the winner was a shoo-in to take the title. And that's why were like that.

Before the race, speaking to Jeremy, I had said: "Fine, if he wins and I finish second, he'll gain five points, but I'll still have a five-point lead with several races left which means there will still be everything to play for."

I think that kind of reasoning proves how, at the end of the day, we were relaxed, even if, at heart, we weren't as calm as we wanted to make out. The tension of the race itself was massive.

Beyond my lead in the standings, which, after Biaggi's fall, had become even more solid, what really mattered was that I had reacted straight away and that I had responded very well to the problems I had experienced at the Sachsenring.

And this was all thanks to Jeremy. The combination of what happened at Suzuka, where I won a very difficult race by digging very deep, and my conversations with Jeremy had produced a very positive effect. Jeremy's attitude infected the whole Yamaha team from the moment he arrived in Sepang for those tests in November 2003. Thinking back, I suppose Jeremy could have begun by talking about the bike's problems – and there were plenty at that early stage. There was a lot of work to be done, and a good part of it needed to be done immediately.

Honestly, when I heard him on the phone, I expected him to say totally different things. I imagined he might say stuff like, "Well, the four cylinders in line aren't doing too well, there isn't enough power, we need to rebuild the frame, the bike uses up the tyres too quickly . . . " I expected him to say all these things that, incidentally, were all true, as I would later discover. If Jeremy had spoken about those issues, I would not have been surprised. They were legitimate comments to make. I might have been alarmed, yes, but I would not have been surprised.

I also appreciated the fact that Jeremy always took responsibility for everything. He did not shirk a challenge, ever. And simply coming out and listing all of Yamaha's problems would have been a way of shifting that responsibility on to others. It would have been like saying, "Well, there are lots of problems, I told you so, if things don't go well it won't be our fault, after all, Yamaha is still Yamaha . . ."

Instead, he simply got on with it and said, "Well, it will be up to us to fix it!"

And I really liked that about Jeremy. He's always balanced, serene, optimistic, measured: both when the bike is going great and when it's not going at all. And that is the way I like to work.

Before Yamaha, I think Jeremy allowed the Honda mentality to infect him a little bit. Jeremy, in the last months at Honda, was starting to think in the same way as Team HRC – winning is logical, it isn't anything to get excited about, it's something to be expected. Jeremy didn't seem to allow himself to get caught up in the excitement of it all, but remained quite detached. But when he arrived at Yamaha, things changed. Or, rather, he went back to being the type of guy he was before the last few months at Honda. He was relaxed and laid-back, but also concentrated and determined.

Jeremy is not one of those guys who comes in, screaming and shouting, causing a stir. But he is always smiling, happy, he doesn't hide his joy. He enjoys himself, in other words, and he does it peacefully. In this way, Jeremy contributes to my own calm outlook and approach to my sport. I need calm people around me. People who will remain laid-back and positive in the pits and low-key outside it. Because I'm the same, deep down.

Another thing I liked right away about Jeremy, and which helped us get along at every stage, was that he is very blunt and direct, just like me. We talk freely and we tell each other the most important things. And that's it. There's no need for us to spend an hour saying what can be said in ten minutes. We don't waste time indulging in idle chit-chat, talking about unimportant nonsense. Jeremy is not one of the guys who hangs around the pits until ten o'clock in the evening, just in case something crops up and there's something to do. He talks, he works hard and, if there are no particular problems, it all ends there. He knows how to leave the office, so to speak. He has the right balance. And that's something I always valued, both in him and in his boys, who then became my own team of mechanics.

Jeremy is methodical and, most importantly, he knows exactly what he wants. That's why our technical meetings have always been very brief. We always know what we need to talk about and we are used to focusing exclusively on the highest priorities, isolating the biggest problem so we can work on it, without being distracted by all the lesser issues. We look at the important factors, we check the tyres, the settings, we compare things, we decide what to do. And that's it. The rest is just pointless chatter. Our concept of motorcycle racing is built on being concise and focusing on what's essential.

Jeremy always has very clear ideas. He thinks, he reasons, he analyses. Nothing gets done until he pronounces his famous catchphrase: "Let's do this!"

I listen. I analyse things too and when I say "OK", we move quickly. Because the two of us always work in perfect harmony. We never doubt each other's opinions. We trust each other. Outside of work, we relax together, and we also manage to have a good laugh in and out of the pits.

Sometimes, during our technical meetings, I notice that, at a certain point, Jeremy stops listening. He may nod along, but his mind is clearly elsewhere, working things out, evaluating solutions. He's already focusing 100 per cent on the job at hand. And I can tell Jeremy's doing this, and I can tell what he's thinking about, just by looking at him, and vice versa, because Jeremy and I can convey what we're thinking through our facial expressions. Then, when one of us has something important to say, we'll talk – in English. That wasn't by choice, we were forced to do so.

"You should learn the technical terms well, and in the meantime I'll make an effort to learn some Italian." That's what he said to me when I arrived at Honda at the end of 1999. I learned all the technical terms, but Jeremy never did learn a single word of Italian. At first he tried, but I could tell that his efforts were not going to get him anywhere. Once he realised that I had learned the technical terms and that speaking Italian was not going to be essential, neither for his career nor for his life, he stopped entirely. Thus, apart from the odd swear word, which he obviously learned from me or one of my friends, he really can't say anything in Italian. And quite often I'll jokingly chide him about his linguistic limitations. And it's the only promise he made to me that he hasn't kept! But to be fair, the same thing happens when I speak English, and sometimes what I'm saying isn't clear or it sounds wrong, and to his credit Jeremy doesn't joke at my poor English, he just tries to understand what I'm getting at. Although I guess he also does this because he knows all too well that if he starts to mock my not-so-great English, I would start making fun of his non-existent Italian!

The boys on the Yamaha team have taken Jeremy's philosophy on board. His way of thinking and doing things is common to all of them. They are very good at what they do, but they are also accurate and concise in the things they say. Jeremy borders on the philosophical in what he says. In fact, within the team, we soon started calling him "the wise man". When I have to make reference to something Jeremy said, I'll say, "As the wise man says . . ."

Other things I like about Jeremy: he listens patiently to what people say, and, a few minutes later, summarises the point, often with a touch of irony. He calls a spade and spade. He's a winner. He has an unquenchable thirst for victory (sometimes he can be worse than me). He wants to win every single race. All of them. He doesn't want to know about problems – he just wants to win.

Naturally, if I lose, it's not as if he'll come to me to complain, saying I should have done better, that I should have done more. He doesn't preoccupy himself with problems linked to my driving style. And that's unusual too. Usually everybody has some piece of advice to give riders. Everybody wants to weigh in on problems that actually should only concern the racers themselves, nobody else. And, many times, it causes problems, this needless interference.

For me, there's a very important rule. Each of us must do his or her job, and the rider's job is to drive the bike on the track. If Jeremy believes we could have all done better in general, obviously he'll say so (and he'll do it with his usual calm, relaxed style, without losing his composure). What he won't do is put pressure on me or bust my balls, like so many people do. He never contributes an ounce of tension to my life. And that's important.

When he started believing in the project, he devoted every ounce of his energy to the cause.

"We have two years," I said as soon as we got together to draw up our master plan. "It's clearly impossible to win in the first season, but in the second we can do it."

He looked at me with a frown. He seemed rather perplexed.

"Let's fix the bike and maybe in seven or eight races we'll be up there in front of everybody else," I continued, outlining my expectations.

Jeremy listened patiently, looking me in the eye as I spoke. Then, he told me what he really thought about our master plan.

"Sure, we can do things that way," he said. "But I think we can win straight away."

"Straight away? You mean in the first season?" I asked. This time I was the one who was shocked. I had never imagined that an engineer would be so explicit and ambitious, particularly when the task ahead was so daunting.

"Yes, straight away," he said.

"You had better explain this to me," I said. I was filled with disbelief. I couldn't believe what he was saying.

"Well, I've never gone into a season without knowing that I could help win the world title," he said. "And I don't plan on doing it now."

It was an interesting point, no doubt about it. His words made complete sense. Well, sort of!

"Look, we can't make the same mistake we made in 2000," he said. "You remember what that was, don't you?"

"Of course I remember!" I replied, a touch annoyed.

"Well, that can never happen again!" Jeremy remarked, ending our discussion.

Back in 2000 we had in fact committed a huge mistake. We did not believe in our chances at the start of the season. We thought the title was going to be out of reach. It was my first season in 500cc and it was the first year we worked together. I was twenty-one years old. We began assuming that it was just going to be impossible to win the title in our debut season and, by the end, we regretted having felt that way. Because, even though we did not try that hard, Kenny Roberts, the world champion, was not that far ahead of us.

By the end he did have a certain lead, but I had not raced to win, I had raced to gain experience. I didn't plan on trying to win the title. And analysing my performances and those of the competition, we both later agreed that we could have won straight away.

Reminding me of 2000 was Jeremy's way of telling me that we had to go on the offensive immediately, from the very first race of our very first season with Yamaha.

"We have to prepare the bike thinking that we're going to win immediately," he said. "From the very first Grand Prix!"

And that idea excited me. Jeremy deserves the credit for making me think like that. True, I had told Brivio during our negotiations that I wanted to win immediately and that I wanted a bike with which I could win at Welkom, in the very first race. But it was Jeremy who turned that bluster into real self-belief. And it wasn't just myself who was benefiting from Jeremy's boundless energy. Slowly but surely, Jeremy did this with everyone at Yamaha. One by one, he stimulated all of them and brought them around to his way of thinking. He pushed the right buttons and found the right motivations for each of the individuals involved in the project.

And that's what happened. He was proved right. We worked

exceptionally well during the winter test season and we won right away, starting from the very first race, in April.

I was very relaxed during my traditional winter skiing holiday in January. Yet, day after day, I became more impatient. I wanted to get down to work.

"Why don't you drive an extra 200 kilometres and swing by Monza," Brivio suggested over the phone one day. "Your bikes have just arrived, fresh off the freight container from Japan. Besides, Jeremy is on his way over, together with the crew, and they are going to start working on them immediately."

There is no need to tell you what my reaction was. As soon as the holiday was over, I packed my bags, fixed the snowboard to the roof of my car and hit the road: destination Monza. Because Yamaha's Italian headquarters were right there, in Gerno di Lesmo, next door to Monza's famous track. And those are also the racing team's head-quarters.

When I arrived I had a few friends with me. I couldn't just leave them behind – they needed a lift home. Thankfully nobody seemed to notice, they were all already engrossed in their work. Walking into the racing department was a thrill. We came in through a side entrance, wandered down several hallways and arrived in the garage area. That's where I saw my bikes and Jeremy and the boys already hard at work. That was my team, huddled around my M1. Not just any M1, like the one at Donington that I saw up close. No, this was *my* M1.

The air was electric, pulsing with expectation. I noticed this as soon as I walked into the room. Normally winter is a quiet time in most racing departments. But this was different. The bikes were on display, emitting a mystical aura. Even as the technicians moved around the bikes, doing the usual tweaks and tests, I could sense some-thing was different here.

As if drawn in by an irresistible attraction, I went straight over to my M1 and climbed on. I grabbed the handlebar, I pushed the brake lever, felt the clutch with my fingers, positioned my feet, felt the saddle beneath me and wrapped my legs around the gas tank. All normal, unremarkable gestures which I had done thousands of times before. And yet, this time, there was silence in the room. Everybody had stopped what they were doing. They were frozen, watching my every move, enveloped in their own private silence. My audience.

I asked to adjust a few things, I had them raise the brake lever and then I just sat there in total silence. Just me and my new bike. My M1. It was a special moment, a different moment. So much so that when I got off I could tell that everyone expected me to say something. I waited a few seconds, I looked around the room. I pursed my lips, cocked my head and said: "Well, from my position there, standing still in the middle of the room, everything looks fine!"

There was an instant of silence and then everyone burst out laughing. Of course, they all realised that the sense of expectation that had come over the room a few minutes before was entirely absurd. What could I say about a bike that was immobile and was just sitting there? But this episode was important nonetheless. It was a shared experience, the first moment of contact between racer and bike. And it was the first real bonding session between those of us who had come over from Honda and our new teammates, the Yamaha guys who had stayed on.

She was a beauty, my M1. This was no surprise; Yamaha bikes had always been beautiful. But this was my M1. This was different, a different kind of beauty. And, even though I knew we would have to modify her tremendously, she appeared to me as a thing of absolute majesty and awesome potential.

Our big debut was scheduled a few days later. Eager to show just how excited I was, I agreed to go to Malaysia one day early. Normally I only show up on the eve of testing, sometimes the night before. But I couldn't help it, I was so excited. Still, it wasn't until I actually arrived in Sepang that I realised just how big the occasion was. There normally aren't many people at the January tests in Malaysia. Usually it's just a few photographers and the occasional journalist. You step into the Sepang track complex and you feel alone, very alone. All you see is the other teams, the rest is totally deserted. You might see a handful of people at the entrance, guys sitting in the shade without getting out of their chairs, looking at you sideways to see if they recognise you.

This time, everybody was there. All the journalists who follow the world championships were there. It looked and felt like a Grand Prix, not a winter test. There was a flood of people and hordes of photographers. And naturally there was a great commotion. I saw cameras and microphones sprouting all over the place, continuously, with Italian journalists pressuring me into organising an impromptu press conference.

This annoyed me. I did not want to face a situation like that. At least not on the eve of my first test. Besides, I had nothing to say about Yamaha, since I had yet to try out the bike. And I certainly did not feel like talking about Honda, because, for me that was all part of the past and I only wanted to think about the future. Besides, I had been on holiday for the previous six weeks and I had detached myself, physically and mentally, from the world of motorbikes. I just had nothing to say.

In fact, I was shocked a few days earlier, when I had heard Brivio talking to Gibo. Brivio was saying things that seemed surreal to me. "The track will be closed, we have it exclusively to ourselves for three days, Saturday, Sunday and Monday," he was explaining. "We'll block off the pits and keep everybody out. We'll also arrange it so we're far away from the entrance of the complex. That way we'll have much more privacy."

All this talk surprised me quite a bit.

"What are they on about?" I asked myself. "What are they so worried about? It's the winter tests . . . there is never anybody there . . ."

Upon arriving in Malaysia I realised just why Brivio was so worried. I solved my problem with the Italian press by deciding that I would not speak to anyone. And then I went down to the pits, the Yamaha pits. I was wearing my Yamaha shirt. It was black, with the word Yamaha on the left shirt pocket. I had on the shorts I usually wear when I'm napping in the motorhome (they're flannel plaid and look rather like pyjamas) and flip-flops on my feet. Yes, I was dressed ultra-casual, as if I were headed for the beach, but then that's standard attire for the winter tests in Malaysia, where the temperature often hits forty degrees in the shade.

As soon as I entered the pits I took a long look at my M1. Then, I began to attach all my stickers, including, of course, the number 46. Brivio had already explained to the Japanese mechanics (those who had not yet met me) that they shouldn't worry if they saw me around the bike. I'm just that kind of racer, I need time alone with my bike.

So of course, my boys, the ones who had come over from Honda, knew exactly what I was like. I go through one of my favourite rituals, the placing of adhesive stickers. Only I can perform this task, it's a matter of superstition. I had brought all of them from home, of course. And in addition to my number, I had included my tax disc, insurance, a logo bearing the phrase "The Doctor" and a picture of my dog Guido. And then, written in Japanese, the phrase: "Go, Rossifumi!"

The Rossifumi nickname dates back to 1994. I invented it, combining my last name with the first name of Abe, Norifumi (Norifumi Abe is a very popular Japanese racer), and it dates back to my early pre-racer obsession with motorcycle sports. In those days it seemed all I did was spend time thinking of motorbikes and watching races on television. I had always been like that, but, in that particular season – the '94 season – my obsession verged on insanity. It was not uncommon for me to watch the same Grand Prix five or six times on videotape.

One day I had gotten up at dawn to watch the Japanese Grand Prix, live from Suzuka. And I was struck immediately by this wild card named Norifumi Abe (also known as Norick Abe). He was eighteen and raced the official Honda NSR 500. She was beautiful: all fluorescent orange, with green rings and numbers. They were the sponsor's colours. Abe had long straight hair and even when he was standing still, he looked like a great character. But most of all, he rode like a madman. He was absolutely fearless. I think that day was the fastest race of his life.

Suzuka is an unusual track. It's a gorgeous for a start, extremely technical, and it's full of secrets. It's not one of those computer-designed tracks. You can really only go fast there if you know your way around, if you've logged a fair few kilometres there already. But you need to know the asphalt inch by inch, learning every turn, every braking point, every little hole. It's a bit like Philip Island, except Suzuka is even tougher. Abe obviously knew that track very well, because he was very fast, despite being a wild card. He was up against the likes of Schwantz, Doohan and Itoh.

His racing style made me think that he was an absolute nutter. He took turns with his steering locked, and often had to keep himself up with his knee. His suit was usually smoking, and he overtook in the most outrageous spots. He gave me the impression that he was racing in his last ever race. Instead, it was his very first race! Three laps from the end, his steering finally gave out and he fell. You could see it coming, to be fair. He was going so fast that, when he fell, his bike rolled off into the distance, smashing into an advertising hoarding on the other side of the track. But to me, Abe was a hero.

That year, from April to June, I got up every morning at 7 a.m. to watch the replays of that race in Suzuka. Every single morning, for two whole months. First I watched the race and then I went to school. That was the genesis of my great and undying admiration for Japanese racers.

Like I said, on my bike it says, "Rossifumi gambatte!" Which means "Go, Rossifumi!" in Japanese. That's because when I first made it up to the world championship, the Japanese racers would always say "Gambatte! Gambatte!"

I was very good friends with Haruchika Aoki and, in fact, he's the one who designed the "Rossifumi gambatte!" logo, from which I had the sticker made. I've always had it with me, going back to my very first race in the world championship. I've used it on all my bikes, from Aprilia to Honda to Yamaha. And the sticker was always the same, just like the original version: yellow and blue.

I should also tell you about another sticker. It's a picture of Guido, my dog, and I attached it towards the back of my bike in 2001, just before the beginning of the Friday tests. It commemorated an important moment: I had defeated Biaggi and went on to win the 500cc. Because it brought me luck, from then on Guido's sticker stayed with me on all my racing bikes. Including the M1, of course.

Anyway, that day in Sepang, 23 January 2004, I stayed with my bike all afternoon and into the evening, well past sunset. I only left when it was dark. Only Brivio stayed in the pits that long that day. And we were there for different reasons. I just wanted to spend time with my new bike, checking and double-checking that everything was in order. And

I think he stayed because he still could not believe that the number 46 was now on a Yamaha. It had been his dream for years and he had worked so hard to fulfil it. And still he behaved just like he did that night when we shook hands, back in Brno, when I told him I was going to join Yamaha. He was still totally incredulous.

"It's true, then, it's all true!" he would repeat after we were left alone in the pits, just me and him. Before leaving he wanted to take one last look, to reassure himself that it was not a dream, that I really was there with him and that the number 46 really was there on the bike. He could not believe it. I enjoyed watching him. Because I too felt an unusual sensation – even for me it did not seem entirely real that I was about to start the season with a team other than Honda.

The next day, as I got dressed and put on my suit, I did everything in a slow, deliberate way. I knew perfectly well that this would be a day I would never forget. I wasn't nervous, however, when I actually climbed on to the M1. My only worry was how she would actually run. I did fear that she might end up being as disastrous as everybody seemed to have predicted.

"It's a totally irrational fear," I told myself repeatedly, though it didn't do much to alleviate my concerns. "Let's just hope it's not a bastard bike."

What I meant by "bastard bike" was one of those insincere bikes, those bikes that seem fine but then cause you to fall as soon as you push them a little bit. Because that's how people had described the M1 to me. In reality, these people were ignoring the tests which Checa had run back in November, which actually were quite encouraging. Instead they focused on the stories emanating from the men who had ridden her in 2003. "As soon as you push her, you fall," they kept repeating. Checa was the most outspoken, but Barros and Melandri agreed with him.

The first lap with the M1 was like a first date. It's more exciting to eat ice cream with a new girlfriend than it is to make love with a girlfriend you've been with for years! What I mean is, everything you do with a new girlfriend is exciting. Your senses are aroused, you pay more attention, you feel more involved. It's the same with the bike, as far as I'm concerned. The slow early lap is far more exciting with a new bike than the fastest lap in a race with a bike you know inside out. That's just how it was with my Yamaha in Sepang. The moment I came out of the pits and approached the M1 was exactly the way I had imagined it, way back when I was choosing between Honda and Yamaha.

I remember thinking back then: "If I choose the Yamaha, it will be amazing when I go and take the first lap in Sepang, in the torrid heat, immersed in total silence, with the grandstands empty . . ."

I had imagined that moment so many times. And that's exactly what it was like. That first lap at Sepang, enveloped in the silent emptiness and the suffocating heat, I felt exactly the sensations I imagined I would feel. Truth mirrored fantasy down to the slightest detail. When I came out of the pit lane and entered the track itself I was looking partly ahead — at the track, the stands, the low palms, slightly burned by the sun — and partly at the bike. I cycled through the gears, I tried the clutch, the brakes, I took the turns and checked for the slightest reaction, the softest sound. It was beautiful, very beautiful.

But then, after the first lap, I began to think about how I felt on the bike, how the engine was reacting and what it meant, how the chassis was holding up. In other words, I was immersed in work. Because if you want to understand the underlying difference between two bikes, even two bikes as different on the surface as the Honda and the Yamaha, you have to push them, you have to go fast, very fast. If

148

you go slow, at best, you can tell if the clutch or the gearbox are more or less stiff, but you don't really get a sense of how the bike handles.

Therefore, after the first lap, when I rode very slowly, I did a session of six laps, pushing the bike more and more. Then I returned to the pits, without saying a word to the engineers. In those six laps, it was all quite clear to me. At first, the memory of the Honda was quite distant, but then it all came back to me and I immediately started making comparisons.

When I stopped on the pit lane, I handed the bike over to Bernard, who was with Gary and Alex, as usual. What we were doing was totally normal, something we had done so many times before at Honda, but now it was different and perhaps a little strange. We weren't at Honda any more. We were Yamaha men now. I went inside, took off my helmet, removed my earplugs and mouth guard. I did everything I usually do after test laps.

But it wasn't the same. There was silence everywhere, I didn't hear the usual sounds you hear in the pits, technicians and mechanics who move around, chat, switch things on and off, tinker with equipment, put tools away. It was an unnatural silence, a weird silence. So I looked up and saw everyone gathered around, totally mute. There were mechanics, Japanese engineers, Michelin technicians, guys from Ohlins, Brembo, the telemetrists. They were all there and they were all staring at me without saying a word.

And suddenly I knew. They were all waiting. All of them, except for Jeremy. As usual, he was getting on with things, because he knew full well what I always did when I returned to the pits. And he, like me, was already fully immersed in work. But the others were all waiting. They had no idea what I was going to do, what I was going to say and thus they had no idea how to behave.

The blinding light that floods straight into the pit area in the mornings at Sepang was gone, the doors having been rolled shut by the mechanics as soon as I walked in. There was an air of intimacy; the only light coming in was from the back gate, for some reason left open. It was already very hot, even though it was still only 11 a.m. and the fans were going at full blast. I took a deep breath, I absorbed the sensations of the moment, digested the ideas I had. And then I began to talk about the bike and its behaviour on the track. The first impression was very good. I thought the M1 went well. It gave me confidence. The front was stable, the engine felt fast, and I immediately realised that, compared to the Honda, the real problem was power delivery.

Still, I had expected such a difficult bike, that I was happy and relieved after this first test. Maybe I was even too relieved. Because after the second test session I realised many more things and there was a real moment of discomfort. Still, at the end of the day things didn't go too badly. I clocked a 2' 02" 75, while Biaggi was at 2' 02" 58 and Gibernau 2' 02" 70. Checa, my teammate, notched a 2' 03" 57!

The biggest problem, at least at this stage of development, was in the engine, as I say, specifically related to the power delivery. In the first session of tests I had used the "screamer" version, which had a violent power delivery, and this was simply inappropriate for the way the bike was configured. In fact, this was part of the problem the Yamaha team had encountered in 2003. The power delivery was so violent with their configuration, that it put the chassis, suspension and especially the rear tyre, under far too much stress.

I also noticed that the M1 did not slide in a linear way. It would sway as it moved along, forcing me to continuously close the gas. This meant that at the beginning you could go fast, but only for five laps or so, because, after that, the tyres deteriorated and the bike's reactions would become unpredictable.

I thought back to the Honda and how, even when the tyre deteriorated, it was still easy to handle. That was the first truly unfavourable comparison I made between the two. That's why, by the third day of testing, I wanted to try the four-stroke irregular combustion engine. The racing department had shipped five engines to Malaysia and I immediately chose the one we had dubbed "Big Bang": the first version of the irregular combustion engine. I immediately realised it was the engine with the greatest potential, although it had one not-so-minor problem: it was slow. And I mean really slow. It was the slowest of all the engines I had, but at least it was easy to handle. And it lasted a good ten laps, which meant that I could go for half a race at a constant speed. This was a decent starting point. I tried not to think of the problem of power versus handling ability because I knew that power delivery was still the single biggest problem.

I had come over from Honda, so my standards were high.

"The Big Bang is the way forward," I told the engineers who had come over from Iwata, following our long final technical briefing. "Let's get rid of the other versions and focus on this one."

As soon as they returned to Japan, they started working only on that one, and abandoned the others.

From the very first test, then, I realised that to win on the Yamaha I had to prioritise handling ability over anything else. This meant we had to maximise the chassis. The Yamaha was slow, but at least it was easy to handle and it took turns very well. Mentally, I made a note that I would have to change my driving style to suit the qualities of the M1. We thus focused on developing the chassis of the Yamaha, emphasising the effectiveness on the turn and the agility in the change of direction. But the way to develop a bike is to improve all its components simultaneously, which meant the M1 needed a softer and more progressive engine. The goal wasn't to go faster – mentally, as I

151

said, I had already accepted that I'd be losing out on the straightaways – it was to perform better on the turns.

I had no illusions about what could be achieved in terms of making the engine more powerful. I understood straight away that we could never have an engine as powerful as the Honda. But it was enough for me to have an engine that did not create problems for the chassis and which allowed the rear tyre to maintain its efficiency throughout the race. In any case, I asked for more power and better performance. I was told that I had to be patient. In the event, the first real evolution of the Big Bang engine only came in March, in our second test at Philip Island. Which was our fourth test overall, a very private session. Yamaha had reserved the whole track for our own exclusive use. And it was one of the best and most significant moments of 2004. At the February tests, performing alongside the other teams, we had been outclassed. In fact, when they were over, I gathered everyone around me and said: "Guys, I think we just came crashing back to earth!"

They were all silent, a sign that they agreed with me. And indeed those tests had been disastrous. I was eleven seconds behind Colin Edwards and Gibernau on their Hondas, after the Grand Prix simulations.

But, as I said, when we returned to Philip Island in March, it was a different story. I finally got my hands on the new version of the engine, which had just been shipped over from Japan. The new propulsion still featured irregular combustion, but it was far more powerful. The engineers had kept their promise. The M1 was much improved: it simply drove better. When I ran the race simulation and we compared the data, nobody could believe their eyes. I finished with a sixteen-second lead over the times Gibernau and Edwards had registered earlier. Not only that, I had turned in an incredible 1' 30" 82 on the last lap! We were euphoric because it was there that, for the first time, we realised we had the potential to achieve great things.

So that test did not just comfort us, it made us dream of a bright future. After a while though, I understood that we could not afford to let ourselves get carried away.

"Guys, let's stay cool," I said. "Let's wait. Let's not tell anybody about this, not from here, not when we return home. Most of all, let's not tell people what our times really were, let's exaggerate a little, make them think we did worse than we really did."

My objectives were twofold. On the one hand, I did not want the race department to let their efforts slide, thinking they could relax because of our good results. On the other hand, I wanted to get to Barcelona and the IRTA tests with everyone convinced that I was facing huge difficulties. It was a strategic choice on my part. But I'm not sure that many at Yamaha understood what I was doing and why I was doing it. I could tell this from the strange looks they were giving me. It reminded me that Yamaha had lost that essential winning mentality in every field, including basic strategy and psychology.

"What do you mean?" somebody asked. "We did well. Why can't we let people know that we're improving? What difference does it make?"

Yamaha were a nice team. I mean, they were good people, maybe too good. They were always smiling. They didn't appear to possess that ruthlessness, that ability to bluff which is often a prerequisite for success. At this point the Yamaha team were just too open and trusting, which is one reason why they were no longer winning races on a regular basis. This applied to all of them, with the exception of Brivio, who understood right away what I was trying to do.

"It makes a huge difference if others know our true situation!" I insisted. "Nobody can say a word about this or there will be hell to pay!"

They continued to look confused, so I had to explain myself.

"Look, if we start to tell everyone just how well we're doing, the others will start working that much harder, particularly Honda," I said. "And we're not here to do Honda any favours, are we? They don't need any more motivation, do they?"

Slowly, they began to understand. Because we knew that Honda were very confident, perhaps overconfident. And that suited us. We wanted them to be too sure of themselves, believing they were miles ahead of us. They were all sure that we weren't going to achieve anything. I could tell how much they were looking forward to dominating the world championship. And, by March, it became even more obvious that they were convinced they were going to run away with the title. And this is exactly why we needed to keep a low profile: we wanted them to continue thinking it would be a cakewalk.

"Let's let them believe that they are the best, that it will all be easy for them," I said and, little by little, the team came around to my viewpoint.

Jeremy, Brivio and I had begun to draw up our strategy. And, in those days, at Philip Island, we were teaching the team how to win. Crucially, it was important to work well not just on the track, but outside it as well. Of course, we knew we could not hide the truth for long. Sooner or later, probably at the IRTA tests in late March, people would find out. And, if it didn't happen then, it would happen immediately afterwards, when the world championship kicked off. But, for the time being, we didn't want anyone to know just how much progress we had made.

For the entire winter testing period, we were never the fastest. Sometimes it was because we were genuinely slower than the others, but there were other times when we purposefully did not try to outrace the competition. Still, our times were not far off those of the top riders. This was important too. We needed to show that we were not that far behind, we were in the rear-view mirror so to speak.

At Yamaha, little by little, they began to understand that nothing should be left to chance, if you want to give yourselves the best opportunity of winning. The Yamaha guys didn't understand that, to win, you had to try and exploit every little shred of advantage that you could muster.

Jeremy had always repeated the same concept to me, ever since we started working together: "It's not our job to have our opponents like us," he would say. "That's not we are paid to do. Our task is to win. And we don't need to be concerned with what the other teams and racers think about us. It's not our problem."

Jeremy was right. If you are happy to be there or thereabouts, somewhere in the top five, you can smile, be nice to everyone and everyone will like you. But we had no intention of settling for the top five. We had a different objective – we wanted to be number one – and, to do this, we had to think differently.

"We have to stop being nice guys, we have to win!"

We would repeat this over and over, ad nauseam. That was our slogan: "No more Mr Nice Guy." Because Yamaha had fallen very, very far behind. And bit by bit, they learned our way of thinking.

Jeremy also restored order to Yamaha. He transferred the Honda mentality to our new team as far as methodology was concerned. First and foremost, he stopped them from tinkering excessively with the bike. He explained that we would make progress one step at a time. We would only change things once we were 100 per cent sure that something was wrong. Honda, for example, wouldn't let you touch anything on the bike. And sometimes, that mentality was very damaging to the team. But, at Yamaha, they went much too far the other way. Thus, we injected a bit of the Honda philosophy into Yamaha's company culture. And we took on board some of the Yamaha mentality. We chose to take the middle road, between the two rival philosophies.

Of course, between the two, I prefer the Honda method. At least as far as important things are concerned. You find one thing, you change it and you stick with it. But before we could get to that point, we had to battle through other problems. The front fork for example.

"How is it possible?" I asked myself. "I brake and I can feel something isn't working quite right."

This bothered me and I could not find an answer.

"It's as if the handlebar moves and the bike slides forward," I explained to the crew. Nobody could offer an explanation.

I carried this problem with me for the first three races. And, to be honest, it did not seem so serious at Welkom. I'm not sure why, but everything went great in South Africa. Many of our defects we only noticed later, they just weren't there at Welkom. Without question, it was an inspired weekend, one of those times when everything went smoothly. But there were technical reasons for this as well. The track is very smooth and there are no sudden braking situations. It was quite different in the next races, at Jerez and Le Mans, when I only finished fourth and had to face a whole series of problems.

Thankfully in the tests we ran immediately after the Grand Prix in France, we discovered just what the problem was: the front fork. It did not work properly and, when I had to brake hard, it would compress the tyre, which then wouldn't be as effective. Nobody had ever thought that if the front fork seized up, the tyres would seize up as well. Who could have ever thought that? But that's the reason why we struggled at both Jerez and Le Mans, even though we still had problems with the power delivery. After running through every possible scenario, we began to work our way through what you might call the impossible scenarios. And that's how we arrived at the front fork. Before, during the initial races, we had tried everything else and were unable to solve the problem.

Ohlins had been a little behind, compared to Showa, also because in the last few years Yamaha riders had not asked for particular improvements in the front fork. The problem was in the way it worked, in the hydraulics. Anyway, once we figured out what caused the instability at the front in braking situations, I began working closely with the Ohlins engineers. And they responded well. They were very good. They doubled their efforts, followed us closely and, with the help of our suggestions, designed a new front fork – one which was really excellent.

When I had first received the M1, back in January 2004, I had immediately got the sense that the riders and the crew who worked on it before were simply confused. They tried to fix it through trial and error, without any logical process. Thanks to Jeremy's arrival, the Yamaha engineers learned a new method of working. It was all about focusing on the problem. We came from Honda, which goes so far as to block the frame in the steering column, to stop people from tinkering with the geometry of the bike. Their philosophy is that, once something works, you don't mess with it. That's the HRC mentality.

At Yamaha they had a chassis that lent itself to any and all types of modifications. Everything could be moved, raised, lowered, poked and prodded. Before our arrival, the engineers and riders were accustomed to repositioning the engine, moving the shock absorbers, changing the inclination of the front fork. In other words, it was a huge free-for-all!

They had the freedom to do whatever they liked. And if you give that kind of freedom and such an easily changeable chassis to people who don't really know what they're doing, their natural instinct is to tinker. And, at that point, you're in serious trouble, because confusion ensues. And that's exactly what Yamaha was facing in 2003.

NINE

They say I'm a lucky boy. That everything always works out for me. That I get all the breaks and that, most of all, fortune always smiles down on me, especially when I've had to make big career decisions. They point out that I've always had the best bikes and that I happened to ride for whatever the best team was at that moment.

Over time, I got used to the barbs. They've been saying that I was privileged and that I had every advantage, ever since the early days, when bikes for me were just a game, back when I was in Sport Production. As I said, I am used to the criticism. And I am used to people being envious of me.

But when people start talking about "teams" I can't just let things slide. It's too important to me. Luck is one thing. It has always been there, it has always been a part of my success. It's a part of everyone's success. Without it, you can't be successful. But luck is something you have to stimulate, something you have to nurture through the choices you make. And, frankly, I've always made the right choices at the right time. And that's why things have always worked out for me. Things work out not just because I'm lucky, but because I plan ahead. I figure out what I want and I go for it. I've always spent a lot of time trying to surround myself with the right people, the kinds of teammates who could lead me to my goals. That's why my victories have never been a factor of happenstance or unforeseen events. Well, almost never.

Most of all, everything has followed from the choices I made. And I chose my teams. They did not just fall into my lap. I wanted them, I pursued them. In that sense I believe I have been a trailblazer in my sport. I am the first racer who made picking the right team his priority. Before me, the vast majority of riders didn't really care what team they were racing for. There was no link between rider and team. That is something I created. When you changed teams in the past, you just switched from one to the other and that was it. You didn't take your crew with you, as I did at the end of 2003. No rider ever tried to create that rapport, that link, that team spirit which I instituted and in which I have always believed. When other racers would sign contracts with new teams, they never asked that their own crew, mechanics and engineers, be allowed to come with them. Or, rather, they might have asked, but it never happened. Until I came on to the scene and made it happen. And this, of course, made history.

Too many riders have an attitude that says, "Well, as long as I'm good, the rest doesn't really matter, all teams are the same." I don't believe that. I always handpicked the people with whom I worked. Conventional wisdom states that this is an individual sport, because you're out on the track on your own, competing against other riders, all of whom are also there on their own. But the truth is that this has become, through years of technological advancement, a true team sport. If the rider does not have a strong group behind him, he may win something occasionally, but he can't achieve the extraordinary, like I have.

So the team counts for a lot. It's absolutely essential to motivate those who work for you, just as it is important to have calm and harmony, with each person knowing their role and their job. And it's very handy to have an adviser, someone you trust, someone to bounce ideas off of, someone who will be there for you in those tight spots. These are the things I have always searched for, going back to my first international adventure, back in 1995.

At the time, the official Aprilia team in 125cc was "Team Italia", run by Domenico Brigaglia. I did not try and get into his team, I wanted to work with Mauro Noccioli. And it was with Noccioli that I won the world title in 1997. I could have stayed with Noccioli in 250cc, but instead I chose to go with Rossano Brazzi. And, together, Brazzi and I won the world title in 1999. My modus operandi did not change once I arrived in 500cc. I picked the team, which, in this case, was Jeremy's team. And I won the world title in 500cc, in 2001. Jeremy's team became my team. And when I moved to Yamaha, I took them all with me. And I triumphed once again.

So you can say I was lucky if you like. But I also think I was far-sighted and courageous. If I have been blessed with having the best at my disposal, it's also because I've known how to identify the best and to pick out the best.

From the very beginning, I learned just how important the group was. When I joined Noccioli's team, I met Mario Martini, who immediately became my mechanic. We began working together the year I competed in the European championship, 1995. He stayed with me until 1997. I had a great relationship with him, one that went well beyond the bike. We hung out together, we talked a lot, about all sorts of things. We were just very close. And it was with him that I began to really understand how important it was to have a close bond with one's mechanics and teammates. After that experience, I always made it a point to have a strong bond with my team. Mauro Noccioli. Rossano Brazzi. Jeremy Burgess. They are the three chief engineers with whom I shared important victories. They were also three very different personalities, with three contrasting philosophies.

Noccioli is a "*toscano verace*", a true Tuscan as we say in Italy. He was close to me in the important early years of my career, when I began competing abroad: 1995, 1996 and 1997, always in 125cc, the first season in the European championship, the latter two in the world championship. By the end of 1994, I had to start thinking about my future. Sport Production was a starting point, not a goal. After winning in Sport Production, it was time to worry about winning with real bikes. An era had ended, in other words. And we needed to start doing things seriously. At the end of the season, I was approached by Carlo Pernat, who was sporting director at Aprilia.

"In 1995 you're going to race the European 125 series," Pernat told me. "If you finish in the top three, I'll guarantee you a spot in the world championship."

Of course, the world championship was my goal, my objective. Graziano followed my career, he advised me on my choices. And he believed that this was a very interesting opportunity for me. And, in fact, it was. Pernat gave me a three-year deal with Aprilia.

Team Italia wanted me, but I asked to join Noccioli's team. I had a lot of confidence in him; we seemed to suit each other perfectly. It was the right decision. My bikes were always fast and dependable. In fact, Noccioli's team often featured bikes that outperformed those of Team Italia, even though they were the "official" team. In the final analysis, my results with Noccioli were very positive. I dominated the Italian championship and I finished third in the European series. And this, as Pernat promised, got me into the world championship, which I won in 1997, the third year of my partnership with Noccioli.

We never argued and generally had very few problems. It's just that, at one point, he changed, adopting a racing and life philosophy that was quite different from my own. Of course, this was something that emerged over time and, in any case, it did not prevent us from reaching our objective, which was becoming world champions.

At one point we drifted apart. He had become a touch too paternalistic towards me and I began to notice that the people who worked for him were the same way. They were always trying to offer me riding tips, how to ride the bike, that kind of stuff. And, to me, that's one thing in which the team should never interfere. Everyone races differently and should be left free to learn on his own. Or, at least, as far I was concerned, nobody was going to tell me how to ride.

And yet we were always discussing how to ride. In those years he was obsessed with the idea that you should always push down on the footrests, so that you could hold the bike steady and control it better. And when something went wrong with the bike, perhaps with the front tyre or in acceleration, he always said that it was because I did not push down enough on the footrests. I'm sure it's a perfectly valid theory and it may work for some, but, since it did not come naturally to me, I did not think I should be doing it. And, besides, I don't think we got any benefit out of it. In any case, that's not the reason why I chose to move to another team when I advanced to 250cc. I had learned a lot from Noccioli and the rest of the team. After all, he was a very good engineer, who knew the engine inside and out. Besides, I had a lot of fun with that team. We had a lot of team spirit and I have lots of happy memories from that time. The 1997 season was sort of my coming-of-age party at international level, the year I established myself on the big stage. And it was also the closing chapter of the first part of my career.

Perhaps that's why I decided to change my appearance around this time. I did it my own way, naturally. With a string of silly choices. Although the first real change was the result of a promise I made to myself during the 1997 season.

"If I win the world title, I'm cutting it off," I decided one day, thinking about my hair. And, to be fair, my hair was too long. I just couldn't commit to trimming it, even though I wanted to. And so that's why I made this solemn promise to myself. Naturally, when I won the title, I had to keep my promise. Of course, to me just cutting my hair was not enough. I also had to dye what was left. And, because of who I am, I dyed it a bright blue colour.

We went to my trusted barber. There were three of us: Uccio, Pirro (another member of my tribe) and me. Pirro also had very long hair; I think he drew courage from the fact that I was cutting it as well. As for Uccio, he didn't really feel like dying it, he was just happy cutting it. But Pirro and I both decided to go for the dye. Our families did not take it too well. In fact, when Pirro got home, his mother actually started crying. In any case, that was the year we started becoming preoccupied with our hair. When we began our semi-annual tradition of changing things around. For us, changing hair colour was like a ritual. I liked to experiment with bizarre colours and unusual haircuts. But still, I think the best arrangement, and, without a doubt, my most famous, was the "Brazzi cut".

Brazzi was my chief engineer when I moved up to 250cc at the end of 1997. It was known as the Brazzi cut because it made me look just like him, when I unveiled it at the Italian Grand Prix in 1998. The "Brazzi cut" consisted of shaving my head with the exception of a sliver of hair at the bottom and down the back of the head. In other words, it was like the ultimate receding hairline, one which went all the way back. To be sure my barber would get it right, I took a picture of Brazzi with me when I went for my haircut. On Thursday afternoon, when I saw Brazzi at the track, he did not suspect a thing, because I kept my cap on. That way he could not see my hair. Or what was left of it.

Friday morning, for the first set of tests, I arrived late, so that I wouldn't raise any suspicion. In fact, I was always late and this made him very nervous (indeed, that was one point over which we never got on . . .). This time, however, I did it on purpose. Brazzi is one of those guys who is always anxious. When I didn't show up, he became very jumpy and nervous and made sure everybody else became nervous and jumpy. In any case, I waited until he got really highly strung before showing up. When he saw me like that, with my "Brazzi cut", he burst out laughing. In fact, we all started laughing. It was a huge shock, but it was also incredibly funny. We laughed so much we almost missed out on the testing altogether.

It was wonderful. One of the many moments when Rossano laughed heartily. I loved making him laugh. In fact, the whole team enjoyed having a laugh together. That's just the kind of team it was. I had a great relationship with Brazzi. Sometimes he was not too easy to get along with. He could be a bit prickly, a bit dour. But it was just a question of knowing how to handle him. Our weekends were an absolute hoot; many times the crew and I amused ourselves just by winding him up. Because he had a low breaking point, he was very easy to wind up. But in the end, he forgave everyone everything, and he and I had a wonderful relationship.

Rossano was the first to fully understand the kind of potential I had. When I made mistakes, as I did in that first year, he would get very angry, because he felt we should be competing for the title right away. I, on the other hand, wasn't taking that season too seriously. I just wanted to enjoy myself, and learn about the tracks and bikes while having some fun. I didn't have any particular goals in terms of results. But he believed that we could actually do it, that we could become world champions. And in that 1998 season I made many mistakes, though one in particular stands out, because it was truly unforgettable.

We were in Spain, at Jarama. I had the fourth best time in qualifying. Back then, I simply was not as fast as Harada or Capirossi. And that would make me very angry. Rossano knew this, which is why, before the race, he took me to one side.

"Look, there's nothing you can do," he said. "Those two guys are faster than you. So don't worry about trying to beat them, just focus on taking home some points. Don't fuck around."

"Fine," I said, even though I had no intention of doing as he said. I was going for the win. And I suspected that Rossano knew this.

"Remember what I said," he added, just to drive the point home. "Don't go after them, don't try to compete with them, just be cool and get the points."

"Yes, Rossano, yes," I reassured him. "I'll go nice and slow. Nice and easy."

As it happened, Capirossi made a mistake on the first turn and I found myself right behind Tetsuya Harada. I was there, relaxed and calm as I'd promised Rossano, but suddenly, at one stage, I felt the urge to attack him, to give him something to worry about. So that's what I did. After a few laps, I passed him. And, almost immediately afterwards, I fell flat on my rear end.

My thoughts immediately turned to Brazzi and what he would say. I was so terrified of what would happen when I returned to the pits, that I actually tried to get up and continue. But my Aprilia was all bent and uneven, I did a few laps, but it became clear that my race was run. It was over. I couldn't stay out there on the track for ever, so I accepted the fact that, sooner or later, I had to go back and face Brazzi.

And there he was. Waiting for me. He was absolutely furious. He was scary. Terrifying. When I walked in, there was a deathly silence. I tried to stoop forward and walk with a limp, feigning some kind of injury. And I tried to look as sad and downtrodden as I could, in the hope that he would go easy on me. I knew it would all be to no avail, but I had to try. I removed my helmet and, as soon as Rossano approached, I tried to mount a credible defence.

"The bike just went, I couldn't keep it together, I don't know why . . ." I stammered.

He looked at me and said: "*In cu' t'a' ne propri capi un cazz!*"

That's not Italian. That's a dialect from the Romagna region. And it's probably best if I don't translate. After all, there might be children reading this!

In any case, his expression was terrifying, his moustache menacing and his eyes fierce. It was a long time before he spoke to me again. The simple truth of the matter was that there was a lot of tension at Aprilia that season. There were three teams, all cordial to each other, but each of us wanted to win. There was a huge rivalry, not just between Harada, Capirossi and myself, but also between Sandi, Noccioli and Brazzi, our respective chief engineers. Brazzi is a real connoisseur when it comes to two-stroke engines, as well as carburation. I've never seen anyone like him. It was always fascinating when he checked the carburation. I loved to sit and watch him work. The team did not talk much among themselves, but they didn't need to. They seemed to communicate without saying anything, like their thoughts were being transmitted through the air. I'd arrive with the bike, Paolo would remove the underfairings, Carlo laid out the tarpaulin, and Brazzi took his trusty small torch and examined the carburation of the bottom cylinder. It was a mystical moment; everyone fell silent. Then he'd get up and we would all wait with bated breath for his verdict. "She's rich," he would say, or, "She's lean," depending on whether there was too much air or too much petrol in the mix. And then he would announce the course of action to take. My bike was always fast and dependable. My rivals claimed that it was because we got the best material and parts from the racing department, but this wasn't true. We simply had Brazzi, who was the best around when it came to tuning a bike. While others always had carburation problems, and sometimes seized up as a result, my bike was always perfect.

My first win in 250cc came at Assen, in Holland. And it was all down to Brazzi. Noale had sent us a new exhaust. The bike did run a bit better with it, but Brazzi was adamant: "We're not using that thing in the race."

"Why?" I asked.

"Because I think it retains too much air, so if the engine heats up, it's going to break," he explained.

I trusted him and allowed myself to be convinced by his judgement. I did not use the new exhaust, whereas the other two Aprilias, belonging to Capirossi and Harada, duly mounted them. And, as it happened, both broke down during the race. My bike, on the other hand, had no problems and so I won handily. This showed that I was right in choosing a man like Brazzi and his team.

When Aprilia first explored the possibility of moving me up to 250cc, they assumed I would stay with Noccioli. However, by the end of the 1997 season, I had made up my mind. And I had seen that Brazzi, more than anyone else, was the kind of engineer who could take me to the next level. I had improved considerably with both Noccioli and Martini in the 125cc category, but I knew there was still work to be done. And, in my opinion, Brazzi was the right man to facilitate my progress through the ranks of 250cc. He was the type of person who gave you confidence, thanks to his experiences and his extraordinary team. I'm not sure why I was so taken with him – perhaps it was because, as a young boy, I had been a massive fan of Loris Reggiani, and Brazzi had been his chief engineer too. Either way, for me, Brazzi was a legend. He had just finished working with Doriano Romboni (another of my favourite facers) in 500cc and was returning to 250cc.

"It's all set, Brazzi will work with Capirossi and you'll move up to 250 with Noccioli," Pernat announced at a meeting.

"I've got other ideas," I said confidently.

"What ideas?" he asked.

"I want Brazzi!" I announced firmly.

So I asked Capirossi what he thought about it. He told me that, frankly, he didn't really mind either way: Brazzi or Noccioli, it was all the same to him.

"Great! In that case, if he doesn't care, I'll take Brazzi!" I thought to myself.

And so I had reached my second objective. Just as I handpicked Noccioli to guide me through the 125cc, so too I was able to select Brazzi for the 250cc.

During the 1999 season I faced another huge decision: stay in 250cc or move up to 500cc with Honda. Once again, I stayed true to myself. I had always believed that teams were crucial and I made it very clear that if I was going to move up, I wanted to be able to choose my own team.

"I don't really mind which bike you give me, even if it's not the 'official' one, I don't care," I told the Honda executives when they came to Rio de Janeiro and offered me the NSR. "However, I'll only join if I get to work with Jeremy Burgess."

I fought to be with Jeremy. I chose him and I made him a condition of my signing. To me, it was a deal-breaker. No Jeremy, no deal. I had met Jeremy at Philip Island in 1999 and he immediately made quite an impression on me. I realised immediately that, with him, given the experience he had, my debut in 500cc would be less traumatic. And, because I said Jeremy was a key part of the deal, a secret meeting was arranged in the pits at Philip Island.

Jeremy had basically stopped going to the Grands Prix. Every once in a while he'd turn up, but such appearances had become less and less frequent. Mick Doohan had suffered a serious accident at Jerez that basically ended his career, so Jeremy and his team were on their own now. His crew had split between various Honda teams, helping one rider or another. He also had the chance to serve as Gibernau's chief engineer, but turned it down. He needed time out, time to sit at home and be on his own.

But he did come to the Australian Grand Prix. He had been told that I wanted him, and HRC had arranged a meeting. He had been away from the track for a while and so he accepted. Our rendezvous was set for Saturday night, on the eve of the race. Around that time, the paddock is completely empty, so it's the perfect time to meet discreetly, without being seen. Jeremy was accompanied by Alex and Dickie, whereas I was with Carlo Florenzano. As soon as I walked in my gaze turned to the "official" NSR. And I immediately asked if I could climb on to it. When the answer was "yes", I jumped at the chance. It was Gibernau's NSR. The other bikes were all covered up; they had left this one out for me. They wanted *me* to touch and feel the bike. And yes, I was only on the bike for a minute or two, but I was quickly seduced by the NSR. And I'm pretty sure I wasn't the first, either.

"Look, I think it's only fair that I tell you that I'm thinking about quitting everything," said Jeremy. His words were a brusque reminder of why I was there. "There is a part of me that would be willing to stay on, but I still haven't made up my mind."

"What does he mean, he's quitting?" I thought to myself. I had worked so hard to get to him and now, all of a sudden, he was telling me he might walk away? It was tough, but there was nothing I could do. He asked for some time to think about it and we had no option but to agree.

"OK, let's wait and see what he says," I told the Honda executives. "But my agreement to join you is subordinate to Jeremy's. Let's wait and see what he says. And then we'll talk."

I said this in front of everyone, including Jeremy. It was my way of letting Honda (and Jeremy) know just how important he was to me.

In reality, the negotiations with Honda had been going on for a while. Back at the end of summer, they had sent Carlo Florenzano to see me.

"If you're interested in racing 500cc, Honda has something to offer you," he said. "You could get the official 500cc."

Every kid on a motorbike dreams of 500cc and, in fact, many times he doesn't even dare to dream about it. I was obviously taken by the idea. I showed the right amount of interest and then bought some time, telling them I had to sort some things out.

My first meeting with the Japanese Honda executives was at the Imola Grand Prix.

"I'm in no rush, I want to become 250cc world champion first," I told them. "Before that happens, I'm not going to decide a thing."

"Fine," they said. I could tell they were annoyed, if not offended. "Just remember we're not going to wait for ever."

I justified myself: "OK, but just remember that if I don't win the 250cc now, I'm never going to win," I said. "Whereas there will be plenty of time to win the 500cc."

At the time, I was nineteen. I had all the time in the world. That's why just as back in 1996 I decided not to go up to 250 without first winning 125, at the end of 1999 I had no intention of thinking about 500cc unless I first became 250cc world champion. Of course, I then won the title and everything became a lot easier. But, even if I hadn't won, I would never have gone back on my word. I would have stayed in 250cc until I finally did become world champion. No matter how long it took.

That's why I lived through the latter part of 1999 thinking about 500cc, even though in the end Honda waited for me. And so the night of the Rio Grand Prix, where we won the title, I sat down with Carlo Florenzano, who represented Honda. This time my mind was clear – all I needed to think of was the future. My days racing 250cc were behind me. When I climbed onto the NSR at Philip Island, it felt great right away, and I understood that my career was going to go even further, much further. After two years in 250cc with Aprilia and Brazzi's team, finishing second one season and winning the title the next, I was about to reach the apex of my sport. All this after just four years in the world championship. And only six years removed from my first ever motorcycle race, back on the Cagiva 125, in the Italian Sport Production series.

Still, I was waiting on Jeremy's decision. Fortunately, he did not take that long to make up his mind. Jeremy dug deep and rediscovered his hunger for the track. Plus, I think he was intrigued by the possibility of starting all over, a whole new adventure, with me. And when he agreed, so did his crew, a bunch of guys who are still with us now at Yamaha. A month later, in November, we were all working together.

The Honda NSR was one of those bikes that made history. It's the bike you dreamed about. I was twenty years old when my dream was fulfilled and I got to ride it for real. I was the reigning 250cc champion and I had just ended my career at Aprilia. I was ready to move to Honda and, finally, live the dream of the NSR.

To be fair, leaving 250cc was not an easy decision. It took a long time before I realised I was finally ready to move on. I first began to think about taking the step up in the second half of the 1999 season, as I was cruising towards the world title. I began looking ahead, wondering what the future would bring. At that time, the future meant moving to 500cc, just as today it means racing MotoGP.

I thought about it a very long time, because I was just twenty years old. I could have defended my title for a few more years, earned a load more money and taken it easy in 2000. I still would have had plenty of time to move to 500cc later. But that's not the type of person I am. I am curious, I always push myself, I always look for new challenges. Besides, it's not every year that you are given the chance to race a Honda NSR 500cc. Not just that, the "official" Honda NSR 500cc. I felt honoured by the fact that Honda picked me, that they agreed to hand over the "official" bike and that they allowed me to put together my own team in Italy, rather than having to join the Team HRC Repsol. In other words, I got everything I could have wanted: the official bike and Jeremy Burgess as chief engineer.

Ivano Beggio, president of Aprilia, and I left each other on a good note. He did not try to hold me back, giving me permission to test the NSR 500cc right away, without having to wait for January 2000, even though my contract ran until 31 December. I jumped at the chance. When I got to Jerez de la Frontera, in the south of Spain, just across from the North African coast, I was incredibly excited. It was wonderful enough being given a chance in 500cc, but the fact that my chance came on a Honda NSR 500 only made it even more special. The feeling was incredible, my skin was crawling with excitement.

Today there is no 500cc category any more, of course, as it's been replaced by MotoGP. The demise of 500cc helped to weed out many problems, but also a fair dose of excitement. Because the simple truth is that no bike in the world can match a two-stroke 500cc. I loved its violent character – it was so intense that you got an adrenalin boost every time you shifted gears. Besides, I was a massive fan, as 500cc had always been the home of the best racers.

I made my debut, at the end of 1999, on one of Alex Crivillé's bikes (he had just become world champion). It was also identical to Mick Doohan's bike, and he had just retired. That NSR featured the four-cylinder – or "screamer" – version, whereas the one I rode in

2001, when I won the title, was somewhat different from Doohan's bike. I had always imagined my debut on an official Honda 500cc as a sort of initiation, almost as some kind of formal ceremony. I had fantasised about it so many times, that I had already played it out in my head.

"When I arrive, I'll see first the Honda trucks," I told myself. "Then, I'll see the bike itself, shiny, every detail glowing. I'll slip right into a perfect organisational machine, with Japanese engineers running around, catering to my every need, and mechanics in white gloves assisting me at every turn."

Well, it didn't work out exactly like that. I arrived in a semi-deserted paddock. There was nobody around. Then I saw a green rental van approaching. I could recognise Jeremy, Bernard (a mechanic from Team HRC) and, with them, a Japanese mechanic. Jeremy was not the most formal type. He was wearing Timberland boots and a horrible jumper, dark wool with ugly rectangles. It was the kind of jumper that I thought no longer existed.

So this was the great and legendary Jeremy Burgess . . . and he looked like a man trapped in a time warp, and a very unfashionable one at that. Jeremy and Bernard and the mechanic hadn't seen me, so I just stood and watched as they piled out of the rental van and opened the gate to unload the NSR 500. One of them had a toolbox, but that was it. Just the bike, a set of tools and the three mechanics. The bike itself looked rather unremarkable. It was black, with orange rings, a grey gas tank and generic fairings. It all looked really cheap and ordinary.

"What's going on?" I thought to myself. "This is the most important bike in the world, I'm here with the most important team in the world and these guys unload a piece of junk like this from a rented van?"

I was horrified. I simply could not believe it. I was very upset. I was mortified. On these things, I've always been fairly unyielding. I demand high standards. The bike has to be in order. It has to be neat, with no stickers in the wrong places. The colours must be coordinated and make sense together. The visual impact must seduce the viewer immediately. To me, this applies to everything I own. But, for the bike, the thing I love more than anything else, these standards go even further.

I guess that's why I was so incredulous when I saw the bike in that condition. It might almost have been funny seeing Jeremy so shabbily dressed, accompanied by the single Japanese mechanic with the crummy toolbox on the ground and the poorly maintained NSR. But it wasn't funny. All I could think was: "And this is supposed to be motorcycling at the highest level?"

And to think that I was so excited for my test, that I even had two suits specially made by Dainese. They were designed by Aldo Drudi and were both yellow with a big Honda logo and a picture of an old Fiat Cinquecento. It was my way of celebrating the fact that I was now on a 500cc, albeit a very different type of "500".

"Well, even if the bike looks like rubbish, I'll still look good," I thought to myself, remembering my beautiful new suits. I leaned over into my bag and pulled them out. As I did this, Gibo immediately intervened.

"Wait, don't you have your Aprilia suit?" he asked.

"No."

"Look, you can't wear those suits. You need to use an Aprilia suit."

"What?" I exclaimed. Hadn't Aprilia allowed me to test with Honda? What was Gibo talking about?

"Our deal with Aprilia is quite clear," he said. "You can test with Honda, but you need to use the Aprilia suit, because that has all the sponsors on it. And they are fully paid up until the end of the year."

He was right. Gibo thought he had told me about this, but, in fact, he never did. And so I knew nothing about the terms of the agreement with Aprilia. This is when I started to panic.

"I can't come this far, this close to the NSR and NOT test it for something as silly as a suit," I thought.

I called a meeting of my clan.

"OK, what the fuck are we going to do?" I said. I was happy for people to brainstorm. After a few minutes, it came to me.

"Guys, somebody needs to go and get my suit and bring it here!"

So I called my friend from Pesaro, Filippo Palazzi. When I got him on the phone, I blurted it straight out, without much preamble: "Look, I need you to go to my house, get my suit and grab the first plane over here, so that you can be in Jerez by tonight. Can you do it?"

"What better excuse is there to get away after all?" I added, knowing that his wife had not wanted him to come see me in Jerez.

He understood the situation, explained everything to his wife (who was, I gather, quite understanding), drove to my house, got the suit and then was off to the airport, getting the first flight to Jerez. That solution was fine for day two of the tests. I still had to figure out what I was going to do on the first day, the day that was supposed to have been my debut. As luck would have it, Aprilia were also running tests in Jerez. So I went to Marcellino Lucchi and asked him for one of his suits. He was so kind and understanding, there wasn't much convincing to be done. He handed it over. The problem was that he is quite a bit shorter than me and I didn't feel comfortable at all in his suit.

"Still, this beats watching from the side of the track," I told myself. I went back to the pits to put on my helmet. Except it wasn't there. It had disappeared. As I later found out, it had been stolen at Milan airport.

My heart sank. I could not believe it. Jeremy didn't say a word, though I would not have blamed him had he made some kind of sarcastic remark. Ultimately, the Honda guys may have shown up at the track looking like bums, but I certainly hadn't fared much better: I had an ill-fitting suit which belonged to somebody else and no helmet.

"What a wonderful debut!" I thought. "What a shitty day!"

I was very depressed. Suddenly, it came to me. The idea that would save my test debut. I remembered that Harada and I had once exchanged helmets. And because Harada was there in Jerez testing himself, all I had to do was to go see him and ask for my helmet back!

That's why if you go back and look at pictures of my debut on the official Honda NSR 500, you'll see that I look fairly ridiculous. The day of the big event, the day which changed the history of 500cc and ultimately played a huge part in the later success of my career, was just a succession of fashion faux pas. From Jeremy's jumper to the ugly NSR 500, to my suit which was covered in masking tape (to conceal the name of its owner, Lucchi) and which barely fitted me and an old helmet which wasn't even mine any more.

At least the bike ran well and I was able to race. Once on the bike, I didn't have time to think about how silly we looked. I told myself, "This is a 500, this is serious stuff, you better just focus on racing."

It's a good idea that I thought that too, because the G-force was ferocious. When I think back to the first few laps on the NSR 500 what I remember most is the adrenalin and the violent jerks every time I shifted, particularly in the low gears.

I thought I had prepared by watching other racers, both on television and in person. But the truth is that you can never actually prepare for the 500cc. It's twice as fast as the 250cc and far more powerful. It causes terror and demands respect. For example, on television I had noticed that 500cc racers rarely went straight after coming out of a turn, they normally wobbled left or right. I had no idea why this was the case. I soon found out. With a 500cc you could not come out of a turn and open the throttle the way you would with a normal bike. The 500cc's front tyre was never on the ground and the rear tyre was all over the place. I understood that the only way to deal with it was to keep it inclined, at an angle, in an attempt to stop it from rising too much. And that's why you saw 500cc guys coming up with such weird (and often illogical) trajectories. It wasn't poor driving, quite the contrary.

I was fast from day one on the 500cc. On the second day – when I finally was able to put on my own suit – I was already clocking excellent times, pole position times, such as 1' 43" 5. I have always been like that on my debuts. I always tried to be fast right away, because I feel that I can take my bike to the limit very quickly. It was the same in 250cc. I pushed my bike immediately and, as a result, I also collected a series of falls. Because that's what happens, you're going very fast, you think you have things under control and that's when you take risks. On the 250, that period – driving on the edge – lasted much longer than on the 500. That's because when you fall off a 500cc bike, you don't forget it any time soon.

The 500cc was so powerful that, if you pushed on the gas too quickly, you simply flew away, there was no margin of error. And, actually, those are the most painful falls, the ones caused by acceleration. This is because the back tyre slides at first and then achieves traction all of a sudden, which makes the bike fly through the air as if propelled by a slingshot. In technical terms, we call it the "high side". And it's not fun.

Still, the NSR 500 was easily the most exciting bike I ever rode. It was a very selective bike, very challenging to ride. If you made the slightest mistake, you'd end up on your rear end. And that's why I can say that few racers were suited to the NSR 500. It really was the toughest bike to master. Either you rode her or she punished you. There was no middle ground.

At the time, I was falling a lot. And for many different reasons. Part of it had to do with my style in 250. In 250cc you can go into a turn bent right over and you can even open the throttle all the way on the turn, accelerating as you go through it. OK, it's not the easiest thing to do but it was possible and many of us had mastered it. You can forget about doing things like that on a 500cc. One of the problems with the 500 is that, at first, you feel totally confident. That's what happened to me. I felt very sure of myself, I pushed ahead, keeping my 250cc style. And, as a result, I kept falling off.

It happened in my second test, at Philip Island. And it was a very bad fall. Gibernau had come up to me before the test and actually warned me: "Look, you bend the bike too much, treat it as if it was a 250cc. You can't do that. You should use your body more rather than bending the bike."

"Gee, thanks, yeah, I'll do that . . ." I replied, not really taking him too seriously. I asked myself, "Who is this Gibernau who thinks he can tell me how race?"

Of course, I paid no attention to him. And that was a big mistake. Two hours later I had a terrible spill. I was going very fast and, all of a sudden, I felt the rear tyre lift itself off the track and the next thing I knew I was flying through the air. It was an incredible flight. When I finally landed it was with the kind of thud I'm sure to remember for a very long time.

And yet, even episodes like that one weren't enough to teach me my lesson. At the South African Grand Prix, I fell once again. This time the steering locked up. In Malaysia I was going even faster and flew through the air again. At that point I began having doubts. I thought about what had happened to me and asked myself where I was going wrong.

"Now it's time for you to really change your style," I told myself.

And, yes, the time had come, though I still did not fully comprehend how to go into a turn on the 500cc. And that was the biggest problem.

On the 500cc the trick is to come in very fast and then brake as much as possible inside the turn. On the 250 on the other hand you want to be braking well before the turn, you don't actually brake in the turn because you want to maintain your speed for the straightaway which usually follows.

But the 500cc is, as I say, a completely different animal. You can't drive it like that because it weighs 130 kilograms and if it stays bent for more than a few seconds, it's easy for the steering to lock, and it's easy to lose traction on the front. The 500cc is also much more stable when braking. You can brake very hard and the front will hold, but if you release the brakes and you're bent then the front loses traction and rises off the track. So you want to go into the turn with a lot of speed, slow down in the turn and then straighten up and take off, because with such a powerful engine, finding power as you come out of the turn is never a problem. But there is a split second when you have to be very careful: when you go into the curve, there is an instant when you don't have any downforce and, if you lose traction, you go flying through the air.

The trick is to try to turn as soon as possible and then get the bike back up so that you have as much of the tyre on the track as possible. That way, if you slide, at least you have some control. Because there is another problem in 500cc. If you are bent and you hit the gas too hard, the bike bucks and – you guessed it – you're thrown through air.

Anyway, it takes time to understand the 500. You have to be very sensitive. It took me a while as well. And, once you do master it, you have to be careful not to become overconfident. The bike will punish you for such arrogance. You have to always be on your toes, metaphorically speaking.

It took me a lot of spills and most of my first season to understand the nature of the 500 and change the way I drove. Sure, I was fast, but that was never a problem. I'd always been fast. By the end of my first year, the 2000 season, I had been on the podium ten times. And I would fall only a few more times, each time because I was too confident.

One of those spills was at Mugello after an epic battle with Biaggi and Capirossi. All three of us went head-to-head and, by the end, we had pushed each other so far that only Capirossi made it to the finish line. Biaggi and I had both fallen.

For me, the turning point came in Valencia. I was the only one left who had a chance of catching Kenny Roberts, although it was all theoretical – his lead was huge. But I fell again in that race. And it was for the same reason: my front tyre lost contact with the track. By the time we returned to Rio, I had finally mastered the bike, I believed I had finally adapted my style to cope with the 500. Of course, by then the season was nearly over. It had taken me nearly a whole year. In any case, it's not as if I never used to fall in the past. Not even in 2001, when I became world champion. That year, I fell three times. Which is slightly more than my seasonal average.

Things changed shortly thereafter when we moved to MotoGP. MotoGP bikes can be driven in many different ways; each rider can have his own style. That's because the four-stroke engine gives you a lot of latitude, as it's far easier to control both power delivery and acceleration. Part of the secret lies in the four-stroke engine, and the electronics are a huge help, too. MotoGP is also far more user-friendly. It's simply easier than 500cc. There are far fewer falls, because controlling the power distribution is simpler. It's also easier to brake. When you do fall in MotoGP, it's always a slide, rarely the sudden jerky motion you often had with 500cc. This is not to suggest that MotoGP is for everyone or even that I'd like to see them on our roads. Yet it's true that it's a far easier bike to handle, compared to the 500. And that's why MotoGP is far less selective.

I'd say that there are a far greater number of racers who can use up to 95 per cent of their bike's potential in MotoGP. In 500cc, I'd say few got as high as 75 per cent of the bike's potential. That's why the races are much more close-run affairs these days.

Like I said, don't get the wrong idea. You don't want to be going on holiday on a MotoGP or driving it around town. Because while the power delivery is softer, it's still a very, very fast bike and one which is extremely complicated to tune.

And that's why, at the end, even in MotoGP some racers do stand out. Because they don't just exploit 95 per cent of their bike's potential. They get pretty darn close to 100 per cent . . .

TEN

Just above my beltline, off to the left, I have a tattoo which is very important to me. It's a turtle. In fact, it's a replica of an anti-stress turtle that Uccio gave me as a present a few years ago. He gave it to me in the early days of my career in 250cc, when things weren't going particularly well. I was quite tense at the time and needed a release.

"You're stressed out," he told me. "Use this."

And he gave me the turtle. It was made of that ultra-soft material which, no matter how you distort or misshape it, always pops back into its original shape. You can beat it, stomp on it, torture it, maybe even microwave it, it doesn't matter, it always bounces back. Drudi copied the design and I later had it tattooed.

It's funny. I feel as if I need this turtle, this slow, deliberate creature, every time I need to go fast. It seems like a contradiction, but it's true. Weird, isn't it?

Another turtle has also played an important part in my life. It became my good-luck charm, following me everywhere, in every single race. It's my Ninja Turtle. My mum, Stefania, had given it to me when I was eleven, a week before my first minibike race.

I have to say, I don't have an innate predilection for turtles. It's just that I became attached to the turtle my mum gave me. And I guess that's when my love of turtles was born – and why I later got the tattoo; although in reality my mother didn't give me the Ninja Turtle because I was about to make my debut on the minibikes – it was just one of those happy coincidences. I remember clearly: Mum had kidnapped me and taken me grocery shopping. We were at the super-market in Pesaro and I saw the turtle. I liked it immediately and began to pester her so that she would buy it for me. It was a typical scene between mother and son.

"Mum, come on, please buy me the turtle!"

"No, I'm not buying it."

"Please, I really, really love it."

"Leave it!"

"Please, I beg of you, buy me the turtle! I promise I'll be good."

"No."

"Please! Please! Please!"

"OK, fine! I'll buy you the turtle, but you'd better behave!"

A few days later I competed in my first race, but the turtle wasn't with me. It was only later that I decided to attach it to my helmet. I had copied the idea from another kid who had a little stuffed animal on his helmet. My turtle had suction cups, so attaching it was not a problem. That Ninja Turtle raced with me – and I do mean literally *raced with me* – until I turned thirteen. After that, when I moved to real motorbikes, I was no longer allowed to keep my turtle on the helmet, so I cut off the suction cup and removed the turtle. But I vowed that it would stay with me.

"You'll come with me wherever I race!" I told the turtle.

And that's what I did. The Ninja Turtle, that very same Ninja Turtle, is always among my personal effects when I go racing. I also have a turtle on my helmet, on the left side, next to the logo on the upper part of the visor: "The Tribe of the Chihuahua".

It's the name of my group of friends, my best mates since I was a child. We've been together for as long as I can remember. Most of them are from Tavullia, the others from nearby. We've always been together. First in pre-school, then at my elementary school, Vittorio

Giunta. Some of them were always in my class, year after year; others came into the Tribe later. When I began middle school, I had to leave them. I attended school in Pian del Bruscolo, near Montecchio, because the school we attended before only taught French as a second language and Graziano wanted me to learn English. I was very disappointed because I was forced to go to another school in another town where I didn't know anyone and also because I had to leave my friends. I was a bit desperate at first. We were apart for only a few hours in the day, in the mornings (in Italy you go to school until lunchtime), but it still hurt. Naturally we spent every minute of the afternoon together.

Those guys were, and still are, my friends. Naturally I've got many friends who aren't part of the Tribe. Because I have a lot of friends, of all different ages, and there are some whom I love as much as those in the Tribe. But the Tribe is something special, something different, something unique. When I'm with them, I don't feel like a celebrity. Nor am I obliged to behave like a celebrity. When I'm with the Tribe I'm neither a champion, nor a star. When I return to Tavullia I immediately find the usual intimacy and I go back to being Valentino and nothing else, I can talk the way kids my age talk, I don't need to be a role model to others. I can be a normal kid. And that is what I miss the most.

It's only when I'm with my friends that I can be considered a normal kid. With them I can talk about anything, without worrying about whether my words will make it into the media or, worse, make it into the media and be used against me. Of course, we often talk about racing and motorbikes, but with them it's just about telling stories, the same way you may tell a story about your colleagues at work or your schoolmates. And I speak to them the way I might speak to my brother, if I had one. Because that's what they are to me: brothers.

Uccio, Pirro, Caroni, Nello, Bagaro, Mambo, the Fuligna, Gabba,

Cico, Secco, Tia Musto, Biscia, Lele, Filo, Yuri, Pane, La Matta, Spugna, Sburo, Pedro, Gabbia and Piwi (the last ones are a bit older). Plus me, of course. That's the Tribe. One day, when we were at Mambo's house in Cattolica, we were on our own, overdoing it, drinking too much red wine and eating chestnuts. One of us came out with the phrase: "We are just like a Tribe."

And so we were. That's why we chose the name of an Indian Tribe. The Tribe of the Chihuahua. And I decided to take that name with me on the racetrack. When I was on the 125, I had a sticker that said "Cosmico!" ("Cosmic") on my helmet and I won the world title with it in 1997. Then, in my first year in 250, in 1998, I stuck a little sign which read "Do not speak to the driver", much like the signs you see on buses. Later, I replaced it with "Tribe of the Chihuahua".

The Tribe is untouchable. For us, friendship has always been a very important value, which takes priority over everything. We've always been united, despite the passing of the years, our growing up, our jobs and the different paths down which life has taken us. I'm always with them when I'm in Tavullia. We're together at night, we go to the beach in the summer and to the mountains in the winter. It was always like that when we were small and it is like that every year.

Our group is made up of people who do the most disparate jobs, at different hours, so there is always someone to hang out with. Many of them work during the day, others work at night. Still others own bars or restaurants or they're waiters. So when I'm in Tavullia, I can be with one group of friends until a certain hour and then, when they need to go to bed, I can move on to another group, which will just be getting off work. (As you've probably gathered by now, I stay up pretty late. And in the morning, I sleep. As far as I'm concerned, there is no such thing as the morning, except for race weekends or other times when I'm stuck with a commitment I can't postpone to the afternoon.)

Sometimes I feel like a fugitive. Fleeing from my opponents and from the fans. But I generally can always handle the situation . . .

Graziano, my dad, has helped me from the very beginning or my career and he often gives me good advice.

My job takes me all over the world, giving me the chance to see some beautiful cities.

The sea in Philip Island, Australia, is not the most welcoming, but the island is a marvellous place to race motorbikes.

I love London. I moved there in 2001 and immediately appreciated the atmosphere of truly multi-ethnic city.

Jerez, April 2005, first race of the world championship. Gibernau left me an opening, on the last turn, and I went for it. My racing is sometimes aggressive, but I always try to be fair.

Opposite: Steve McQueen was a rebel spirit, much like me.

The pits are a special place, that's where we work on the bikes, fine tuning them or solving problems.

Who said you have to be serious when you're working? You have to smile and joke around. Life is much better in a relaxed setting.

I don't like formal clothing, I'm more of a casual type of guy. It suits my style and my character much better.

I'm Italian, which means I love life in the sun and I have a good rapport with the sea. Thus, taking the boat out was a natural match and soon became one of my passions.

My day, usually, begins in the afternoon. It's as if I exist inside my own personal time zone. I live at night, because I love the night. Now, this might make you think I do goodness-knows-what in the wee hours, or that I don't live the life of a professional athlete. It's true, I don't live the life of an athlete in the traditional sense – early to bed, early to rise and all that – but this does not mean that I'm not careful about what I eat and drink or that I don't train. In fact, I train a lot, both in the gym and on the bike. It's just that I go to the gym in the afternoon, rather than the morning. Equally, when I'm training on the bike, down at the quarry, I always go in the afternoon, never at nine o'clock in the morning.

My body has a certain type of metabolism. It is used to living according to a different body clock. That's why, even if I'm travelling all over the world, I don't experience jet lag and I rarely go to bed before 3 a.m. It's much more likely that I'm just tucking into bed as people are leaving for work. As I say, I have a special relationship with the night. I like moving in it, living in it, thinking in it, relaxing in it. The night fascinates me, because it's the period of least confusion. The world calms down, it goes quiet. And, besides, I'm Valentino Rossi. I'm wanted . . . I'm a fugitive.

Yes, I'm always running away from my beloved countrymen. The Italians. I'm proud to be Italian, I'm proud of our merits and I regret our shortcomings. Italians are exceptional people. In every way. Even when they start loving you. Because that's actually when problems can arise – if it's you that the Italian falls in love with. Italian people are warm, empathetic, spontaneous. But they can also be excessive, oppressive and disrespectful. I don't know who said that Italians will forgive everything except for success. Whoever it was, they were right. Because it's absolutely true.

After the 1997 season, I could tell I was becoming popular. Year after year, that popularity turned into fully-fledged love. They're in love with me now and, as a result, since the 2004 season, I've been a man on the run. And there's no escape, no end in sight, because wherever I go they find me. There are simple things, the little pleasures in life, which I simply can't engage in when I'm back in Italy. I can't go to the bar and have a cappuccino, because I would not be able to drink it. To be fair, I can do it in Tavullia, but that's the only place. If I go more than a few kilometres in any direction from the centre of town, that's it, everything changes and I become, once again, a hunted animal.

I can't walk into a store, look at something and decide what I want to buy. In fact, I can't stop anywhere, not even at a petrol station. If I stop, I'm screwed. Somebody will recognise me (Italians are exceptionally good at recognising people), make a lot of noise, call other people and then, before I know it, I've been swallowed up by the crowd.

If I schedule a meeting with someone, we have to meet in a secret, out-of-the-way location and, even then, we can't linger. I can't go to a restaurant if there are too many people inside. And if I do go, I can't go at a normal time, say eight o'clock. I have to go later, much later, when people are leaving. And I can't sit where I like, I have to hide away in a corner, in the shadows. As for places like cinemas or the beach, forget about it. They are just always off-limits.

Having said that, I do mix with people. I do it because I like doing it. It's just that I wish I could do it as a normal person, because, deep down, I am a normal human being. This is part of the reason why I have to live at night. It would be that much tougher during the day, with all those people about. Plus, I don't like the traffic, the chaos, the noise, all those people running all over the place, stressed out and out of breath. The night is different. Everything is softer, there are fewer people around and you are much more free. It's like a parallel dimension. The world is different at night. Everything is different. That's why I've assimilated the lyrics of a song by the Italian artist Jovanotti, "Gente della notte" ("People of the night"). It has become my personal anthem. Jovanotti is one of my favourite singers and I find myself agreeing with him on most things. I love his work.

What else can I say? The night is my reality. And I don't change just because Grands Prix are scheduled during the day. My way of being and living is reflected in what I do during races. I don't really change. Obviously, I don't go to bed at dawn, but let's just say that when I do, finally, go to bed, there aren't many people around. Everything is better at night in the paddock. There is silence, the people have disappeared and, with them, the chaos. I can wander around freely, most of all I can enjoy the empty pit area and my bike. Yes, my bike. Because at night I often slip into the team garage. At some races I do it every single night, because I love being with my bike.

My night-time activities can be traced back to the years racing in 125cc, and are directly tied to my passion for aesthetics and the stickers, which would later become my obsession. I don't leave anything to chance when it comes to choosing the colour or the stickers for my bike. That's why I've always been central to any and all discussions when we were deciding the aesthetics of my racing bikes. I've done it always, with every bike, at every level, with every team. And, naturally, I still do it today. Nobody has ever been allowed to attach a single sticker to my bike, unless it was the logo of a technical sponsor.

Until a few years ago I was totally inflexible about this. Now, Roby takes care of the number: he attaches it because then he needs to cover it in transparent paint. But apart from this, which is primarily a technical procedure anyway, I take care of everything else to do with the stickers. And this takes time and planning, which is why I started going to the garage at night. During the day it is packed with people.

There are mechanics, technicians and others around. I would just get in the way, if I wanted to get near the bike just to check the stickers.

As I got older and progressed from 125 to 250 and then to 500 and on to MotoGP, I maintained that passion for aesthetics and stickers, as well as the habit of dropping in on the team garage at night. I enjoy the bike during the day obviously, but my relationship with the bike is so special that I can spend hours with it, just looking and admiring it, making sure that everything is in order. Those are very personal moments which I find difficult to describe. The Japanese guys, both the executives but also the engineers never knew this, not the guys at Honda, not the ones at Yamaha. I don't think they would really understand. They would probably view it as a waste of time, since I don't actually do anything concrete. I never touch anything to do with the bike itself, beyond, obviously, the stickers. And yet I find it hard to explain to an engineer that I enjoy simply being near the bike, even when I'm not doing anything. It's a complicated concept to explain: the risk is that people will think that you're crazy.

During the day everything happens so quickly, frenetically, neurotically. However, there is a sacrosanct moment when I need to step away and isolate myself. Once my commitment to the team is over, usually around 5.30 p.m., I retire to my motorhome, relax and take a nap. It usually lasts a couple hours and then I go out.

There's always something to do after dinner. Of course, the range of options depends on how many friends are around. I really start enjoying the paddock around ten o'clock at night. Before going to sleep I check on the bike again and then I go into the team motorhome, which serves as an office. Now that I'm at Yamaha, I have an office all to myself. That's where I keep all my race gear. I do this for two reasons. My own personal motorhome is an absolute mess, nothing more fits in there and I probably couldn't find anything amid all the junk. Plus, the office is where I change into my racing suit before going out on to the track. Thus, at night, after going to the pits to see the bike, I go make sure that all my stuff is where it should be: gloves, suit, socks, boots . . . everything needs to be perfect, because I just don't have time in the morning to hunt around for stuff.

Because I wake up late, I'm always late getting to the garage for the first round of open testing. It's just like being back in school, when I was always the last one to arrive.

Thus, each morning I have to follow a very precise routine. I'm like a robot, everything is the same each day. Because the truth is that I need to be like clockwork. I just don't have the time to think. Somebody generally comes to wake me up – usually it's Jeremy, because he doesn't trust my ability to wake up on my own! I then get up, wash my face (my eyes are still shut at this point) and try to stay awake as I ride the scooter from the motorhome to the pits. I then go up to the office and get dressed. There too everything is done mechanically. It takes the slightest hiccup to throw everything off, forcing me to be late to the testing.

Going back to the Italians, while it's true that sometimes I get annoyed with their insistence when they come and hunt me down, I recognise that it's partly because of me and the way I am. I am the kind of person who puts others at ease, who makes them feel like we've known each other for years. They think we're friends, that we can laugh and joke together as soon as we meet. Because Italians love doing this.

So everybody thinks they know me well. Nobody approaches me with a degree of detachment. When they see me they want to hug me, grab me, touch me, squeeze me.

There are all sorts of "types".

There's the guy to whom it would never occur that maybe you don't feel like laughing and joking at precisely that moment. No, he appears and does his little shtick, one question after another, telling you things you never asked to hear.

Then there is the worrier, who usually wants to come and sit down next to you, asking you how the bike is, the one who really cares about the standings, the opponents, who gives me all sorts of advice on how to ride in the next race.

There's the sensationalist, the one who runs over as soon as he sees you. He hugs you, grabs you, pins you down and then calls his friends who arrive by the dozens and repeat the same routine.

The souvenir hunter makes me feel like an animal in the zoo. He observes me, he photographs me from a nearby table or from the sidewalk. Ever since somebody had the bright idea of putting cameras in mobile phones, my life has changed, and not necessarily for the better: there is no such thing as privacy any more, ever. Anyone can spy on you, take your picture or even shoot a video of you. I truly loathe this, because the mobile-phone-camera maniacs have no compunction about stopping you, passing the phone around among themselves and snapping away from every conceivable angle in every conceivable pose. They don't ask permission. And, if they do, and you say "No", they just go and take your picture anyway, perhaps doing it secretly, which I believe is worse.

The disrespectful type has no idea what privacy is. He'll come right up to you when you're at dinner with friends, or on a date, without thinking that you might need some time to yourself once in a while.

There's the moraliser, who comes up to you, interrupts whatever it is you're doing, puts his hand on your shoulder and says: "Goodness, you sure lead a nice life, you make all this money, you do fuck all and you get to travel all over the world! Life is good, isn't it?"

And finally, there's the jealous one and here you have to be very careful, because it only takes a split second for an Italian to turn you from God to Satan in their minds. And if they change their minds about you, they're very unlikely to forgive.

Having said that, when the Italians love you, they really love you. They transmit so much warmth, they really make you feel special. And that's why I always try to do something a little different at, say, the Italian Grand Prix. And that's why I still love my countrymen. It's just that I wish they were a little more polite.

I try to be open with everyone, to give everyone a smile or a second of my time. But I also need moments of quiet and intimacy. If, everywhere I go, I am spied on and watched as if I'm living in a goldfish bowl, life quickly becomes oppressive. The pressure is constant and it never goes away. And this is part of the reason why I decided to take a break from Italy and go live in London, a city I've always liked. In April of 2000 I became a resident and went to live in a very nice area near Piccadilly. London is a truly multi-ethnic city. People go there from every corner of the world. It's as if the whole world is in one city. And I love that. Because of all the different cultures in London, you always learn something new, whether it's a new trend or a new idea. But the really big difference, for me personally, was the way I was treated by people on the street.

As soon as I arrived, I immediately appreciated the fact that I could go around without being stopped. Nobody recognised me, and this was something totally new for me. And it was wonderful. After a few years though, things have begun to change, although it remains a far cry from Italy. In London I can relax a bit for two reasons. First, fewer people recognise me and, second, they are far more respectful of my privacy and my personal space. They may give me a compliment or let me know I'm appreciated, but they're not oppressive.

In London I can live a normal life, I feel on a par with everybody else. I wait in line, I don't have it any easier to get into nightclubs or restaurants, I struggle to get a cab late at night like everyone else. I can wander around for hours, whether in the park or in the shops, buying a new shirt or a pair of shoes. And this is all wonderful. If anything, when I do have problems, it's because I'm recognised by the Italians who live and work in London. The good thing is that, after a few years in Britain, they too tend to adapt to the local way and are somewhat more reserved.

As soon as I arrived in London, I had to fit in. And that meant finding the right places to buy things, to figure out how to get around, and the right restaurants to eat at. Because eating well is important to me, like most Italians. And, in England, it's not always so easy to eat well! Thankfully, London is an exception. There is such a blend of different races and cultures that you can find almost any type of cuisine in the world.

At first, I rented a home, though now I've bought one. And near my first house there was an Italian restaurant that we discovered one night. It was called Il Duca and the food was excellent. And that's where we met the chef, Michele.

Because he was a chef, he knew his way around. He gave us the low-down on which places to check out and which ones to avoid. And so, most nights, before going out, we would swing by the restaurant and get some advice. Michele was an absolute nutter. He was always on his motorbike: every night and every morning he commuted an hour and a half to get to the restaurant, since he lived outside the city. And, at the time, he rode a Yamaha R6.

Given the climate, it's not always easy to ride a motorbike in London. Doing it every day, the whole year round, seemed crazy to us, because London is usually cold and rainy. And Michele was very fast when it was wet, and sometimes things did not work out so well. In fact, he banged up the R6 quite badly, just after buying it.

Once, we were in the square in front of my house, right near the restaurant. I tried his bike and, naturally, it was one of those typical London days. It was dark and rainy, even in the middle of summer.

When I returned I said: "Look, today is not a good day to be out on the bike. This asphalt is no good, the tyres have no traction, it's very dangerous!"

Just then we saw a pizza-delivery guy fly past us on an ancient Kawasaki 350. As he came round a turn on the wet asphalt, his foot-stand hit the pavement and he took a right wobble but, amazingly, he didn't fall and even kept the pizza boxes upright!

I often wondered about the pizza-delivery guys. To me, they are fantastic riders. They'll overtake you on the wet, in traffic, on cobble-stones, they can handle any situation. And they're always fast. I think some of them are wasted talents. In fact, the pizza-delivery kid on the old Kawasaki 350 might have potentially been faster than me!

Every year, the British Grand Prix organisers put together a special event for me to meet my fans on the eve of the race. We meet in Leicester Square, a place known for its film premieres and therefore quite familiar to actors and show-business types. In 2004, there were so many people there you would have thought there was a Hollywood star somewhere around, rather than little old me . . . And then there is the British Grand Prix itself. To me, Donington feels like home, because of the crowd support I get and the incredible scenes under the podium. It feels like Mugello to me.

There are also times, however, when I realise that there are some people who are celebrities, like me, and have an even tougher time of it in the media and the public eye than I've had. Vasco Rossi is certainly one of them. Vasco is an Italian rock star and one of my heroes. In fact, he's the only true, legitimate Italian rock star. He has gotten three different generations to dance, sing and fall in love, among them, my father, Graziano thinks Vasco is more famous than me, that people follow him around more. I don't know. Vasco and I lead similar lives and think the same way, at least on certain issues. He too is under tremendous pressure. In fact, because he's a bit older, he's been dealing with this situation for longer.

Vasco and I see each other regularly. We don't have a set schedule, but we've agreed to get together from time to time. And we always do it secretly. I go see him in Bologna, at his recording studios, which are also his sanctuary. It's a great place, comfortable, relaxed and private. Sometimes one of my good friends will come along, because when I say "I'm going to see Vasco", there's always someone willing to hide in the boot of the car or strap themselves to the roof, just so they can come along. But that would be abusing my friendship, so usually it's just a few of us who go see Vasco. In fact, most of the time, it's just me and Uccio.

When Vasco is on his own, when he's relaxed, free from pressure, he's one of the most incredible people you'll ever meet. He's pleasant and funny.

Many times, when you finally do get to meet your heroes, it's a burning disappointment. Because if there's someone you admire and you meet them at the wrong time, you get a wrong impression. And that unfortunate coincidence colours the way you view them, it affects your opinion of them. You may think they're rude or haughty when, in fact, they might just have been having a bad day, or a bad time of it lately. Or perhaps you had built them up too much in your own mind and they didn't meet your high expectations. I know this well because the same thing happened to me. Or, rather, its inverse. There are people who used to like me but then, when they met me, I was having a rough time or I was dealing with other problems and thus couldn't give them enough attention. And, as a result, they changed their opinion about me.

Yet I've had plenty of time to get to know Vasco and to understand him well. He has a magnetic personality, he's very sensitive and treats everyone the same. And you love talking to him because he's fun and interesting.

We met when he was involved in 125cc with his own team. We were introduced and he told me that he had been following my career. As the years went by, our relationship blossomed. These days we regularly text each other. He always compliments me after races and if he has a new song out, I'll send him my critique.

In 2004 we did something that I thought was a lot of fun. In my spare time, I write for *Rolling Stone* magazine (the Italian version) and I interviewed him. It was the first time I ever found myself on the other side of the barricade, as the one asking questions, rather than the other way around. Naturally I was entirely unprepared, so I decided to improvise. Yet I still think I came up with some good questions and he really sat and thought about the answers. I remember that I had one burning question.

"What's the first thing you do when you write a song?" I asked. "Do you just grab a piece of paper and pen and churn out something like 'Alba Chiara'?"

In truth, I knew Vasco couldn't answer this question – from a creative point of view. Because you're entering a subject – of talent, creativity, art and inspiration – that can't be described. Nor can it be summoned on command. Some moments happen spontaneously and that's it. It just comes to you. It happens to me the same way when I'm on the bike, during a race. In any case, he started talking, one question led to the next and by the end we couldn't stop. We were in perfect harmony. And it was beautiful. Yes, he and I are definitely on the same wavelength and we always have a lot of fun.

It was thanks to Vasco that in 2003 I was privy to a strange and wonderful experience. I went to San Siro (home of AC Milan and Internazionale football teams), to see him in concert. Because, as usual, I was late, I missed the start. I found a spot just in front of the stage and, after the first song, Vasco saw me.

"Tonight, among us, is the greatest motorcycle rider of all time, Valentino Rossi!" he announced, and 80,000 people started screaming. It was wonderful. Not unusual, because it has happened before, but that time it was special – it was an entirely different kind of ovation. Being Valentino Rossi has side effects. You can live many wonderful moments; it's not just about the problems. Among the good bits, one of the best is definitely the fact that you get the opportunity to meet people who were – or still are – your heroes. Just as Vasco is to me. And now, after all these years, I can say that Vasco is not just my hero, he's my friend.

In many ways I'm a true Italian. But perhaps my most "Italian" quality is superstition. I have always been very superstitious. Incredibly so. I don't know if it's something that was transmitted to me when I was young or whether I was just born that way. I remember having always been superstitious to the point where it affects my friends and everyone around me. I have all the classic hallmarks of superstition, plus some that are specifically linked to racing. I don't have amulets or charms, like others do. If I have something with me, it's because I like it. But, at each race, there are things I do which are part of a ritual.

Getting dressed is one such thing. It happens the same way, every time. There are some items of clothing – shoes, shirt, polo shirt – which I regularly wear and have a very specific significance. I always recognise what I need to wear at a certain moment. For example, if there is a pile of ten identical shirts in my closet, I always know the one I need to wear that day. And, when I'm at a Grand Prix, everything needs to be laid out in a certain way, in a certain order.

But the most important element is what we call my "official Kabbalah". It's a ritual which has to always occur in the same place, with the same people. The same five people who were there the very first time. You see, it all started years ago, when I was in 250cc. One night, some friends and I went out to party and had a few drinks. The next day I left to go race in a Grand Prix. And I won. Before the next race we didn't go back to the same bar and things went badly: I fell.

"We need to go back to that bar, otherwise it's bad luck!" suggested one of my friends, who was also very superstitious. And so we repeated the ritual. And it worked well. Thus, the Kabbalah was born. And because once a Kabbalah starts, it cannot be stopped, this ritual continues as it has done for years. On the eve of any race, at a time which can vary but which is always in the middle of the night, we meet up at a friend's bar. Sometimes it's closed, but that's not a problem. He'll open it up for us, it's too important. We always have the same drink, seated at the same table.

To do this, I'll even fly back from London. The ritual is valid regardless of whether it's the eve of the Grand Prix or the eve of a series of Grands Prix (for example, if I have to go to Asia, where we race on three consecutive weekends). If for whatever reason, my four friends and I aren't together when we decide it's Kabbalah time, we start calling each other up. And it doesn't matter if it's the middle of the night. As soon as you hear the word – "Kabbalah!" – even if you're asleep you get up, get dressed and leave the house. It doesn't matter if you're with your wife or girlfriend.

If we're all there (me, Uccio, Alby, Palazzi and Piwi) and if we repeat the various parts properly and none of us gets anything wrong, the Kabbalah works. When things haven't worked out on race day, it was always because something went wrong in the Kabbalah ceremony. Perhaps one of us was missing, or somebody else sat at our table or someone took a girl along. That's another rule: you can't bring a girl-friend to the Kabbalah. Neither a long-term one, nor an occasional one. It's a mistake that I too have made.

Once, in 2004, a friend of ours showed up who wasn't part of the Famous Kabbalah Five and sat down without warning. The next race went badly. We thus decided that we could never allow this to happen again. If a girlfriend or a friend shows up, we simply say, "Sorry, you can't sit down." And we really are sorry, but the Kabbalah is the Kabbalah. We have thousands of rituals. Some are constantly evolving, others have remained unchanged. But the Kabbalah is sacred.

Sometimes I think that the wives and girlfriends of my friends really hate me. And I know why. It has nothing to do with the Kabbalah, because by now they're used to it. If they hear the phone go off, they just roll over and go back to sleep. The real problem is that every time I go back to Tavullia, there is no question that my friends and I will get together for a night out. And the problem is that my friends use me as an excuse to stay out late. Today they say this to their wives and girl-friends, a few years ago they'd say it to their parents.

"Look, Vale is back!" they'll say. "That means I need to stay out with him and the others!"

Wives and girlfriends don't complain, at least not officially, and probably, I suspect, because there would be little point in doing so. Amazingly, they don't even rebel when my friends use up their holiday days to come to the races. This happens at every Grand Prix on a rotational basis. I always have friends there. Still, the women under-stand. When one of them comes out with us, she may get tired, but she never says anything. Because, after all, every time I go back to Tavullia, it's an excuse for the Tribe to reconvene. We'll meet up at someone's house or go out to a bar or restaurant. We do the same stuff everybody else does.

But there was a time when we were really wild. We were always out on our scooters, which had "jumped up" modified engines. And we got into all sorts of trouble. We did all sorts of things, though our passion for motors in general was overriding.

At one point, we put together a pop band, and we would regularly get together to practise. Biscia was on the drums, Lele was on the guitar and Omar was the lead singer. I would be on the other guitar. I have always loved music, though my passion for the guitar has waned over time. Still, I love all sorts of music and have a wide-ranging collection.

In any case, the point of all this was that we were a group, a united group, and we were always together. And we still are today.

It might be a function of where we were born and raised. Tavullia is on top of a small hill, long and narrow, 165 metres above sea level. It's in the province of Pesaro, not far from Rimini on the Adriatic coast. It has a population of around 5,000 and the town is basically a bunch of homes huddled on top of this hill. The surrounding land looks like a series of green waves heading out to the coast. Which, by the way, is very close. On a clear day, you can see the Adriatic Sea. If you're ever there, you'll know you're in the right place when you see the lamp-posts, each adorned with the number 46, my number. You'll see the number everywhere, in bars, shops, on scooters and cars.

There are no tall buildings in Tavullia, it's a quiet place, where things like family, friendship and solidarity are valued above all else. In Tavullia, if you buy a new car, you pay for everyone's drinks. And you always greet each other if you're driving, whether in a car, on a motorbike or on a scooter, which means there is a constant honking of horns. The sports bar, our strategic command when it comes to planning our gags, is next to City Hall and across the street from the elementary school where the Tribe was first formed. Right near there is the church, where Don Cesare, our local parish priest, resides.

Don Cesare is legendary. And he's one of my biggest fans. He's close to the whole parish so I've known him for a long time, although I am certainly not a model parishioner. At one point, Don Cesare started behaving strangely, at least for a parish priest. He started watching all the races on his own, in the sacristy. And if they clashed with Mass or services, he would postpone the religious service to accommodate the Grands Prix. He says he always needs to be fully concentrated when watching me race. And, if I win, he starts tolling the church bells immediately. Don Cesare became a racing fan thanks to me, by following my career. He doesn't like to leave Tavullia, because he wants to be close to his flock, but in 2003, he made an exception. At the age of eight-two, he joined my Fan Club and went to see me race in person, in Germany. Today I always go and see him. I love talking to him, he is truly an incredible person.

Just to the left of my old school are the headquarters of the Fan Club. Its full name is "Valentino Rossi Official Fans Club Tavullia". And it's run by Flavio Fratesi and Rino Salucci. It was created in 1996 and in 1997 became the Official Fan Club. It's my only Official Fan Club and I want to keep it that way. Flavio started coming to see me race way back in 1994 and 1995, while Rino would take Uccio along. From 1997, the group started travelling abroad for every race. And now, wherever I go, there are always people who follow me. It's a minimum of thirty people.

But don't get me wrong, I'm not claiming that I'm responsible for Tavullia's love affair with the motorbike. It had been like that for years before I was around. Tavullia's always a haven for local motorbike enthusiasts – Flavio's father had founded a motorbike club that was one of the most active in the area. Then, when I started racing, it turned into a really popular movement. Because of my character, I always ensured the Fan Club didn't become too serious and remained something fun and relaxed.

The Fan Club organises away trips and parties, but it also deals with more important things, like charity. All our revenue, in fact, goes to charity. I never wanted to publicise this because I believe charity ought to be done privately, without fanfare. And it should only be done if you feel strongly about something, otherwise you're not being genuine, you're doing it to win acclaim or promote yourself. Flavio, who is the real "engine' of the Fan Club, says that I'm the one who keeps everyone together, but I think there is a spirit of solidarity there which brings us all together. We are all equally important. We all get along and have fun and, thanks to this, we've come up with a whole bunch of ideas, some of them pretty cool. For example, I have a tax disc and insurance certificate on the bubble of my racing bike. I've had it since my days in 250cc. These are exact replicas of a "real" tax disc and insurance certificate, just like the ones you'd find on a roadbike. The one thing which changes is the name of my "insurance", which is always linked to my chief engineer. In 250cc, it was Rossano Brazzi Insurance. When I moved to 500cc, I signed on with Jeremy Burgess Insurance Aldgate, in homage to the Australian town near Adelaide where Jeremy was born. I duly list the period of cover as well, of course. It corresponds with the length of the world championship and, like any respectable insurance policy, I make sure it doesn't lapse. You never know . . .

ELEVEN

The police in Tavullia knew us well. They saw us nearly every day. Which was pretty much every time they stopped us. Our relationship was very simple: we ran and they chased us. Sometimes we got away, usually they caught us. It was a bit like playing "cops and robbers", except this was for real. They were cops and we were – well, we weren't robbers, nor were we hooligans. We didn't steal and we didn't even commit crimes. At least not proper crimes. Our "crime", if that was what you wanted to call it, was the fact that we used the streets of Tavullia as if they were a Grand Prix circuit. And, admittedly, our scooters, all of which had been modified and "jumped up" with loving care, were rather illegal. But that was it.

Naturally the police understood the situation: we were a bunch of hyperactive kids with a healthy passion for scooters and for racing. We didn't really do anything wrong, beyond the odd Highway Code violation. Besides, we were likeable. After all, why else would they lecture us so patiently? True, they would usually sequester our scooters, but we knew they had no choice and we knew how to accept defeat. And when we got our scooters back, it would all start from scratch, with us racing and them chasing.

There was definitely some reciprocal admiration between us and the police. Because, frankly, we weren't bad. Deep down, we were good kids. And we were busy kids, especially once we started middle school. We spent all day on the scooters, every day. We began with the scooters and later moved on to the Apecars. Even when we were only eleven years old, too young for scooters or any kind of motorised road vehicle, the seeds of mischief had already been planted. We were already looking forward to what we knew would be an incredible period in our lives, that magical time when boy and machine become inseparable. Because, in Italy, you can legally drive a scooter at the age of fourteen. And we knew that was right around the corner.

In middle school, the differences between boys and girls run very deep. Girls are ahead in terms of development, so they tend to spend time with older boys, ignoring their classmates. The problem is that if you're a boy, you're rather stuck. Your female classmates aren't interested in you, older girls are not an option (because they chase guys who are even older, guys with cars) and neither are younger girls. Because, let's face it, if you're thirteen you can't really be dating a ten-year-old! And so, we basically had to wait until we were old enough to see younger girls (or, until the younger girls were old enough to see us, depending on how you look at it). That's why we decided to devote all our free time to scooters.

We got involved in all kinds of shenanigans with our scooters. We always loved bikes and races, and we loved the taste of a challenge. My friends and I belong to that generation which, between the ages of fourteen and eighteen, lived for scooters. It was a passion we all shared, every single one of us.

Motorbikes have always been my single greatest passion. As I mentioned earlier, I learned how to ride a minibike before I learned how to ride a bicycle. So, for me, turning fourteen was a huge event. I could not wait, because it meant I could legally roam the streets. Of course, I had been out on the scooter many times before, usually taking Graziano's Benelli. It was a strange scooter because it would fold up neatly. Graziano used to keep it in the boot of his car and he would use it to drive around the paddock when he raced in the Supertouring series. Sometimes I used it as well. It was green and black.

My generation witnessed the emergence of scooters over the old, cycle-driven 50cc bikes like the Ciao and the Bravo. I would dream of having a Ciao with the front fork of the Bravo, like the ones which some of the older kids in the Tribe rode. But when I turned fourteen, all of a sudden scooters came on to the scene. They were beautiful. Our dream was the Aprilia SR, which looked just like a MotoGP bike. Indeed, you could order the special replica versions. Uccio had the "Reggiani" replica. My bike on the other hand was a yellow and purple Viper. I too had wanted the "Reggiani" replica, but, by the time I turned fourteen, it was no longer available (Uccio was a few months older and thus got his before I got mine). So I took the Viper. The first time I saw a photograph of the Aprilia SR was in the pages of *MotoSprint*, and the first time we saw it for real was in the shop window of a store called Champion, in Pesaro. We had actually organised a tour to visit the Champion store and see the Aprilia SR. We left Tavullia and went to Pesaro by bus. I stood outside the shop window open-mouthed, nose pressed against the glass, tongue out, drooling at the sight of that scooter. Yes, it was that beautiful.

When the time came time for Uccio to get his Aprilia SR, both Graziano and I went with him. Graziano had borrowed a van and we had to drive all the way to San Marino, because the bike had sold out in our part of the country. The van we had borrowed didn't have any kind of strap or support in the back, which did pose a bit of a problem on the way back. So we made the best of it. Uccio and I put down the stand and, for the entire journey, stood in the back of the van, holding it up with our hands, making sure it didn't fall. You could say that he and I were the straps that day. Needless to say, we were thrown all over the place in the back of that van, but we gladly put our bodies on the line to protect the bike.

I can't really overstate how important the arrival in our lives of scooters at the age of fourteen turned out to be. One by one, the members of my Tribe reached that magical age. In the space of two months, we must have added ten scooters. Some of us had the Vespa 50, others the Yamaha, the Aprilia . . . what they all had in common was that they had all been modified. For whatever reason, you could do so much with these scooters in terms of modifying them and giving them a bit of extra kick. The first thing you did, the minute you got home, was remove the dampeners so that you could go faster than the 45 kilometres per hour allowed by law. I don't know why the government even bothers to put such a limit on those scooters, since everybody simply removes the mechanism that enforces the restrictions.

But that was just the first step. From there, we would change everything. We'd change the cylinders, the carburettor, the clutch, the exhausts, the suspension. And then, of course, there were the tyres. We used Japanese IRC tyres, which held the road exceptionally well, allowing you to go that much faster on turns.

We got to the point where each of us had a trusted mechanic who could supply us with the gear we needed. I would go to a place called Motor House Energy, in Misano, which belonged to Alessandro Ugolini, better known as "Sgana", a guy who had raced minibikes with me. He was the guru of scooters. As a result, my scooter was always there, in his racing department.

We reached such a level of sophistication that every few weeks we had to either change the chassis or the engine. That's because our scooters easily reached 100 kilometres per hour, which, as you can well imagine, made them pretty fragile. After modifying the scooters we naturally had to go test them, so that we could fine-tune them. And then, once that was finished, there was only one thing left to do: race them. Yes, race our scooters. That's what we did. All day. Every day. It went on until we turned eighteen. Until then, I was always on the scooter, racking up more and more kilometres. I practically lived on that scooter.

This was also due to the fact that my parents separated around that time and I went to live with my mum in Montecchio. This meant that when we returned home after a day out, I always had an additional five to six kilometres to cover on my own, the road from Tavullia to Montecchio. It's actually a nice drive, uphill one way, downhill the other. It's not that long, but it's medium-to-fast, with nice long curves and the odd straightaway. Legend has it that I learned to ride there, on the Montecchio–Tavullia road. That the fact that I rode that stretch on my own without any reference points, without having to follow the rhythm of another rider, taught me how to get ahead – and stay ahead – when racing.

Either way, we were always out and about. And we would always compete. We would fix a finish line at a place to aim for. It didn't really matter where it was or what we would do once we got there, the whole fun was getting there, because we transformed the journey into a genuine race. Of course, as soon as we arrived, we would turn around and go back. It was all about the journey, not the destination.

Back then, the legend of the "Panoramica" had already taken hold. The Panoramica was a road some 22 kilometres long, and as the name implies, it has a panoramic view, as it hugs the cliffs above the seas. It runs from Gabicce Monte to Pesaro, linking the regions of Marche and Emilia Romagna. It's a tight, winding road. A gorgeous road, and for us it was a racetrack. It consists of alternating uphill curves, some narrow, some wide, and there is a constant change of elevation and rhythm. There are moments in which you are surrounded by greenery, tall trees and lush vegetation, others in which the sea looks so close that you feel you could reach out and touch it (in fact, the beautiful view is often distracting and, potentially, dangerous). It was the focal point of the area, even back when Graziano was a boy. He too had raced along there with his friends, a group which included Gibo and Aldo Drudi. Today you can no longer race along the Panoramica. It's simply too dangerous. You run into the absent-minded guy who'll do a U-turn with a van, or holidaymakers in a caravan. There are too many cars and, besides, it's full of cyclists. Back in my time, however, it was often nearly deserted and we took advantage of it as much as we could. And yet the sad thing is that they're thinking about putting speed bumps there too, on the Panoramica. To me it would be a scandal, a sacrilege. Like putting speed bumps at Assen or Donington.

Our days were rather simple: school, lunch, Panoramica. We'd meet up in the early afternoon, fill up our tanks at the twenty-four-hour service station near Gradara and then it was just us and the 22km of open road on the way out and the 22km of open road on the way back. There were days when I'd complete four or five *"panoramiche"* in a single day.

My big advantage was that I could take advantage of several different groups of friends. After school there were those who already had jobs and would go racing on their lunch breaks. Then in the afternoon, others would arrive. In the summer it was even better. From the Panoramica we would go down to the beach and stay there until sunset. Every so often one of us would get to the beach with blood-red arms, the typical symptoms of those burning spills on the asphalt. It was always the same story: "Get in the water and you'll disinfect it!" I never knew if it worked. I just knew that the salt water caused an initial burning followed by a general numbness. After a few hours in the sun, you were good to go.

We did have some ground rules for our races. We had a self-enforced limit on how fast you could go on the straightaways (the turns, however, were fair game) and crossing into the opposite lane was strictly prohibited. We always rode in the right-hand lane and, if anyone crossed the white line, there were serious penalties. Unlike many Italian kids of that age, we made helmets mandatory from day one. In that sense, we were very clever.

We had some neat touches, like wheelies, for instance. We were always up on one tyre. There were times I returned home at night with sore arms for that very reason. Speaking of nights, that was a whole other story. We would all be home for a quick dinner and a bit of tuning on the bikes. But we didn't stay too long because most nights we would have another rendezvous at "Pistino", an area in the nearby town of San Giovanni in Marignano, near Cattolica. Because the Panoramica was for the daytime, but nights belonged to the Pistino. It was basically an industrial park with factories and warehouses. We had turned it into our own Grand Prix track with the paddock, car park, finish line, turns and straightaways. And then, of course, there were all the spectators, including many girls, who came to see us.

When the world championship came to Misano, just a few kilometres away, there were people who would go and steal the advertising banners from the track and install them at the Pistino. Thus, as you cruised through you could see these racing banners, advertising all sorts of official sponsors, just like at the "real" track. Our track was very technical, with a fast "S" and beautiful turns. I remember, there was one part, a fast left turn, where you had to go out on the actual street for a few metres or so. It was the only dangerous part of the track but, come to think of it, it really was bloody dangerous. We took some pretty nasty spills, but in general things went very well.

Those were great races and we took them very seriously. At its height, there were as many as two hundred people there, including kids from all the neighbouring towns. Some guys got so into it that they looked like professionals, bringing their modified Ciaos over on little trucks. Of course, we would get regularly raided by the police, who used to come in and sequester everything. There were times we managed to escape, and others where we got busted. Ultimately, it was the constant raids that decreed the end of the legendary Pistino. The demise of the Pistino was truly the end of an era.

I was very fast on the Pistino and on one occasion I raced there to see how well I had recovered from a broken wrist I suffered in 1995, when I was racing in the European series. I had actually fractured it racing motocross, which wasn't the cleverest thing to do. In the standings I was third, but a gifted Czech rider, Yarda Hules, was right behind me. It was a tricky time. I had to be careful not to concede any more points, since I needed a top-three finish to move up to the world championship.

So what did I do? Did I take it easy? Did I go meditate and prepare myself mentally and spiritually? No. This is me, remember? I went off and raced motocross with my friends. To be fair, I raced quite a bit of motocross back then. This time, however, it was a mistake and I paid a price for it.

I was cruising around the motocross track when I got to the ramp for a jump. I was in second gear, but I should have been in third. I lifted my foot to shift, but the gear did not bite and I remained in neutral. But, by this point, I was on the ramp. So I took the jump in neutral and, naturally I was thrown forward. It was quite a tumble and I fractured my wrist. I immediately thought of the European 125 series and, most of all, the world championship.

I skipped my race in the Italian championship and went to see Doctor Costa. My next European series race was in Portugal, at Braga, so I had a bit of time to prepare. He put on a hard cast so that I could race. On the eve of my departure he looked at it again and said: "It looks fine to me, but you've lost muscle mass in your arm . . . I'm not sure you're going to be strong enough to race. Why don't you go and find out?"

"OK, but how am I going to do that?" I asked myself.

I was sixteen, I didn't have a licence to ride a motorbike on the streets and going on the track was obviously not an option. Yet I couldn't miss that race in Portugal, because I simply needed the points.

Suddenly, it all came to me: "I know, I'll go to the Pistino!" I got my aquamarine Zip out of the garage and made my way to the Pistino. My Zip was beautiful. I liked it so much that I still have it, somewhere in my garage. The Aprilia was too heavy, so I had replaced it with a Honda ZX and, later, with the Zip. It was a very competitive bike and I loved it. My version was the "Zip Fast Racer" which, naturally, I had modified to the point that it wasn't far off a MotoGP bike. Well, almost. At the Pistino I would be able to drive and see just how bad my wrist was. I took it very seriously and was totally concentrated. That night, at Pistino, I didn't just race around the track: I set the track record.

"All set, I'm fine for Portugal," I told myself, as I returned home.

And, in Portugal, I grabbed third place, which was enough to move to the world championship the following season. So if I made it to the world stage at the tender age of seventeen, some of the credit should go to the Pistino.

Still, our greatest adventures were on the Apecar. I was the first of the Tribe to get an Apecar. It all happened because in winter, no matter how cold it got, I never wanted to leave my scooter. I was freezing and often got rained on. There were advantages too, especially the twenty minutes I would save compared to the time it took for the bus to take me to school. That's partly why I didn't want to take the bus. It would have meant getting up at the same time as my mother, who would have nagged and nagged ("Hurry up", "You're late", "Eat your breakfast", that sort of thing . . .).

By taking the scooter, I got a full extra ten minutes of sleep, which I thoroughly enjoyed. And my school route was planned perfectly. On the Montecchio to Pesaro route I was faster than the bus. The route took me between eleven and twelve minutes and, if I found a truck, I could shave off a few more seconds, riding up behind it and using the lack of air resistance to "slingshot" past. I would leave home at 7.57 a.m. and get to school at 8.10. Of course, in spite of all this, I was still always the last guy to make it to class!

The real problem was the cold – this was undeniable. And we often had to adapt to tricky situations. For example, when we had to meet up with girls, we'd go out on the scooter with our puffy winter coats, wool scarf and heavy gloves. We'd stop a few hundred metres away from the rendezvous point and we'd change. Literally. We'd put on Barbour jackets, those thin leather gloves and the trendy wool hats. That way, we looked better for the girls.

"Aren't you cold?" they would ask.

"No, what cold?" we'd lie, freezing our buns off. "It's just an impression, it's quite pleasant and crisp, actually."

My parents, however, were less amused. They did not like the idea of their son freezing every single winter day.

"Well, maybe we could get you an Apecar," Graziano said one day. That way, he reckoned, at least I'd have some protection from the elements.

"What are you talking about?" I said. "Can you imagine? Me, on an Apecar? It's a very bad idea."

And I was rather horrified. The Apecar did not have a good image. It was the kind of thing pensioners might use. Or a labourer who needs to take something in the flatbed. It was not something for kids. And it certainly was mighty uncool. But Graziano went ahead anyway. And I got an old Apecar, in fact, and it turned out to be as old as I was, a 1979 model. Thus, I was the first of the Tribe to drive an Apecar. I showed up with it in Tavullia and there was a moment of rather embarrassed silence. They were all shocked. I stepped out and my friends began inspecting it, with total bemusement. It had drum brakes that were all rusty and a manual windscreen wiper. My friends were by no means convinced, but every night I would show up in my Apecar which was nice and cosy inside and they would freeze their bums off on their scooters. I thus started a trend. Within a year and a half, a dozen or so of us had Apecars. And, naturally, we treated the Apecar the same way we treated our scooters. With lots of love, and a little bit of technological injection. Yes, we modified the Apecars just as we modified the scooters. They became race vehicles.

There was one important difference, however. Apecars are big and bulky, so they simply don't have the grace of scooters. So we changed the rules of our races. We decided that, from now on, in Apecar races just about anything went. You'd still be racing, but it would be like bumper cars, you were free to ram the opposition.

"We're protected, we won't get hurt," we reasoned. The idea seemed brilliant to us at the time. And thus our endless duels began, with us ramming each other in the Apecars. Naturally, they got banged up, collecting an impressive series of dents and welts. Given the amount of punishment the Apecars took, we had to take some precautions, such as tying one of the doors shut. This was because the Apecar chassis was so prone to losing its shape (let's just say it's not exactly a Deltabox!), and what we found was that once this happened at the next bump, the doors would often fly open and, occasionally, fly off.

But if our outer chassis was basically a complete wreck, inside many of the Apecars were little gems, thanks to our modifications and tinkering. Mine, for example, started with the original 50cc engine and eventually became a 140cc! And if the police loved to take away our scooters, they were equally fond of the Apecars. Uccio holds the record: his Apecar was sequestered six times. But I have my own distinction. My Apecar was impounded the very same day that the police let me have it back for an earlier infraction. One Saturday afternoon I went to pick it up. That same Saturday night, they took it away once again.

When I still had my arm in a cast, I couldn't ride, obviously, but I still wanted to watch the action. So I decided that Uccio would give me a lift in my Apecar. This was rather more complicated than it sounds. First of all, the Apecar's front cab is very tight. It's just not built for two. The only way to get two people in there is if one steers and the other brakes (there was a front brake and a back brake, though the front brake did not actually do anything). This is obviously far from ideal. On top of that, my arm was in a cast and so my range of movement was somewhat limited. Uccio and I got in there and we must have looked rather ridiculous. Because of the cast, I had to keep my arm up over my head and the cab was so cramped that we were practically embracing as we drove along. It may not have been a pretty sight, but it at least allowed us to go from point A to point B.

The fact that it was all a moot point because two minors were not allowed in an Apecar at the same time hadn't occurred to us. At best it seemed like a small detail. We made the mistake of passing a patrol car and, soon thereafter, we realised we were being followed. The siren wasn't on, but the lights were flashing behind us.

"Well, I guess we're busted, slow down," Uccio said, visibly saddened.

"No, screw that, let's run for it, get us out of here," I said.

"What do you mean, where are we going to go, looking like this?" he aid.

"Who cares?" I replied. "At least we're trying something. We're busted anyway. We have no licence plate, no insurance, we're underage, the engine has been modified . . . we might as well try."

And so we did, although our escape did not last long. As you might expect, the police caught up with us right away. And they weren't happy. Not one bit. Their steps were slow, ponderous. You could tell they were really angry.

"Where is the licence plate?" one of them asked. "And where are the insurance papers?"

"Ummm . . . they're at home," I said.

"OK then, you're coming with us." They took my Apecar away and drove me to the police station. As for Uccio, they simply left him out there, by the side of the road. I remember looking in the rear-view mirror and seeing his face, surprised and saddened, as we drove towards the police station.

The Apecar was taken for a whole month. To get it back, I had to show up at the police station with my parents. And they were not happy either.

"Why can't you be good?" my mum kept repeating. "Why can't you drive more slowly?"

"Yes, Mum!" I reassured her. "Got it! Yes . . . drive slowly . . . OK!"

Graziano, on the other hand, was so angry that he did not even say a word.

Naturally, that same afternoon I was back on the Apecar. We were planning what to do that evening, when somebody suggested bowling.

"Yes! Great idea!" we all shouted. "Let's all go bowling!"

There was one problem. The bowling alley was in Rimini. And we were in Tavullia. It was me, Pirro, Uccio and Nicola and we decided to take the Apecars. I was with Pirro, Uccio was with Nicola. We were two terrible crews. I should point out that the four of us did have a bit of a history whenever we went out. We never returned home without having something happen. Maybe our scooters had fallen apart, or maybe we were stranded without petrol or maybe the cops had taken our transportation away (again). Whatever the case, the four of us never seemed to make it back together. Without question, we were the most dangerous in the whole Tribe, especially when it came to anything related to Apecars or scooters.

The drive out to Rimini was rather uneventful. True, we had rammed each other several times and whacked each other with the doors, but it was relatively low-key. The return leg was going to be different.

"OK, let's make this interesting, let's make this an official race!" one of us said and we all agreed.

I couldn't tell you exactly why, but, this time, we really did go wild on the drive back. It was still Pirro and me against Uccio and Nicola and we really were all over the place. We raced side by side, we banged into each other repeatedly, we zigzagged through traffic . . . At one point, we came to a red light and we faced off, trying to out-psyche each other, as we revved our engines as hard as they could go. It felt like the starting line of a Grand Prix. We had not even realised that, in between us, there was a nice middle-aged man with his family in a green Lancia Dedra. When the light changed and we roared away, he was absolutely terrified.

We continued our mad run until, at one point, Uccio and Nicola drove me off the road. I would have been fine, had it not been for the fact that my back tyre had gotten stuck under the guard rail. The Apecar was on its side and this was a bit of a problem. One door was facing the ground and so obviously could not be opened. And the other door had become deformed following another whack earlier and it simply would not open. We were trapped.

217

Fortunately, Uccio and Nicola, who had gone ahead, began to worry about us and they returned to the scene. They found us still busy trying to get the door open, pushing and pulling as best we could. Eventually, with their help, we found a way to open the door. We then got the Apecar back on its wheels, hopped back in, and resumed our incredible race. We rammed each other a few more times for good measure and then ended up at a service station, near Riccione. This was where we would meet before going nightclubbing. The older guys would come here to grab a few drinks or maybe try and get some kind of VIP pass for the club. Shortly after our arrival, we were confronted by the now familiar sign of flashing lights: the police.

"Uh-oh, they're here for us," Pirro said, his voice shaking, as we saw the silhouettes of two cops get out of their car and make a bee-line for us.

The car park by the service station was quite big and there were people everywhere. They were all watching us, perhaps delighting in the fact that we would, once again, be thoroughly humiliated. I'll never forget the way the two cops approached us. I really thought they were going to kill us.

"Guys, what the fuck are you doing?" the first one shouted, wasting no time. "I have never ever seen anything like it. You were playing bumper cars on the public highway at eighty kilometres an hour, ramming each other like morons. What . . . are you crazy?"

"Well . . . actually . . ." We tried to muster some kind of reply, but without success. And then things went from bad to worse.

"Wait a minute!" one of them said as he took a closer look at the Apecars. "These engines have been modified!"

"What? Have they?" I tried to gloss over it. "Well, maybe a little bit, but just a tiny bit . . ."

I was royally screwed. Our engines weren't a "tiny bit" modified, they were totally hopped up. My engine, which was supposed to be 50cc, was actually 140cc. We were cornered, with no way out.

A crowd had gathered and the people in the service station began chanting: "Let them go! Let them go!"

But they didn't. They called a tow truck and had the Apecars taken away. Including my Apecar of course, which I had just picked up that very day.

While I was watching it disappear up the road, thinking I wouldn't be seeing it again for a while, this strange-looking man came up to us and turned to the police.

"What have these guys done?" he asked.

Before they could answer, Uccio jumped in.

"And you? Who the fuck are you?" he shouted. "What the fuck do you want from us?"

"I'm a plain-clothes policeman," he said, icily. And then we knew our goose was cooked, as they say.

"Oh, great!" I sighed, letting my head drop. Nothing could save us now. We knew what would happen. Our Apecars would be sequestered, we would get a hefty fine, a long lecture and then we'd be grounded for a long time. A very long time. And that's what happened.

Of course, we still had the small matter of getting home. We were, after all, in Riccione.

"Excuse me, but what are we supposed to do now?" we asked the police, hoping for some kind of merciful gesture, like a lift. "How do we get home?"

One of them nodded towards some unspecified spot to his right.

"Over there," he said. "The train station. Take a train."

A brilliant idea, at four o'clock in the morning. We checked the train schedule and, predictably, there were no trains until 7 a.m. We couldn't just sit in Riccione for another three hours. We did see some homeless people huddled in some cardboard boxes doing just that. The thought of asking them if they were willing to share their cardboard boxes with us so that we could get a little bit of sleep did cross my mind.

"Let's just take a cab," someone suggested. So we began to count our money, discovering that we had 11,400 lire between the four of us. That's slightly more than five euros. I didn't expect that would get us very far, but it was worth a try. We found a cab and I approached the driver.

"Hello, pardon me, could you perhaps take us as far as Cattolica?" I asked in my most angelic voice.

"How much money do you have?"

"Oh, something in the region of eleven thousand lire . . ."

"For eleven thousand lire I'm not even driving you around the block."

So much for that idea.

"OK, now what?"

We debated calling our parents, which, I suppose is what responsible kids would have done right away in this situation (then again, if we had been responsible we would have never been in this situation). But that was easier said than done. My dad was at a race and my mum was away. Pirro's parents were in Canada, Uccio's dad was also at a race, along with his mum. Which left just one option: Nicola's father.

"Nicola, you call him," we said.

"OK, suit yourself," he said. "If you really want me to I'll call him. I'm sure he'll come down immediately. Just bear in mind that when he does come down, he'll probably do so with a shotgun."

And so that quickly eliminated the "call-the-parents" option, which probably should never have been seriously considered anyway.

"Now what?" we all asked ourselves. We looked at each other knowing there was just one option left: hitch-hiking.

This was actually where our luck finally changed. We were out there by the side of the road with our thumbs ready to shoot up every time we saw headlights approaching. Still, we were sure nobody would pick us up. What kind of a nutter gives a ride to four teenage boys at 4 a.m. on a Saturday night? Desperation was setting in when, suddenly, like a gift from God, someone stopped. Someone we knew. The guy who owned the service station in Tavullia. He had recognised us and was more than happy to take us home. He saved us from a twenty-kilometre walk home, but he could not save us from our parents, who nearly killed us. We all paid dearly for it. Graziano kicked my butt and my friends did not have it any easier.

I had to eventually let go of the Apecar because the seat broke. I did drive it until the last possible moment, even when it was falling apart to the point that, towards the end, I had to sit on the battery because the seat, which was loose from its moorings, had flown out the window during one of our more intense races. Because the battery was much lower, I couldn't see properly out the windscreen and, to others, it would have looked as if the Apecar was driving itself around.

"This is absurd, I can't go on like this," I told myself.

One day I was on my way home and I decided to show off my parking skills with a very sophisticated manoeuvre. I came down the hill towards my house in neutral, thinking that all I needed to do was brake at the exact right time and the Apecar would magically slip into its parking spot. It wasn't the smartest thing to do.

I had picked up a lot of speed when, all of a sudden, one of the tyres hit the pavement, sending the Apecar hurtling through the air. I rolled with it, of course, as if I had been in a giant cardboard box. Our flight down the hill was interrupted by a parked Jeep, which we struck at some speed. We rolled a little further until the Apecar came to rest on its side. I was a little groggy, but I was fine. I opened the door, which was facing straight up to the sky, and crawled out, as if I were coming out of a submarine. Imagine my surprise when, just as my head and torso began to poke out of the Apecar, I realised where I had landed. I was just in front of my mum's kitchen. And she was there, staring at me, while cooking her minestrone.

She was wide-eyed and shocked, as was I. Her expression was somewhere between incredulity and anger.

"Are you hurt?" she said. She was, after all, my mother.

"No, I'm fine," I said, using my most reassuring smile.

"OK, in that case, come in and set the table," she said. "Dinner is ready . . ."

I smiled broadly, both outwardly and inwardly. Because I understood how wonderful my mother was. And how hard it must have been for her not to get angry and blow her top.

"OK, I'll fix the Apecar and be right over," I said, as I tried to get it right-side up, with all the wheels on the ground, rather than up in the air. I was in quite a rush, because I didn't want the owner of the Jeep to show up. He was sure to be cross because I had no doubt damaged his car. I needed to get out of there as quickly as possible. Just then the door to the Jeep opened. There I was, wondering that the owner might show up, and it turns out that he had been in there the whole time! He was shaking all over, terrified.

"A-a-a-re you OK?" he stuttered in a trembling voice. His face was all white, his breathing irregular.

"Yes, everything is fine," I said, reflecting on just how bizarre and incredible the scene was.

I righted the Apecar and slipped into the house. And then I burst out laughing. I had gotten away with it. The funny thing is that the guy in the Jeep was so terrified that he didn't even ask about damages. Maybe it was because he forgot. Or perhaps because he simply didn't want to. Either way, I never found out exactly what he was thinking.

Over time we calmed down. All of us. I started racing seriously and my life changed radically. My friends still come to see me race, the Tribe mixing freely with the Fan Club and both sets mix with my other friends. But there is no question that we are not as wild as we were. We've all maintained our passion for motorbikes, even though, of course, I've managed to turn mine into a profession. But that's work, and that's on a racetrack. Taking the bike out on roads is a totally different proposition. The funny thing is, I only got my motorcycle licence at the age of twenty. I have to admit, I was a bit scared out on the road. There are too many dangers that a motorcyclist simply can't control. Motorbikes are just too fast. Cars and trucks too often simply don't see them. And, if there is a collision, the motorcyclist always comes off worse. And that's when you can get really hurt. That's why I waited so long. I might have been racing 500cc professionally and I might have been an absolute daredevil on the scooter (not to mention the Apecar), but I simply felt I wasn't ready to take a proper motorbike out on the road.

At some point, however, the urge became too much. And so I got my licence. Still, I try not to overdo it. I use my motorbike a bit differently, without going over the top. Indeed, I should say "my motorbikes" in the plural because I have quite a few. Open up my garage and you'll find an Aprilia RSV 1000, a Honda CBR 600, a Honda CBR 900 Fireblade and a Honda VTR 1000, plus a Yamaha R1, a Yamaha XJR 1300 and another special "supermotard" which the Yamaha engineers and mechanics constructed for me. And then there are all my dirtbikes, which I use at the quarry. I've taken these bikes back to the Panoramica several times in recent years. But I've never overdone it. It's just not worth it. And if I had a magic wand and could have one wish granted, I would take Mike Hailwood with me on the Panoramica. Yes, we'd have a nice adventure on the Panoramica. As far as I'm concerned, Hailwood was the greatest ever. Back in his day, many races were run on urban circuits, which would have made him perfect for a road stretch like the Panoramica.

I'd also love to go for a ride with Wayne Rainey. But, with him, it's more of a competitive thing. It would be great if we could square off one-on-one, with the exact same bike and tyres. Rainey is one of the riders I admired the most. In his day, Yamaha was much slower than Honda and yet he always went for it, he always believed utterly in himself. And, even though he was very fast, he hardly ever fell, so he was always in it at the end. There is no question that he and I have very different personalities, but for me he was one of the all-time greats. Rainey and Hailwood: those are the guys I'd look to measure myself against. And I like the idea, because taking on Hailwood indirectly means taking on his contemporaries, Agostini and Reed, while facing Rainey involves competing with the likes of Schwantz and Doohan.

When I use one of the roadbikes, my style of driving is very different from what it was back in the scooter days. Now, I enjoy the bike in a different way, appreciating different elements and aspects. I can enjoy the bike even driving slowly, even if I'm not running away or chasing an opponent. Of course, this may also explain why my relationship with the Tavullia Police Department has improved tremendously.

If I once used the Panoramica and the Pistino to have fun while training – or to train while having fun, I never quite knew which! – then when I grew up I began to frequent another somewhat unusual place: the quarry. The quarry was Graziano's idea. And, actually, the quarry is just that: an *idea*, or, better yet, a way of thinking, a philosophy of life, based on riding sideways. In fact, Graziano calls it "the sideways philosophy". And it's not just about motorbikes. Graziano is the ultimate guru of "the sideways lifestyle".

According to his way of thinking, one should always ride sideways. He adopted this philosophy when he was himself racing motorbikes and he upheld it when he moved to cars. You see, when he was a young man, before I was born, he had developed a training method to help build his speed. He would use a Honda XR 500, which, back then, was a four-stroke version of a motocross bike. He kept the spiky front tyre and, on the back wheel, used a normal smooth road tyre. He would then go to the beach, where the sand remains humid and, therefore, more compact. And he would practise driving sideways, slipping and sliding, learning to control the bike in precarious circumstances.

When I was young I really liked motocross, but Graziano did not agree. He said that motocross was dangerous, especially for fast racers, and that you learn a type of racing which was useless for those who wanted to race on a track, because, in motocross the track is filled with things like jumps, holes and canals which simply aren't there in track racing.

And so Graziano immediately tried to get me to do something different. He explained his philosophy and the benefits of it. And he's right, you do learn a lot, particularly in terms of controlling the bikes. That's why we began hanging out in quarries. They are the ideal place, because they have a tight, compact ground, but they also have things like truck-tyre tracks, which are perfect for sideways racing. In our area, in the hills outside Pesaro and Tavullia, there are plenty of quarries and we've tried out about ten of them. We had to change them regularly, because we kept getting kicked out. Then we found one that we could call our own. We don't use it during the week, which is fair enough. I mean after all it is someone's workplace. We do drop by at weekends, with the owner's permission, and then we feel at home.

At first, some ten years ago, we were a group of ten people at most. Now, without even realising it, there are so many of us that we've had to put up chicken wire to limit access, because at one point there were so many people it was getting dangerous.

I start riding in the quarry the week after the last Grand Prix and I don't stop regular workouts there until the week before the start of the new world championship. We've had some incredible times at the quarry. We've organised real championships, endurance races or even just head-to-head action. We even have our own version of the Superpole, like at the Suzuka Eight Hour Race. I love the fact that at the Superpole you start off on that ramp, almost as if it were a rally. You get up there, you wait a second or two to be introduced and then you're off.

That's what we do down at the quarry. It's just that, as a stage, we use one of those devices to weigh trucks. It's a ramp that takes the trucks up to the weighbridge.

With the advent of modern technology, we've greatly improved organisation as well and we now have transponders and computers that can constantly update our times. It's a very technical course, it's fast and it's fun, you're always in third or fourth gear. There are some brilliant braking opportunities and you ride sideways and accelerate at the same time. There is just one jump on the whole course, but it's low and fast and fits in nicely.

And, if you're still not satisfied, we also have a speedway oval there. We only use bikes whose back tyres are road enduro tyres, because motocross tyres create little tiny holes that make it more difficult to slide and ride sideways. The front tyre, however, is always a traditional motocross tyre.

The best bikes for the quarry are the cross 450 four-stroke. We always use those, but in the early days we would visit every junkyard around to find old chassis or abandoned bikes that we could then turn into "specials". We found all sorts of stuff, including some really, really old bikes. One season, we raced with XT Yamahas, XR Hondas and even a Cagiva Elefant. You need a four-stroke bike, because the two-stroke's power delivery simply isn't right on that kind of terrain. I love riding like that. I really enjoy it and it's also a useful way of training. In fact, it's the basis of my training regimen. I have a very detailed programme which I follow. I'll do fifteen laps, trying to maintain the same pace and always working on controlling the bike as it slips and slides.

Of course, over time the quarry has become like an amusement park, though, for me, it's like a gym, an essential component of my training. It was at the quarry that I really refined my sensitivity on the bike and my ability to control it while allowing it to slide. Because, when you're sideways, you don't have the same traction which means you need to know how to control the bike.

Those sessions at the quarry were especially important in 500cc, because that type of bike really does slide a lot. And it was also useful in MotoGP, particularly the first two years, when the bikes tended to slide a little more than they do now. In fact, I developed my style for entering turns on angle on the Honda RCV at the quarry. Because, ultimately, when you think about it, it's a similar type of ride. At the quarry, you need to gauge the petrol as you accelerate and allow the back tyre to slide both going into and coming out of a turn. The only difference is that on the track it all happens much faster, but the principle is the same.

For a time, we even used quad bikes. I got really into quads, I used to race one that had a two-stroke Yamaha RD 350 engine. It was very fast – even too fast, you might say. I got rid of it after a nasty fall. How bad was it? Let me put it this way: I was going so fast that the quad broke in two and I still don't know how I managed to escape unscathed. I quickly decided that quads were not for me. And I switched my attention exclusively to motorbikes.

TWELVE

I have always liked the Suzuka Eight Hour Race. I have been fascinated by it ever since I was a child. I was a big Japanophile back then, I was attracted to everything that happened there. I liked the Japanese riders, their helmets, their suits and, of course, their bikes.

Besides, Suzuka is a legendary track and the Eight Hours is a legendary race. In addition, when I began asking Aprilia to enter me in the race, I also wanted to race, at least once, on a Superbike. And maybe this is why, at one point, I began to really push for this.

It started when I was in 250cc and Aprilia began producing the RSV Mille; I'd speak to Jan Witteveen, the engineer responsible: "Please, Jan, let's put together a team and go out there, to Suzuka," I would ask him, time and time again, trying to convince him. He simply didn't want to know. And he did not mince his words either.

"Look, if you put our bike in the Eight Hours, it won't even last eight minutes!" he said and this pretty much ended the discussion. It was enough to convince me that perhaps we should stay home after all.

So I didn't raise the issue until a few years later, when I was in contract talks with Honda about moving to 500cc. I asked them if I could enter the Eight Hours. They certainly did not expect such a request from me, but they were delighted. In fact, their eyes lit up. None of the top guys ever wanted to do the Eight Hours and would regularly come up with the most unusual and far-fetched excuses just to avoid it. That's why the Honda guys were overjoyed that I was actually volunteering for it. And so they signed me up for it in 2000 and 2001.

Only later did I realise just how physically brutal and devastating the Eight Hour race really is. At the time I was just excited.

My friends and I dubbed the first trip to the Eight Hours "The Japan Road Trip" in a spirit of entertainment and adventure. I was twenty-one years old back then, and I was joined by Uccio, Alby, Gabbia and my physiotherapist Marco Montanari.

It was eight days of delirium. It began with laughter and the usual enthusiasm of a road trip. It ended with the biggest drunken night I can remember. Not that I remember too much of it. I blame the Japanese riders. And myself, of course. Honda assigned me Colin Edward as a teammate. The tests went very well, I liked the VTR 1000 a lot. I was coming from the NSR 500 and I found the VTR 1000 a tasty yet submissive bike, easy to handle. It went where I wanted it to go and did everything I asked. And it slid a lot, which I absolutely loved.

When we left for Japan, I dubbed myself "The Master", not in an arrogant sense, but because I had been going to Japan since 1996, and now I felt like I knew my way around and thus would make the perfect tour guide. My first task was explaining to them just why the Japanese are different from the Italians. For example, I wanted to prove just how kind, gentle and respectful the Japanese were. And the way I did it was by harassing the staff at our hotel and encouraging the others to do the same. The idea was that no matter how badly we behaved, they would still treat us well.

"Just smile and everything will work out," I told my friends.

They learned very quickly. They said hello to everyone, smiled and basically did whatever the hell they wanted for five days. In that time, we stayed five to a room, and we ate, slept, used the pool and never paid a single penny for anything. We were really shameless, we really took advantage of them. We would come down for the breakfast buffet and be as rude as possible. We would jump the queue, grab whatever food we liked, sit wherever we liked and be as rude as we liked. And, of course, we would always leave without paying and usually after having made a mess. To us it was an experiment. We aren't rude guys in real life, but we wanted to see how far we could push them before somebody kicked us out (or kicked our butts). Instead, nothing happened. They figured we were guests of Honda and they simply watched us, without any kind of reaction. We got away with it!

Another interesting experiment was on the way to the racetrack. There was always a roadblock, where you were supposed to show your pass. I never did, because I didn't have one. And I didn't have one, because I never asked for one. But that was all part of the plan. There were seven of us, crammed into the rental car. We would rev the engine annoyingly and drive on the hard shoulder, jumping the queue. When we got to the roadblock, we would stop as if to show our passes and then quickly drive away in first gear all the while shouting back insults. And nobody came after us!

That was the fun: taking advantage of these kind and respectful people. In fact, they were too respectful, at times they even annoyed me. They would just sit there. They wouldn't react, they didn't know what to do, they're simply not prepared for situations like these. They didn't expect to meet nutters like us. Of course, we exploited it as much as we could.

Our other favourite pastime on that trip was stealing. We would steal from the various shops around the racetrack. We would only steal little things of course: stickers, gadgets, toy cars. Cheap stuff, nothing expensive. But that was also part of our sociological experiment. You see, in Japan there is no such thing as theft. It simply doesn't happen. People leave their front doors open, their cars unlocked. And, for them, it was unthinkable that someone might come and steal anything.

We really wanted to try their patience, test the outer limit of what they could stand. In the end, however, we got a bit discouraged. We would walk up to the cash register and put things in our pocket in plain view, without any intention of paying for them. They would just look at us, without saying a thing. It was weird and unsettling. So much so that, at the end, we would give back what we had stolen or we would pay for it.

Eventually we realised that we had gone too far. It happened in 2001. Being superstitious, I took it as a sign. I had never won anything in Japan, not in 125, not in 250, not in 500. And the Eight Hour Race went badly as well.

"Let's try to behave well," we told ourselves. "Out of respect for Japan, let's stop being Italians!"

And so we did. In 2001, we didn't steal anything. And I won both the Grand Prix and the Eight Hour Race. And so we put a halt to our experiments.

The Eight Hour Race is extremely tough. Not just the race itself. For a rider in the world championship adding long and tiresome events to an already busy calendar is quite a burden. First of all, before the race you need to go out there and do at least two tests, in June and July because the race is in August. And that's another thing. Nobody wants to race in August, during the world championship's all-too brief summer break. Still I was eager to do it back in 2000.

The Eight Hour Race is a bit like entering a parallel dimension of racing. It's surreal and totally different from what we Europeans are used to. The organisational set-up is massive and only once you're inside the system do you really appreciate how highly regarded the race is in Japan. There are a number of internal teams: people who only deal with engines, others with fuel, others still with tyre changes. It's an incredibly expensive race, precisely because it's so complex. Not to mention the fact that it's really hard. There are two riders, but you drive for four hours each. It's about twenty-seven laps each, every hour. And August in Japan feels like Malaysia, with high heat and humidity.

Honda take it so seriously that they organise separate training sessions in the racetrack's park every morning. I should point out that Suzuka is a city devoted to engines. You could live in there, if you wanted, without ever needing to leave. Everything is there: hotels, restaurants, shops, even an amusement park. And then there is the park itself, all around the track. It's a beautiful track, although over the years it has become very dangerous for motorbikes.

In the race itself, I was shocked at how quickly everything is done. As soon as you arrive at the pits, you leave your bike to your teammate and you are led away by a team of people who immediately strip you naked. They then take you into the back where there are these small pools full of huge ice blocks. The first time you see the ice blocks, you think the Japanese are either going to kill or torture you. Instead, you realise that it's the very shock of the cold ice to your system that allows your muscles to recover quickly. The strange thing is that you get used to it and halfway through your turn on the bike you start fantasising about the ice blocks, thinking of them almost like a mirage in the desert.

While you relax with the blocks of ice, another crew dries your suit. You are then taken to a small infirmary where you are hooked up to an intravenous drip to replenish the lost substances. When you stop the first time you imagine that you're actually going to get a proper sixty minutes of rest. Big mistake. Because they shuttle you from one place to the next and everything has to happen according to a very strict schedule. And, under those conditions, an hour goes very quickly.

It's funny, when you're on the track your hour goes by very slowly, when you're back in the pits, it goes by in a heartbeat. It's an infinite race, long and terrible. You have to be strong both mentally and physically. And, at least in my case, you have to do it while your friends are back home, relaxing on the beach!

The most prestigious team always gets 11, because it means 1 plus 1. The best and the best. That's why Colin and I had 11. I was number one in 500cc and he was number one in Superbike. What's weird is that the second team didn't have number 22, they had number 4, 2 plus 2. I never really understood why that was the case.

In 2000, the three HRC teams were me and Colin, Tohru Ukawa and Daijiro Kato, and Satoshi Okada and Hideki Itoh. All three were very good teams. When I was competing, the top ten bikes were all official and each had good riders. The problem is that once you get past the "official" racers on their "official" bikes, the standard really drops. And that's a problem, because the race becomes very dangerous. Someone like me, who'll be driving along at pace, will suddenly encounter bikes who are so slow they appear to be coming towards me.

Some of the riders are little more than amateurs, so you never know what they're going to do or what trajectories they'll take as you try to pass them. This really bothered me, even in the tests. The total lack of safety is incredible. Suzuka does not have a parallel road for ambulances and that is certainly not reassuring. In addition, because testing at Suzuka is so expensive (an hour there costs as much as a whole day in Europe) you tend to test continuously, without stopping if someone falls. And the Japanese riders are constantly falling off their bikes, which means the track is littered with fallen Japanese bikers. They don't even remove the bikes from the run-off area.

I raised this issue with the team, but they told me not to worry –

it's just the way Suzuka is. Colin was chosen to ride first and so they took me aside and gave me some pointers.

"Be careful, because most falls happen at the start of the second hour, just as you'll be coming on," they explained.

"OK, I'll go slow," I said, already imagining a track covered in bikes and bodies.

"Also, whatever happens, don't leave your bike," I was told. "Even if you fall and damage the bike, please try and bring it back to the pits."

There was a reason for this. Because it's such a long race, there is always a chance, however slim, of making a comeback. That same year I saw Isutzu fall, damage his bike and push it heroically all the way back to the pits, amid a standing ovation from the crowd.

After the first hour, Colin came back in and handed me the VTL. We were third. I immediately got the sense that everyone was really slow. And they were. Within five laps I was in first place. And then it happened. I fell, breaking part of the handlebar. I walked the bike back to the pits and the team changed tactics. They refuelled and said: "OK, you're going back out and doing another twenty-seven laps because we've lost four or five laps and you need to make them up."

I wasn't too happy; but I went back out there. When I returned, we were eighth and I was exhausted. I wanted to drop out right there, but they wouldn't let me. Instead, I was sent to the back to receive my IV drip, something I really didn't want, either. But there was nothing I could do, just as the needle was about to go into my arm, I saw a huge commotion on the monitors. Colin, my teammate, had taken a massive fall, the left half of the VTR was missing.

"Yess!!!" I said, making no attempt to hide my elation. With Colin's fall and the damage to the bike, surely we would have to drop out of the race. Which meant that I could avoid my IV drip and go home. Of course, the Honda team wanted us to go on. I begged and pleaded and eventually convinced them that we should just give up and walk away. And so we did. Late that night, after dinner, we were back in the hotel when we ran into Itoh.

"You're not going to bed, are you?" he said. He convinced us to join him at a party in honour of Ukawa and Kato who had won the race. We were sceptical. We didn't think the Japanese would have any idea how to party, but still we accepted. When we got there it was incredible. They were all drunk. It was a beer-drinking contest. Two guys squared off in front of a full glass of beer and, whoever finished first, won. The loser had to stay on and challenge others. This worried me a bit. As did the fact that there were buckets set up all around the tables. I knew what they were for.

Crivillé and Gibernau were there too. Crivillé was there participating in a scooter endurance race. I know it sounds bizarre, but he had asked for the NSR 500 with which he became world champion in 1999 and the Japanese had told him, "OK, but only if you come to Suzuka and compete in our 50cc scooter endurance race." And the poor guy accepted just so he could have the bike. Needless to say, every morning when we would see him on those ridiculous scooters we would make fun of him no end! And as for Gibernau, he was the benchwarmer, the substitute. Honda kept him around in case any of the official riders got injured.

Anyway, I foolishly accepted the challenge of the beer-drinking contest and I got drunker than I have ever been in my life. Not that others, particularly the Japanese, were doing much better. We would pass out from time to time only to awaken and do something predictably dumb. Like when I ran around carrying Ukawa on my shoulders, looking for the toilet. Or when one of the women fell in the entrance to the restaurant and just stayed there. She just could not get up. And then, of course, there was Kato, who vomited all over the table and then fell asleep in his own vomit.

Noboru Ueda, Norick Abe and Makoto Tamada were there too, although they hadn't raced, but the wildest were Okada and Itoh. The Japanese definitely overdid it, but then so did we. When it was finally time to leave, we couldn't find our driver. Alby went to look for him and found him in a closet, vomiting into a bucket. He was barefoot and we never found out why (nor did we ask him to be fair . . .). Anyway, this guy was in no condition to drive, so we hunted around for some-one sober-looking. In the end, it was Ueda who took us back to the hotel. I passed out as soon as I got to my room. Alby was so alarmed that, as I found out later, he became convinced that I was dead! Alby tried to listen for a pulse but apparently couldn't hear anything. Or maybe he just got bored. Bottom line, he also passed out.

Before we knew it, it was morning and we had to leave for the airport. Uccio and Alby dressed me and loaded me on the bus to the airport. I was in a very bad state. Just before getting on the bus, they had left me for a minute or so leaning against the bus. When they came back out, they couldn't find me. I'd fallen into a flower bed, out of view. It took them a few minutes of panicked searching to establish my location. Of course, I was told all this later, I don't remember any of it, as you'd expect. Still, it was a great party. And the Japanese folks did surprise us.

The following year I could happily have done without the Eight Hour Race. But unfortunately it was in my contract now, there was nothing I could do to get out of it. It also came at the worst possible time of the season, just after I had finished a lowly seventh in the German Grand Prix. But instead of a nice holiday, I had to go back to Japan. I really did not want to get on the plane. But little did I know that not only would it be a wonderful experience, it would mark a seminal moment in my career.

Our VTR was red and white and my teammate was, once again,

Colin. At first, they thought of pairing me up with Kato, but he was a Dunlop man and I was with Michelin, so instead he got Ukawa. There were three official Honda teams: me and Colin with number 11, Barros and Okada with number 4, and Kato and Ukawa with number 33. It actually was a very strong field that year. Even though I had arrived in a rotten mood, I found that I was flying along. I was regularly a second and a half faster than Colin, despite the fact that, ultimately, the VTR is practically the same bike he rides in Superbike. Colin would go look at the monitors, see my time and say something like "fucking speedy Italian mafioso". I think he liked having a fast teammate, even though perhaps my performances hurt his pride a little bit!

I recorded a time of 2' 07" 5 in the tests and that was an absolutely monstrous time back then. Everybody had taken notice. I was confident going into the warm-up on Saturday morning. As soon as I hit the track I found myself battling with Hitoyasu Isutzu on the Kawasaki, and Yukio Kagayama on the Suzuki. I passed both of them on the downhill straightaway but then I realised that my brake lever was too close. I tried to adjust it, but I forgot for a split second that the lever on my 500 worked in one direction, but on the VTR it was the opposite. So, instead of fixing the situation I only made it worse. My braking was terrible and, naturally, I didn't take the turn and hit the protective wall, flying through the air like puppet.

I was still flying through the air when I heard two loud noises, one after the other: "Bang! Bang!" It was Isutzu and Kagayama. They had done exactly what I did, banging into the same protective walls. We were still down there, in the gravel, when another rider flew through the air and joined us. A little truck took us back to the pits. Along the way Isutzu told me why he crashed.

"I looked at you and noticed that you weren't braking," he said. "So I said, until he brakes, I'm not going to brake."

"Well done!" I said smiling, while thinking to myself, "Look at these three imbeciles."

I had hurt my neck, but was cleared to race. I didn't push it in qualifying and finished second. That was good enough. But I did ask if I could go first, partly because I wanted the experience, and partly because I didn't want to be racing in the final hour, which is at night. The Eight Hour Race ends at 7 p.m. and in Japan it's always dark by 6 p.m. I did not want to race at night, which was simply too dangerous. In fact, Jeremy agreed: "At night you don't use your motorbike to race, you use your motorbike to pick up your girlfriend." Sound advice.

The start of the race is actually quite unusual. You're on foot in front of your bike inside a little circle, while a steward holds the bike for you. The engines are off. You don't hear anything, not a peep, until the spectators begin the countdown, from minus 15. When it gets to zero, you run to the bike, turn on the engine and take off.

I was up against Okada, Kato, Akira Ryo and Isutzu. Colin had to face Barros, who was our toughest opponent because he was in great form at the time, not to mention that, like us, he had the official Honda. I started well and handed the bike to Colin with a ten-second lead. But Colin struggled against Barros and he was unable to maintain the lead I had built. By the fourth hour, we had lost some thirty seconds. But Colin's performance was partly due to the fact he was unwell, because he doesn't handle the humid heat well at all. Jeremy too had noticed it commenting: "Looks like the Texas Tornado is just a light breeze today."

I didn't think it was so funny. I didn't want to lose at all. I worried that if we lost Team HRC would try and make us return next year and do the whole thing over again. That's why when Colin handed the bike over again I told myself: "OK, now I'm going to pull out all the stops,

I'm going to take chances and risks. Because it's the only way to win and avoid having to come back here ever again."

I did take a lot of risks, but it paid off. After my hour, our lead over Okada was back up to fifteen seconds. When I handed over the bike, I grabbed him by the shoulders and said: "You'd better win this, because I don't want to come back!" That was my single biggest preoccupation. Suddenly, there was a stroke of good luck, at least from my perspective. Okada came into the pits, Barros got on and the crew started the procedure to change the tyres. To do this, the bike should be in neutral, but Barros made a mistake and put it in gear a split second too early. This slowed everything down, costing them another good forty seconds.

So I began to relax. But not for long. An engineer came up to me with a very worried look on his face.

"We told you not to push the bike hard in the final hours," he said. "The way you drove, we're lucky the bike hasn't fallen apart!"

And this really worried me. It's true that the engineers had told us to take it easy, not to grind the gears, not to take the bike to its limits. On the other hand, I was obsessed with winning and that's why I had pushed it so hard.

"Shit, if the bike breaks now, we've got to come back next year," I thought. "That would be horrible."

But the VTR hung in there. In his weakened state Colin was still losing three seconds a lap, but he had the situation under control. And we won. I was ecstatic; we both were. We hugged each other, shouting; "We're not coming back! We're not coming back! We're not coming back!" We were so happy that this had been our last race.

This time, we didn't do any partying. I was demolished. Exhausted. Fried. I stayed in the hotel. I was much too tired, I had nothing left after those four hours. It literally took me months to recover and my arms ached until the end of the year. The Eight Hour Race is really four races in one, that's why it's so brutal. And that's why it's a lot easier for the Superbike guys, since their bikes are smoother, softer, a "sofa" as Colin calls them. There is no way a MotoGP bike could have held out so long.

I was very fast in the 2001 Eight Hour Race. And the success stayed with me. On that trip I truly realised just how much strength I had inside me. Things were rough in the 500cc series, for sure, and I was a little demoralised and yet things went fantastic for me at Suzuka. I don't know what it was, but after that experience I really started flying in the 500cc. And I ended up winning the world title, my first at 500cc and in fact the last ever 500cc world title. It was also the first world crown I would win with Honda. I would win two more, in 2002 and 2003, both times with the RCV four stroke.

THIRTEEN

CAPITOLO TREDICI

I have been through a similar growing experience, in terms of my profession, to the Eight Hour Race, albeit in a different context. Back in 1998, I was making my debut in 250cc after winning the world title in 125cc the previous season. Many important things happened that season and, looking back, it really was a career crossroads for me. I learned a lot and I also got into a fair bit of trouble. I think it was the season where I really matured and went to the next level in this business.

I had dominated at 125cc level. That season, I regularly won and put on my little gags, which people seemed to really enjoy. And as a result, my popularity was sky-high for a 125 rider. Yet when I got to 250cc a large section of public opinion and of the Italian press seemed to forget what I had achieved in 125cc. They didn't seem to care that I had won eleven races and secured the world title with a lead of around one hundred points over the runner-up, an astronomical feat.

"Now he needs to become great in 250, it will be much tougher, he'll start to learn many things. And he'll have to stop being the court jester." This is typical of the idiotic things that were said about me at the time. And they said other things, too, like, "He'll have to become an adult now." But few people actually stopped to point out that I was making my debut. Or, for that matter, that Aprilia was so much stronger than everybody else that season that the world championship was really a three-way race between the three Aprilia riders: Capirossi, Harada and me. Therefore, finishing third in 1998 was the same as finishing last. And many times it was I who finished third, which meant I was disappointing everyone. Never mind the fact that in Harada and Capirossi I was up against two older, more experienced guys, whose bikes were just as good as mine. Nobody seemed to take that into account. All they could do was point out my shortcomings.

Apart from the competition with Harada and Capirossi, my main problem was that I had difficulty in learning how to handle and tune the 250cc. I simply didn't have control of the bike in difficult situations: when the bike would slide, for example, or when the steering would lock up. Compared to the 125 I simply didn't have the ability to react and correct my mistakes. And, on top of that, the 250 moves much more than the 125, and it took some time to get used to it. The real problem, however, was this: I was unable to settle for the results I was getting. I didn't *want* to settle. I wanted to go fast, always, even when it would have been smarter to play the points and ride tactically. And that's why I fell so often.

When we arrived in France, at Le Castellet, I was already tense because Harada always seemed to beat me near the finish. Sometimes he'd push really hard early on, hoping that I would make a mistake. Other times he would go slow, let me get in the lead and simply follow me, marshalling my movements and trajectories. And then he'd pass me on the last lap. Sometimes that's why I fell. I would try to stay ahead of him. I did not want him to pass me like that in the final lap. And so I made mistakes. And it really bothered me the way he always seemed to outsmart me.

Ultimately, his tactic wasn't unique and others employed similar moves in other races. I myself did exactly the same thing many times, both in 250 and in 500, and especially in MotoGP. But that season, 1998, I decided that I would do things differently. I would be the one to sit and wait. And so the Grand Prix became a lot like a cycling race, both of us waiting for the other to "pull" him to the finish line. Like he had done before, Harada tried to take off immediately, but he realised he would not be able to do this. I was close, very close. So he let me pass. And then, a few laps later, I let him pass. But he did not want to be in the lead, so, after a while, he pretended to make a mistake on a turn, taking it too wide, and letting me pass.

You can easily tell when somebody does that because they have made a mistake, or if they're doing it on purpose. And Harada had not made a mistake; he wanted me to be in the lead. So I passed him, because it was inevitable, but then I began to slow down, downshifting whenever possible. And he did the same to the point where we almost reached a standstill.

Capirossi, who was far slower than both of us in that race and was already five seconds behind, caught us and passed us. He had no idea what was going on, but I'm sure he couldn't believe we were making so many mistakes. He did not enjoy it for long, because Harada and I immediately took off, passed him and arrived together at the finish line where Harada beat me. Many were outraged and some journalists went wild. They said I had no respect for others, especially Capirossi.

I never understood their reaction. I was trying to win, plain and simple, and when you try to win you have to do whatever it takes (apart from cheating, obviously). I ran my race. Capirossi simply didn't have the right pace that day and this had nothing to do with me or the kind of race I was running, which was a result of the tactical duel with Harada. I didn't want to humiliate Capirossi. And, incidentally, he could have exploited our mistake and hung on to the lead after passing us. After all, it would not have been such a strange thing. Harada went on to lose the title that year to Capirossi precisely because of such stupid tactics. Because he spent so much time trying to neutralise me, he often ended up penalising himself, thereby giving Capirossi a big boost.

I had already noticed this during the winter tests. Harada had decided that I was his enemy and so he immediately played all sort of games to try and intimidate me. At the third race, in Jerez, Capirossi beat me after a long, hard duel. Harada's engine seized up, so he dropped out early, but while he was still in the race he did everything he could to slow me down. And afterwards, I saw him beneath the podium. He was applauding Capirossi, whom he was complimenting for having defeated me. This was clever of Harada. He had found the right ally because, in the end, he's the one who got screwed. In any case, Harada was very fast in 250cc. He had an unusual style, one which, in certain conditions was very effective. If you left him on his own, he was very difficult to contain. And that's why I tried to stop him, to slow him down. The problem is that I took too many risks to do this and suffered too many falls.

As the season went on, the tension increased. It all came to a head that summer at the Grand Prix in Imola. I was stressed that I had fallen in the previous Grand Prix in Brno and the pundits were having a go at me.

"See? He's struggling now!" they would say, almost with glee. "He's gone up a level and he can't handle it!"

That's the kind of rubbish I had to put up with throughout the summer. And I was getting very angry. But that's the thing with anger. You can either make it work for you or let it drag you down. Thankfully, I'm an optimist, and I was able to do use my anger in a positive fashion.

"I'll show you who Valentino Rossi is," I told myself as I prepared for the Grand Prix.

I was so concentrated that I won hands down. And then I won every single remaining race that season. It was the turning point of my career. In Barcelona, I dominated and set a fastest lap record that was only beaten in 2004! I also won in Australia and Argentina. I finished the season in second place, behind Capirossi. Incidentally, the race in Argentina will for ever be remembered for the row between Capirossi and Harada. I wasn't involved, but then again, I was given strict instructions from Aprilia not to get involved.

"Don't worry," I said. "I'll win the race and leave the two of them behind, they can sort out the title situation themselves."

It wasn't a joke. It was a way of expressing just how confident I was. Even though I started poorly, I caught up with Capirossi and Harada and stayed right on their tails. Both were quite fast that day and I began to worry a little bit. I had promised not to get involved in their title duel, but the way the race was going I might have to if I was to get any points at all.

I waited: Capirossi first, Harada second. Two or three laps from the end, I got fed up and decided to go for Harada, whom I managed to beat on the inside. Now, it was just me and Capirossi. I remembered the instructions from Aprilia. So I told myself: "OK, they don't want me to interfere. So I'm going to try to pass Capirossi. If I succeed, I'll take off and win it. If I don't succeed and it's half a lap to the end, that's it, I'm stepping aside and letting those two sort it out."

On the second-to-last lap, Capirossi made a mistake, almost exactly where Harada had committed his blunder. I made him pay immediately. I passed him and won the race. I was quite proud of myself, I had run a good race and managed to win without getting involved in the Harada v Capirossi controversy. Just as Aprilia had ordered me to do. I only saw what happened later between Capirossi and Harada on television. Everybody was tense at the end. All year long the spirit had been good, but now it was falling apart. And it really should not have happened like that, because we enjoyed a great season, not least for the fact that we finished first, second and third overall. And yet things weren't right. Capirossi and Harada had been having rows all season. And between Harada and myself, things weren't great either, we had been at each other, whereas Capirossi and I tended generally to get along.

The Aprilia pit was split into three parts because, while we were all Aprilia, we were split between my team, Capirossi's team and Harada's team. There were big panels separating the various teams, and each panel was adorned with the image of the rider. As soon as I walked in, I could tell something was going to happen and I knew that I needed to remain calm. You could read it in people's faces. It was as if we were preparing to watch a fight.

And then Harada walked in. He walked straight towards the big dividing panel with Capirossi's face on it, and punched it, knocking it over. That's right. Harada PUNCHED THE PANEL WITH CAPIROSSI'S FACE ON IT.

I couldn't help myself. I thought it was hilarious and I let out a giggle. Then, when Harada's wife showed up, she began abusing Capirossi, calling him all sorts of names, while Tetsuya just sat and watched! Now I really couldn't contain myself. This was too funny. So I tried to focus on something else, like removing my suit.

Somebody stepped in between Capirossi and Harada's wife and, for a moment, everything seemed calm. But it was just the intermission before round two. This time, it was the mechanics. We heard everything: toolboxes being kicked, wrenches being thrown around, shouts and insults. We could hardly not be privy to the whole charade; after all, we were right there in the middle, with Capirossi's people on one side and Harada's people on the other.

"You're bastards! You and Capirossi! Bastards!" was the cry from Harada's camp.

"There was plenty of room out there! It's Harada who's an idiot!" was the reply.

It was a bad scene. And very embarrassing. For a while, the situation between the riders did not improve. The problems at Aprilia continued for a very long time, even after I had left. I myself attribute the problems to Carlo Pernat's departure. Pernat had left following a row with team owner Ivano Beggio. Pernat was clever, experienced and well respected by all. When he left, all sense of discipline left with him. Pernat could solve any problem and he was sorely missed. He was the one who kept the three "official" riders – me, Harada and Capirossi – in check. He was the one who made sure we weren't at each other's throats. And when he left, it all fell apart.

For me the latter part of the season proved that I was growing. Capirossi and Harada had pushed themselves hard all year. They were benchmarks of 250cc, yet, by the end, I was defeating them regularly. I was now certain that I could handle 250cc. And that's what I did the following year, dominating the season on my way to winning nine races.

I have many wonderful memories of 1999. Not only did I win the title, I also made the decision to move to Honda at the end of that season. Capirossi had moved at the end of 1998, immediately after the row with Aprilia. That was understandable. It did set up a certain rivalry between us, however. Even though Capirossi's main beef was with Aprilia, not me, I was the Aprilia front man. Of course, the Italian press did not waste this golden opportunity to fuel this supposed rivalry: Honda and Capirossi versus Aprilia and me.

The Honda was a very good bike that had raced well ever since we first saw it in the winter tests. Team HRC had had a difficult year in 1998 and they were keen to bounce back. To be fair, I think in 1998 they were mostly guilty of being over-creative. They had designed a weird-looking bike with strange lateral radiators in an attempt to make the bike smaller. Instead, all it did was make it more difficult for the engine to cool.

Anyway, because Honda had disappointed in 1998 and I was still on the Aprilia, my detractors returned to their usual games, saying that I was lucky, that I got all the breaks, that I always had the best equipment. They even suggested that Aprilia had sacked Capirossi just to make way for me because they had somehow decided that I needed to win the 1999 world title. Instead, far from being a cakewalk, it was a hard-fought season. Capirossi and Ukawa on Honda, Shinya Nakano and Olivier Jacque on Yamaha . . . I had plenty of competition, particularly since the season did not begin well.

I had a problem with an electronic valve in my first race and finished fifth. In the second, at Motegi, it rained heavily and I was seventh. Capirossi, on the other hand, finished first and third. All I can say is, thank goodness I won in Jerez, as this helped to close the gap a little. That win was very important for my confidence, so I decided to go out and enjoy myself a little. We went into town, where there was some kind of big village fair, lots of people and stands and noise. Unfortunately, I drank a little too much and couldn't find my way back. I was rescued an hour later, after search parties had been sent out to find me. I had been wandering around on my own, totally clueless.

Anyway, immediately afterwards we went to France, at the Paul Ricard circuit, where I was about to win with a huge lead when my chain broke. I revved the engine, I could hear it reacting, but I didn't budge an inch. So I looked down to see what the problem was. We were using a new chain, a narrower one, and it had simply slipped off. I tried to put it back, but I couldn't. So I collected a big fat zero while Ukawa, who won, gained forty points on me. I was so angry that, from that moment on, I drove myself as hard as I could and, in the end, it worked. I became world champion. I was able to channel my anger in the right way, turning all that negativity into something positive I could use during the race.

I think back and I realise that at a certain point my career accelerated and I never looked back. One day I started going fast everywhere. And I mean *everywhere*. I gained a consistency I did not have before. Unbelievably, there was the odd race where I was even faster. Where something inside me made me even better, capable of reaching new heights. I can't predict when it will happen. And I don't know what makes it come out. I just know I have it inside me.

It's certainly not a case of me sitting back, all relaxed and then just turning on when I absolutely have to. Not at all. I always try hard. It's just that, sometimes, everything clicks and I go to some higher plane of racing. And, after the race, I return to my usual level.

It's temporary, I'm already at my limit, or, at least, I'm where my limit should be and yet, though it's hard to explain, I can actually go beyond my own limits, and when this happens I can overtake dozens of people in just a few laps, close a gap or impose a pace which would normally appear unthinkable. Good examples of this are the Grands Prix of Catalunya and Australia in 2003.

At the 2003 Australian Grand Prix I was very fast, I was ahead, I was leaving Capirossi way behind. We were still in the first part of the race when I was made aware that I was now second. I was still in the lead, but I was in second place because I had been given a ten-second penalty for ignoring the yellow caution flags. Yes, the silly caution flags which the stewards, for reasons known only to them, insist on putting in invisible places, where nobody can see them. The same thing had cost me a win at Donington a few months earlier.

"Enough!" I told myself. And, from there, I went on a tear. Without realising it, I started going *even faster*. I gained back nearly a second per lap, and, by the end, I was once again in first place. I had made up the ten seconds and there was still time to increase my lead. It's not as if I had been biding my time before my penalty that day. I wasn't planning on saving myself for the end. No, I was going as hard as I could. It's just that, afterwards, I went even harder, crazy as it sounds. I turned my rage into pure speed. Most riders can't do that. For them, rage just raises the level of tension and increases their chances of making crucial mistakes. I'm like that too – some of the time. Qatar in 2004 is a good example of that. I remember, I was absolutely furious because Honda had filed a complaint and I was forced to start from the last row. In just a few laps, I had come back up the field into fourth place. I should have calmed myself down and waited for the right moment. Instead, I fell. Looking back on it, that was a moment of uncontrollable folly. Normally it doesn't work that way. Normally I can control it. Or, at least, my brain can. And I'm thankful for that, or else I'd really be in trouble! And the 2003 Australian Grand Prix was the only time it happened on a Honda. It was my fastest ever race with the RC211V. And it was probably my best race ever with Honda. But if I'm being honest, at 125cc I never had moments like that. It did happen in 250cc, of course, such as in 1998, the season when I progressed the most and when my riding style matured, the season when I went very, very fast. And that season it was particularly special because that magical spell lasted for four races!

Still, when I think about my favourite races, the ones that gave me the most satisfaction, I have to rank the 2001 British Grand Prix near the very top. It was a stressful period for me because Biaggi and I were neck and neck for the world title. I should point out that Donington Park is one of my absolute favourite tracks, and 2001 was the year I really started to appreciate its finer qualities. On Friday, I had fallen during the tests at over 200 kilometres per hour. I came into a turn a little wide, the steering locked and that was it: I fell and rolled far away from the bike. I got up straight away, but my bike fared rather worse. It bounced all over the place, hitting hoardings before being catapulted through the air and eventually crashing to earth in a crumpled heap of metal.

On Saturday, it started to rain during qualifying, just as I was turning in my fastest lap. As a result, I couldn't turn in a decent time and started in eleventh place, with Biaggi in pole position. It wasn't the best of build-ups and I had very few certainties when the race began. Yet, little by little, I climbed up the field. I started passing riders with ease, always in the same place, braking just before the "S" after the Dunlop Bridge. I sailed up the standings, until I approached Barros, who was second. Then I passed him too and came up behind Biaggi. And at what was now my sweet spot – the "S" after Dunlop Bridge – I overtook him as well, with a good two laps to spare. I had begun the day thinking that my chances of success were very slim, since Biaggi was in pole and I was eleventh. I had ended the day surprising everyone, starting with myself. And, as you know, when it comes to my ability, it takes a lot to surprise me.

FOURTEEN

My mum has seen far too much over the years – first following Graziano's career, later mine – to know that there are some things that you just cannot ask a racer, even if you are his mother. And that's why Stefania (or Stefy, as I call her) is not one of those mothers who calls you up and says: "Please, take it easy out there, speed kills."

It wouldn't make much sense, would it?

She uses different expressions that are nonetheless significant. For example, she'll call me and say, "Hang in there!" Or, on a more general note: "Be careful!" And, of course, there is her favourite: "Be a good boy!"

I always talk to her when I'm at a Grand Prix. She'll come to the big races, and she has always been there when I won a world title, no matter how far away it might have been from home. It may seem strange, but while my conversations with Graziano are often centred around the emotions and sensations we might have felt during the race, with Stefania the talk is often, how can I put it . . . technical.

For example, I'll tell her: "Stefy, I had some problems braking today, I stiffened the front fork . . ." Stuff like that. I might talk to her the way I would talk to Jeremy. And she'll say stuff like: "When I was watching you on television I noticed that when it was changing direction the bike looked a bit imprecise."

Like I said, sometimes she's the technical one. And, of course, other times the stuff she says proves that she is not really part of the MotoGP world . . . but it doesn't matter, she's a lot of fun.

Let me tell you a secret. *Every* rider is scared at the start of every race. There are no exceptions. And that's good, because, in this sport, fear can save your life. Of course, you trust in your own ability and in your "best friend" – luck – which you hope will always be at your side, but you need to know how to use fear. Because fear can be a precious ally.

You hear people say: "You guys, you go so fast, you're all crazy!" It's the kind of comment that, after you've been racing as long as I have, you no longer find funny (in fact, it was probably never funny in the first place). More importantly, this is the typical comment an ignorant person might make. Only those who don't know this sport could conclude that us riders are all crazy or stupid because we go so fast. In fact, at the highest level, this sport is a form of art, like playing the piano, composing a song, writing a poem, painting a picture. Or playing football like Ronaldo or Zidane. Riding a racing bike is an art. It's something you do because you're attracted to it, because you feel a passion for it from deep within. Some people have it, some people don't. And for those who have it, winning a world title is like a singer-songwriter having a smash-hit single or album.

Naturally, I can understand how, from the outside looking in, one might form the impression that the people in this business are mentally unsound. Even I sometimes find myself watching a race, screaming, "Wow, this guy's a real lunatic!" Because when you're on the outside, you see a totally different world. Your perception of speed is completely different and you can't understand how someone can handle a bike at certain super-fast speeds. But when you're actually on the bike, you have the opposite sensation. You have the impression that everything is happening in slow motion, that it's all far slower than it really is. That's because speed is something you learn to live with, something you get used to. And it's relative. If you're standing still by the side of the road and a car zooms past you at 50 kilometres per hour, you think, wow, that's really fast. But if you were in the car, watching the person at the side of the road, you'd think everything was moving by pretty slow. Sure, when you go into a big turn at 200 kilometres an hour and you feel the bike moving and there doesn't seem to be enough asphalt for you to turn, that's when you realise you are going very fast and your situation is rather dangerous. But a rider has mechanisms to deal with this.

Of course, there are irresponsible racers, just as there are irresponsible people. But the real racer is rarely like that. He knows exactly what he's doing. He thinks and uses his reason. And it's the thinking racers who get results. Irresponsibility leads nowhere.

You are constantly telling yourself: "This is dangerous, I'm not going to do it." Or, something like, "I could go a tiny bit faster but if I do that it's riskier, and there is a greater chance I'll make a mistake, so it's best if I keep my speed."

You're always making decisions like that. You have to know your limits and those of your bike. Because the guy who wins in this sport is rarely the bravest. It's usually the one who knows his limits, who can judge what is possible and what is impossible. And the guy who wins is usually the one who knows how to adapt to whatever the conditions are at that particular time.

That's why your sensitivity in handling the bike is so important. Honestly, sometimes I feel as if it's more dangerous for me to take my mum's scooter down to the local supermarket when it's winter and its tyres haven't warmed up, than it is to ride in a Grand Prix. Because in a Grand Prix I know that I'm using the right equipment. That's why on the road I'm always cautious. I don't go fast because the conditions to go fast aren't there. It's not just about having a big engine. A racing bike on a track is far safer than a roadbike on the road. To me that's obvious.

So that's what I mean by knowing your limits. It's having a sense of how far you can push yourself in relation to the equipment you have. It may seem banal, but I think it's the single most important thing. Because the sense of limit is ultimately all about your ability to read and evaluate situations. And that is invaluable in any walk of life.

Motorbikes remain dangerous if you don't have a sense of their limits, but there was a time when they were far more dangerous than they are today. Today everything is geared towards safety, or at least being as safe as possible. Even though fear will always be a part of it, there are things that can be done to make it safer. Starting with the tracks themselves. Because they are the single most dangerous elements.

It's like when you ride out on the road and you find an obstacle that shouldn't be there. When racing we should always make sure that there are no obstacles, particularly in the faster tracks. When I ride, that's the one thing that truly scares me.

Well, that, and the possibility of touching another rider, which is more of a factor at the start. But ultimately, it's about control. And I get the sense sometimes that our world, in some ways, has lost that control. In April 2003, at Suzuka in Japan, there was a tragic event, one which had a massive effect on MotoGP. Daijiro Kato died after a tragic accident.

I don't think certain things happen by chance. There is always a message behind every event. Even a tragic event. And I think I know what the message was in this case: we were all overdoing it.

When a racer dies on the track, it leaves its mark on everyone, wherever they may be. It doesn't matter who they are. We've lost a guy who shared the same passion, who felt the same emotions when looking at a motorbike, who put up with the same burdens, who took the same risks, who accepted the same lifestyle the rest of us had. When things like this happen, your first reaction is incredulity. It can't happen. But you know that not only can it happen, it does happen. And it can happen anywhere. We riders all know this, but the rest of the time we don't think about it. Nobody wants to think about it. Our brains simply ignore that outcome. And there is nothing wrong with that. Quite the opposite, it's right and it's necessary that it be like that.

Nobody knows exactly how it happened. Or, at least, nobody will say exactly how it happened. All we know for sure is that Kato's death was caused by a wall – a low wall, but one that should not have been there. Not so close to the track. And certainly not so poorly protected. Because the spot where Kato came off the track does not have an adequate run-off area, especially if there is a series of low walls lying in wait . . .

If they had an adequate run-off area, if they removed those walls, things should have turned out differently. The impact would not have been as violent. Beyond things like fate and the imponderable, it's absurd that in this day and age a racer can die from colliding with a wall. And this has nothing to do with what the rider is thinking or what Kato was thinking. Because this kind of thing can happen to anyone, anywhere, any time. Particularly on a dangerous track like Suzuka.

Many of us had been saying it for some time. Suzuka did not have the safety prerequisites necessary for this sport and for these bikes. I said it back in 2001, at the Eight Hour Race, even though back then I was a Honda pilot racing on a track owned by Honda. Don't get me wrong, I really like Suzuka, I think it's a magnificent track. But it's very dangerous and it would have been a big mistake to put it back on the race calendar just because of its glorious history.

At that time, we racers were not organised. We weren't part of any discussions; everything was decided without our input. That was before we formed the Safety Commission. Before that date, the rider's opinion was entirely irrelevant.

We riders formed the Safety Commission as a result of Kato's death. And we now have a voice. We elect our representatives who raise our concerns. When we talk about safety it's essential that the riders be the ones making the decisions. Because only we know certain situations, only we know the tracks inside and out. We see things that you wouldn't notice if you do a lap in a car or a scooter.

You want to know how dangerous a wall is? Go close to one on a MotoGP. At 250 kilometres an hour. Then you'll begin to understand. Since the introduction of MotoGP the problem hasn't just been speed, it has been acceleration. The sheer power of the bikes, combined with the electronic precision available now, change both the rider's reaction times and those of the bikes. Previously, at Dorna, they had no clue about any of this. Because they never rode those bikes on those tracks the way we do. And, if they did, they certainly did not ride them at the speeds we reach.

If there is a legacy of Kato's tragedy, it is that the accident brought the riders together. It gave us a bit of unity. We racers could now sit at the table with Dorna and the constructors. And they would have to listen.

In 2002, the era of MotoGP began. It was a radical change compared to the 500cc era. Everything became more technology-driven. There was more enthusiasm too, probably because there were new horizons, new opportunities. The 500cc bikes had reached their maximum potential. Their development had been stationary for the last few years. But with the arrival of MotoGP teams and constructors began putting more money into the bikes, and the new technology brought more challenges and more opportunities. And more costs, too. It has become a vicious circle. More tests, more investment, faster bikes, better performances. Everything bigger, better, faster, more. And that's why Kato's accident, in my opinion, was so significant.

I see it as a warning, which goes something like this: "You're awash with money, men building ever improved motorbikes, everything grows, the fans go wild, but now this is the bill . . . please come back down to Earth and restore some sanity to the sport."

Sure, accidents can and will happen. That day, at Suzuka, we riders knew nothing about it. We saw the yellow flags, but that was it. They cleaned up the track and we went and raced on.

The Grand Prix should have stopped. There is no question, no argument about that. But they didn't stop it. And this was a huge mistake. We riders protested, we got angry. As far as we were concerned, the race went ahead for one reason, and one reason only: television rights. They had been sold and satellite time had been purchased. For Kato, stopping would not have made a difference. The fatal blow that struck him was so strong that he practically died right there, on the track. They resuscitated him and got his heart going, but in terms of his spine and his brain, lethal damage had already been done. And a few days later, his heart also stopped.

As soon as we created the Safety Commission, one of our first demands was to change the rules regarding the suspension of a race or testing. From now on, it will be suspended if there is an accident during racing or testing that requires doctors to intervene directly on the track, or if a rider is unconscious after an accident or if, in the doctors' opinion, a rider is seriously hurt.

In any case, after the race, we all noticed that something was wrong. And yet, if they knew, nobody told us exactly what had happened. Paco, Dorna's chief press officer, simply said: "Kato fell, the helicopter took him away."

And that was it. Those words can mean everything or they can mean nothing. And, when you're there, you never imagine the worst. That's why we celebrated on the podium, it had been a wonderful race, particularly for us, the Italians, I was first, Biaggi was second, Capirossi was third. And nobody had told us the full story. I think I can speak for Capirossi and Biaggi when I say that the mood would have been very sombre if we had been told what had happened. We certainly wouldn't have had even the most low-key of celebrations. They only told us afterwards, once we were off the podium. And even then, all they did was say, "It's serious." We began to sense more during the press conference, but even then all we got was half-truths and partial explanations. So I went to the Mobile Clinic, wanting to know more. And, again, neither my physiotherapist Marco Montanari nor Doctor Costa seemed to want to give me the details about how badly Daijiro was injured.

"He's got badly hurt, but we'll see . . ." That's all they would say. That's all anybody said. Eventually we forced them to tell us. Kato was in a deep coma.

Kato and I had a good relationship. I liked him a lot. The last occasion we had spent time together was in March, when we had toured Honda factories all over Japan. As part of the tour, we met many factory workers. I raced with him in both the MotoGP and the Suzuka Eight Hour Race.

A few weeks after the accident, the championship moved to South Africa and we lived through another surreal weekend. Everybody had the stickers with number 74. They were on bikes, suits, helmets. Everywhere. It was the least we could do.

I had a strange experience that weekend at Welkom. During the first round of testing on Friday morning, while I was out on the track, I saw in the distance the silhouette of a racer. The closer I got, the more he came into focus. And the more I saw that it looked like Kato.

Yes, it was Kato. Except it wasn't. It was Ryuichi Kiyonari, another Japanese who had replaced him for the MotoGP. His suit was identical and for me it really felt like a flashback. We were all seeing things that weekend. Including me.

FIFTEEN

They made the first move. Ferrari's officials suggested that I try their car at Fiorano. Obviously I accepted their invitation right away. And it was an incredible experience.

My test with Ferrari was a genuine test, in that it wasn't a reward or a favour, or some kind of publicity stunt. It was the real deal, the real car, identical to the one Michael Schumacher and Rubens Barrichello would drive at Imola a few days later. I had engineers, mechanics, the whole crew. The computers were running, the telemetry was being analysed in detail, technicians and mechanics basically treated me exactly the way they would have treated a Formula One driver who was testing the Ferrari.

Like I said, they did not do this just for my benefit. They wanted to put me to the test, wanted to see me at the wheel of their car, to understand what my potential might be. And, when it was over, they told me, fully and frankly what they thought of my driving.

Funnily enough, the first time I was linked to Ferrari, things went rather differently. It was back in 1998, the year that Ferrari invited Biaggi to test the car at Fiorano. At the time, it was huge news and it was talked about for a long time. Now, given my rocky relationship with Biaggi, the press wanted to know what I thought. Maybe I'd give them a line. "Would you have wanted to be in his place?" they asked.

"Well, yes, of course I would have liked to test the Ferrari," I said straight away.

"We're not Avis [the car rental company]," the president of Ferrari, Luca Cordero di Montezemolo replied when asked about it.

To be honest, his words hurt me.

It's not as if I had said, "Please ask Montezemolo if he'll let me try his car." All I said was that, if the opportunity were to arise, I would be delighted to take it. But he came out and said that Ferrari was not a car rental agency. Fine. It ended there.

I was nineteen, my first year in 250cc after winning the 125cc title. Maybe that's why I never fell in love with Ferrari, though I never had any particular dislike for them. It's just that I never supported a team, I supported a driver. And as a boy, I had liked Ayrton Senna, Nigel Mansell and, later, Jacques Villeneuve. And, at the height of his career, Villeneuve was the arch-rival of Schumacher, and therefore of Ferrari as well.

In any case, six years later, it was a different story and a wholly different situation. In March 2004, I had dinner with Stefano Domenicali, Ferrari sporting director, the night of the Australian Grand Prix, the opening race of the F1 2004 world championship. We were all relaxed. We complimented each other, we were upbeat and enthusiastic. I loved the day we had spent together out in the paddock, surrounded by all the Formula One cars.

We talked about everything. But at one point the conversation slipped over to the issue of cars. I told him that as a child I had raced kart and that I had always loved cars and that, for a while, I dreamed about becoming an F1 driver. I also added that, as I grew older, I had developed a love for rally cars and that I had competed in a few of them, including one that was part of the world championship series.

"Why don't we arrange a test?" he said all of a sudden. Domenicali seemed cool and relaxed.

"With the Formula One?" I asked. I wanted to be sure that I had understood correctly.

"Yes, in Fiorano," he said.

"Really?"

"Really!"

"Why not?"

"Look," he explained. "I'll tell you right away, it won't be easy, but I'm going to try and arrange a real test. I'm going to ask the president, Luca Montezemolo, directly. We'll do it in Fiorano, because logistically it's the easiest to arrange. I just need to see what the president says."

It was the highlight of a day that had already been very memorable. It had all begun when Yamaha arranged some tests at Philip Island. They were on a Monday and, because Melbourne isn't too far away, I decided to fly over a few days early to catch the Australian F1 Grand Prix. Domenicali heard that I was out there and invited me to watch the race with him. And I accepted, also because – believe it or not – I had never seen an F1 Grand Prix arena in the flesh.

Once we arrived in the paddock, something unusual and unexpected occurred. The whole F1 world seemed to welcome me with open arms, starting with Bernie Ecclestone. I had only ever met him once before, but, right there in Australia, he started to show me around the pits, introducing me to people. Everywhere we went, there were mechanics, technicians, engineers . . . they all came over to shake my hand. And the ones from Ferrari, like those from Minardi, were so warm and friendly that they really struck a chord.

I would never have expected a welcome of that kind, not in Formula One, which I had always regarded as a colder, more clinical, more detached world than our MotoGP universe, and especially towards someone like myself, the star and symbol of MotoGP. Instead, so many of them came over and said they watched MotoGP whenever they could and that they were real fans. It was both pleasant and interesting, particularly for me as I love the technical side of things and, of course, I love cars.

After dinner that night, Domenicali and I left each other without making any specific promises, beyond the fact that we would speak again as soon there was an update. We both agreed that we would have another think about it.

I actually had to start thinking about it right away, because I realised that it could potentially create problems for me with my employers. It did not take him long to get back. Just a few weeks.

"From our perspective, we can do this test," he told me over the phone. "Tell me when you're free and then we'll make it happen."

I reiterated that I was excited to do it, but then we both started thinking about how it could be done. The main hurdle was the fact that my sponsors and Yamaha's sponsors were direct rivals of Ferrari's sponsors. If we weren't careful, we could upset a lot of people. And that was the last thing we wanted to do.

I also thought of the press and all the problems the journalists would create.

"The only way to do this is to maintain complete silence," I said, after we had discussed it thoroughly. "Complete silence to me means that we don't tell anyone."

Ferrari agreed. The date of the test was another problem. We fixed a date on the Wednesday after the South African Grand Prix. And so, after Welkom, I flew back to Italy and a day later I was on the road to Maranello. The organisation of my test with the Ferrari F1 2004 was perfect, every tiny detail was catered for. We arrived secretly. I was with Uccio, Gibo and Arnaldo Cappellini. Graziano joined us later.

To give you an idea of how secret we kept things, very few people in the Tribe knew about it. I had not even told my closest friends. Obviously, Brivio knew nothing about it. As for Mum, I told her I was going to Milan for the day. We arrived at the Modena exit on the motorway, parked our car and found a guy from Ferrari waiting for us. We climbed into a car with tinted windows, specifically chosen to maintain maximum secrecy. We drove to Fiorano, arriving directly at Ferrari's private test track. The security was so tight that Ferrari decided that we would sleep at the track. This way, nobody would have seen us at a local restaurant, we wouldn't need to register with any hotel and nobody would see us cruising around Maranello. We would be in and out without a trace. We would be like ghosts.

We had dinner and they gave us a tour of their assembly line. That night, before going to bed, they took me to see the cars. I got into the cockpit; they prepared the seat. They immediately explained how it worked, all its characteristics and details. They had prepared the "fourth car" for me. It's a "real" car, just like the others. It gets assembled and put to one side, but it's nevertheless ready to race.

Ferrari had arranged for us to sleep in the house in the middle of the track. It's a large house, filled with photographs, paintings and memorabilia. There were so many precious objects that left us all enthusiastic, open-mouthed. It was like spending the night in a museum.

"We're not done, let me show you the best part," our guide said at one point.

He took us down a set of stairs, opened a door and we found ourselves in Enzo Ferrari's office, where everything has been left intact, just the way he left it when he passed away. In that office, it's still 1988, from the desk, to the chair, to the lamp, to the old-fashioned telephone. It was really impressive. I never thought I'd be so affected by such a sight. We went to sleep very late and that was part of the reason: we were all energised by the situation and the atmosphere. The next morning, when I stepped out into the pits, I was dressed up as Michael Schumacher. I had his suit and his helmet. I discovered that the boys in the pit crew had taken bets on my performance. Some wagered that I would not break the "one minute" barrier. Doing a lap in less than a minute is a bit of a benchmark at Fiorano. It means you're relatively fast. Many did not think I could make it, certainly not in the first test. I was ready for the challenge.

The driving position immediately struck me as very weird. On a motorbike, you have so much freedom of movement, whereas the cockpit of an F1 car is like a little cage. Your legs disappear down what looks like a black hole, you're basically tied to the seat. And then you don't move any more, at all. You're stuck. You're so low to the ground, that all you can see is the steering wheel and the track. Your eyes and the top of your head are the only parts of your body that stick out above the cockpit. At best, you might catch a glimpse of the front tyres, but you can only really guess that the front of the car is there, because you don't see it. I understand why you're so low to the ground. The lower you are, the better the flow into the air box, above the driver's head.

I wanted to make sure that everyone knew it was me and not Schumacher, so I purposely messed up the start . . . Just kidding. Luckily, F1 cars have a system which corrects your mistakes. It won't let you stall the car, the RPMs stay up and you're free to try again. And so I did. First gear, second gear, third gear and I arrived to the first right turn and . . . went into a tailspin. Yes, even in a Ferrari I had kept up my tradition of inauspicious debuts.

Because I was going slow, I managed to get back on to the track and start all over again. I remained in contact with the pits via radio and kept going. I did three laps and I was starting to have fun when I went into another tailspin. This time it was on a big, fast turn. At Fiorano there is a quick right and then an even quicker left. It was when I went into the left that I spun again. All this despite the fact that

I was clocking 1' 15", which meant that I was going very slow. This time the engine stalled. They came to fetch me in a four-stroke quad. In the pits an engineer came to speak to me.

"Look, this car is built to be driven fast," he said. "If you're not fast, you can't drive it. It's made to go fast, understand?"

That was one of the first lessons I learned. A motorcyclist at the beginning struggles to understand that you shouldn't brake before a turn and then go in. You need to break once you're "in" the turn. You've got to come in on a full throttle and then slam hard on the brake, going into the turn at a high speed. That's the only way you can do it properly. In effect, F1 calls for the opposite. Understanding how to brake was the toughest part. And I think it's the toughest thing for any rider to learn.

Braking in F1 is so powerful it's scary. And it's made even harder because you have to know how the car relates to the aerodynamics. The spoilers are crucial. The car drives a certain way based on the weight above its spoilers. Their downforce is often twice or three times the weight of the car. A Formula One car weighs 550 kilograms. It's incredibly light. But I already knew this from having visited BAR Honda. I had walked around it and, when I tried to sit on the tyres, it slid away under my rear end. I also enjoyed putting the car in neutral and then pushing it with a single finger. It was so light it moved immediately, with the slightest effort.

When you brake, you need a strong leg. When I saw the telemetry, I began to understand how Schumacher generated twice the force I did when braking. The F1 cars are made to go fast and you can only make them work properly if you go fast too. At 300 kilometres per hour, you have 1,500 kilograms of downforce, which means the faster you go, the more stable the car is. That's why you need to stop the car when it's still going fast. That's the only way to handle her, because of the enormous weight around the tyres. If you slow down too much, you're no longer able to brake, because the car becomes lighter and, at that point, you spin out. Just like me!

The display on the steering wheel showed the temperature of the tyres relative to the minimum range of work. This means the tyres did not have enough traction.

"Let's put on the intermediate–hard ones, otherwise you'll never get the tyres up to the right temperature," the engineers said.

And at that point, the ones who had bet against me were no doubt smiling to themselves. They're all good guys on that team. And I enjoyed spending time with them. I played along whenever I could, when they thought to themselves: "This guy wants to do a lap under sixty seconds and he can't even get the tyres to the right temperature."

With the intermediate tyres I drove much better, but I still wasn't able to fully race down the straightaway. Sometimes, even if just for an instant, I'd relax my foot on the gas, so my acceleration was a bit jerky. It was a scary experience, at least at the beginning. Formula One is something you have to get used to.

I have always been convinced that riding a motorbike is tougher than driving a car. And I still think that. I do, however, think that the adjustment for those of us coming from motorbikes is enormous and you have to learn things you would have never imagined. It is just a question of technique in the end, but it's daunting nonetheless. For example, there's the issue of the muscles in your neck. The speed at which you turn a corner is so great, that your neck muscles have to sustain an incredibly intense load. This means you have to do a lot of specific training in the gym. Otherwise, you just can't do it. Having said that, the arms have it very easy, because the cars have power steering. You can turn the steering wheel with one finger, just like the Fiat Panda!

Fiorano has two sequential turns which are both very fast. One to the right, and one to the left. You go through them so quickly that, at first, you don't even realise you're changing directions. By the time I realised what was going on, I was already beyond the ideal trajectory. At first, I simply had no idea how to go through the two quick turns. The car has so much downforce and is so fast that I didn't even see them coming.

"This car is faster than my brain!" I told myself at one point. It all happens so quickly, you get a strange sensation, and you can feel the car hanging in there, but if you so much as a blink the turn is over. It's gone. And you may well be in the gravel.

My fears regarding the secrecy of the whole affair were justified. The chaos broke out earlier than expected, around lunchtime. Because somebody inside Ferrari had spilled the beans, tipping off the press. We were on our lunch break, sitting around a nice plate of pasta. We were relaxed, we were watching sports highlights on television. And, already, the first item on the news was, "Valentino Rossi is testing the Ferrari at Fiorano!"

"Noooo!!! What the . . ." I was gutted. "We've been so secretive that even my own mother doesn't know I'm here and now the whole country knows?"

Word had gotten out. Someone had spoken. And this had ruined my test. Right after the announcement there was a whole crowd of people outside the gates, including many journalists. My win in South Africa had generated a lot of attention in Italy. I was very much the man of the moment. Plus, the Imola Grand Prix was just a few days away . . . Honestly, my day had been ruined. The television reporter seemed to know more than I did. According to the report, I was going to do many more laps in the afternoon, from 2 p.m., right up until dusk. I was too shaken to do well.

Meanwhile, my mum managed to get in touch with me.

"Where are you?" she said immediately.

"In Milan!" I replied.

She knew perfectly well I was lying.

"Well, yes, you're right, I'm in Fiorano . . ." I admitted.

"Today you really came out of it looking like a big piece of shit," she said.

We waited around for Schumacher to arrive, around 5.30 p.m. We chatted for a while, took a few photographs together and it turned out that I only had another hour or so on the track, late in the afternoon. Yet bit by bit I started to get somewhat more confident. I began to adapt to the car. I had put on the slick tyres and started driving well. And fast: in my last session, I clocked 59' 10"!

Which meant that someone had lost their bet . . .

SIXTEEN

CAPITOLO SEDICI

Journalists are like women: as soon as you're successful, they flock to you.

It's not like I have anything specific against women. That's not the case at all, and I don't really wish to generalise about the press either, but, with the passing of time and given my own experience, I've noticed that these two "species" have much in common . . . (Though, at least, women are more interesting!)

I have not always had an ideal relationship with the press. Perhaps it's because I'm jealous of my privacy and the press tend not to respect it. Probably it's what happens when you're a famous person and it's inevitable that they'll want to use you for their own ends, twisting your words and your actions. Maybe the reason I don't always have a great relationship with them is because I know that they don't really care about me as a person, just as a racer. Or maybe many of them have simply never liked me. After all, I've never liked many of them. Or perhaps it's because I always say what I think and, often, it's a mistake to do that when you're in the public gaze. The one thing of which I am certain is that throughout my career they have never forgiven me anything. Not one thing.

At first, when I was on 125cc, everything was great. Then, when I moved up to 250cc, things began to deteriorate. I am always open to the press, though I've had run-ins with a few of them. It may seem unusual, but, by nature, I am open. I actually enjoy talking and even debating with the press.

So, unlike many other racers, I always allowed the press to work. I've always given them plenty to write about. And, perhaps, that's why some of them went too far. If I didn't talk, if one week I chose not to give endless interviews, it may have been because I had nothing to say, or because I was busy, or because I had already spoken to that particular journalist dozens of times, or maybe because, at that particular time, it was best to keep my mouth shut.

And yet the Italian press decided to complain to Yamaha and to the sponsors, on the eve of the 2004 French Grand Prix, because I had, for once, dared not to meet the press that Thursday. I just wanted a day off, believe me, I was really shattered, and talking to the media uses up a lot of energy. And yet they turned my one absence into a huge affair.

Looking back on it, I think the truth is that the Italian media were spoiled. I had treated them too well, if you know what I mean. I was too available to them, I never turned them down and I never failed to entertain them. So when I did turn someone down, it was turned into this big charade.

In 2003, at Valencia, on the eve of the final Grand Prix, one journalist actually threatened me because I refused to grant his paper an exclusive interview. It was a delicate time. It was the weekend in which Honda were scheduled to announce our separation, and I figured it would be best to keep quiet. My management team and I decided that, because there had been no official announcement, it was best not to speak openly to the press. Or, at least, it was best not to grant an exclusive to one media outlet. That way, we thought we could avoid being trapped by the kind of question that can potentially create problems. So because I did not grant this journalist his precious exclusive, he decided to physically threaten me.

"You're not going to do the interview with me?" he hissed. "Great. I'll just wait for you outside and we'll see . . ."

I looked at him with my hands in my pockets. And simply walked away.

In any case, when I did get to the world championship, I had the tendency to speak my mind without thinking of the consequences. And, as I learned over the years, there are always consequences. When you become a public figure, you have to think that everything you say will be used and, in the worst cases, abused. My words have been twisted many times. Perhaps more than any other rider. I always used to pay close attention to what people write about me because I care about those who read the articles – the fans – and yet at a certain point I simply gave up. I stopped reading certain newspapers because too often they just follow the prevailing wind.

When I arrived on the world stage, part of the Italian press really did not like me. Perhaps it was because I was never particularly obsequious. Naturally, it bothered me when people wrote nasty things about me, but I never kissed anyone's butt. I try to foster a real relationship with people. I am very transparent. I say what I think and I do what I say. And I do not kiss anyone's arse.

In time, the press and I came to establish a cordial, working relationship. When we did argue it was because I saw things that had been written or said with the obvious intent to attack me or use me in a certain way. One thing they frequently do is to write not what I said, but what they wish I had said. They push you, so that they can get the "line" they want. They need a certain word, a certain phrase, so that they can write what they want or get the headline they want. There came a moment when I realised that, no matter what I said, they would use my words in the way which most suited them. I understood that if I wasn't careful, I would cease being myself and become whatever they wanted me to be. At least in the eyes of their audience.

As I learned, there are many factors that can poison an article.

Beginning with the personal antipathy or sympathy one might have for a certain racer. Newspapers are now poisoned by their business needs. That's why they hardly ever tell the truth. One thinks of a newspaper as a tool to find out what is happening, to learn, to understand. But in reality, they exist as vehicles for companies to increase revenues. And therefore all that matters to them is selling more and more copies. And what suffers as a result, is truth. I paid for this directly and personally early in my career, when I was still young and inexperienced.

I had lots of fans at the track – because those who love this sport have always loved me – but some Italian journalists never missed a chance to attack me. That's why the Italian press has often been against me. Just think back to what happened in 1998, when I made my debut in the 250cc, or some of those issues with Harada and Capirossi or, better yet, most of my run-ins with Biaggi, up in 500cc.

I never understood just why, once you become a celebrity, you have to start living with the daily nightmare which is your image. You have to always worry about what's right for your image and be careful with what you say and do. Many times, the things I said have caused problems, mostly for myself. Being Valentino Rossi – Valentino Rossi the celebrity, that is, which is basically what I am when I'm racing or doing interviews – has many advantages and privileges. But there is also a very high price to pay for this popularity. And that's why I'm reluctant to trust someone who doesn't consider me for what I am – a person – but only for what I represent.

From afar, you tend to think that someone like me is free to do and say whatever he likes. That's not true. It's very rare that I can do what I want, given the amount of commitments I have, all the requests I receive and the fact that my presence and behaviour can have huge implications for me.

I want to be myself, I don't want to play a role and so I try to protect myself, but it's far from easy.

The real problem is manipulation. Everything I say is thoroughly analysed, interpreted, judged and, most of all, used by someone. And how they use it depends on their agenda. I know this happens to everyone who has ever lived in the proverbial "goldfish bowl", but I have always suffered from it and mentally it affects me more than most. And I have always fought hard not to be used like this; I have done everything possible to keep my private life private. I have always tried not to give in when faced with injustice. And those who know me are aware that this has been my greatest success: I've managed to remain myself, always and everywhere. And I've done it despite my popularity, which became, for me, very oppressive.

I am Valentino Rossi. And I want to be a person, not an icon.

I was born on 16 February 1979. My father is Graziano Rossi, professional racer, both motorcycles and cars. My mother is Stefania Palma, surveyor with the town of Tavullia. I was a relaxed child, or so my mum says. She told me that nobody ever complained about me when I was in playschool, neither the teachers, nor the mothers.

I would build miniature racetracks when I was a little boy and race toy matchbox cars along them. Later, when I learned to ride a bicycle, I always did so with my knee sticking out. But that was back when I was a child. Back when I was good. When I was well behaved. I turned wild once I got my hands on a vehicle with two wheels and an engine.

I am Valentino. Graziano chose that name for me because he wanted to honour the memory of his best friend, who drowned at sea, near Pesaro, at the age of eighteen. The fact that St Valentine's Day is just two days before my birthday was also a reason.

Number 46 originated when I raced minibikes. I was on a team with two kids from Gatteo a Mare, Marco and Maurizio Pagano. They are the brothers who lent me the Aprilia 125, which I used for my debut at Misano. All three of us had number 46 because we raced in three different categories. They too loved Japan and Japanese riders. One day we were mesmerised by a wild-card entrant at the Japanese Grand Prix who pulled off the most amazing tricks and seemed to have no fear whatsoever. He was number 46. And from that day on, so were we. For me, that lasted until I moved up to the Italian championship and, later, the European series. But when I finally made it to the world championship, I was asked to choose a number. I discovered that 46 was Graziano's number when he won his first Grand Prix on a Morbidelli 250cc, back in 1979. Which was the year I was born. That's why I decided that I, too, would be number 46. For me that number represents my career and, partly, my life. It certainly symbolises my massive, incredible, adventure.

And it reminds me of the day it all began. The day I came to a fork in the road, so to speak, and had to choose which way to go. Four wheels or two? Kart or bike? I chose two wheels, motorbikes. I chose to try the Aprilia 125 and, later, I began competing. And I continued competing.

My first victory was over my parents' fears. My second over the lack of faith in my abilities.

It's true, I did well in school. And, yes, there were many other things I was good at. But I wanted to race. Fast. Very fast. And that's what I did.

Just think, what if I had never raced motorbikes. How things would have been so different. Just think, what if I had never tried it.

Valentino Rossi – at a glance

Nationality: Italian
Date of birth: 16 February 1979
Place of birth: Urbino
Height: 182cm
Weight: 68kg
Residence: London
Race number: 46
Race Team (2005): Gauloises Yamaha Team
Championship competition class (2005): MotoGP

Career summary

	500cc/MotoGP	250cc	125cc	All
First Grand Prix	2000 – South Africa	1998 – Japan	1996 – Malaysia	
First pole position	2001 – South Africa	1999 – Malaysia	1996 – Czech Republic	
First race fastest lap	2000 – South Africa	1998 – Malaysia	1996 – France	
First podium finish	2000 – Spain	1998 – Spain	1996 – Austria	
First Grand Prix victory	2000 – Great Britain	1998 – Holland	1996 – Czech Republic	
Grand Prix victories	53	14	12	79
2nd positions	18	5	1	24
3rd positions	9	2	2	13
Podiums	79	21	15	115
Pole positions	30	5	5	40
Race fastest lap	45	11	9	65
World Championship wins	5	1	1	7

Career statistics

Season	Category	Starts	1st	2nd	3rd	Podiums	Poles	Bike	Points	Position
2005	MotoGP	16	11	3	1	15	5	Yamaha	351	1
2004	MotoGP	16	9	2	–	11	5	Yamaha	304	1
2003	MotoGP	16	9	5	2	16	9	Honda	357	1
2002	MotoGP	16	11	4	–	15	7	Honda	355	1
2001	500cc	16	11	1	1	13	4	Honda	325	1
2000	500cc	16	2	3	5	10	–	Honda	209	2
1999	250cc	16	9	2	1	12	5	Aprilia	309	1
1998	250cc	14	5	3	1	9	–	Aprilia	201	2
1997	125cc	15	11	1	1	13	4	Aprilia	321	1
1996	125cc	15	1	–	1	2	1	Aprilia	111	9

2005 MotoGP

	SPA	POR	CHN	FRA	ITA	CAT	NED	USA	GBR	GER	CZE	JPN	MAL	QAT	AUS	TUR	VAL
Qualifying	1	4	6	1	1	3	1	2	1	4	4	11	7	3	2	4	
Race	1*	2	1	1*	1	1*	1*	3	1*	1	1*	–	2	1	1	2	

	Bike	Pole positions		Wins		2nd Place		3rd Place		*Fastest laps		Points		Position	
Summary	Yamaha	5		11		3		1		6		351		**Champion**	

2004 MotoGP

	RSA	SPA	FRA	ITA	CAT	NED	BRA	GER	GBR	CZE	POR	JPN	QAT	MAL	AUS	VAL
Qualifying	1	1	4	3	2	1	8	2	1	3	2	3	23	1	2	3
Race	1	4	4	1	1	1*	–	4	1	2	1*	2	–	1*	1	1

	Bike	Pole positions		Wins		2nd Place		3rd Place		*Fastest laps		Points		Position	
Summary	Yamaha	5		9		2		–		3		304		**Champion**	

2003 MotoGP

	JPN	RSA	SPA	FRA	ITA	CAT	NED	GBR	GER	CZE	POR	BRA	MOT	MAL	AUS	VAL
Qualifying	1	2	5	1	1	1	3	4	4	1	3	1	3	1	1	1
Race	1*	2*	1*	2	1	2*	3	3*	2	1*	1*	1*	2*	1*	1*	1*

	Bike	Pole positions		Wins		2nd Place		3rd Place		*Fastest laps		Points		Position	
Summary	Honda	9		9		5		2		12		357		**Champion**	

2002 MotoGP

	JPN	RSA	SPA	FRA	ITA	CAT	NED	GBR	GER	CZE	POR	BRA	MOT	MAL	AUS	VAL
Qualifying	1	1	1	1	1	4	1	1	6	3	3	2	6	8	7	6
Race	1*	2	1*	1*	1	1*	1*	1*	1*	–	1*	1	2	2	1*	2

	Bike	Pole positions		Wins		2nd Place		3rd Place		*Fastest laps		Points		Position	
Summary	Honda	7		11		4		–		9		355		**Champion**	

2001 500cc

	JPN	RSA	SPA	FRA	ITA	CAT	NED	GBR	GER	CZE	POR	VAL	MOT	AUS	MAL	BRA
Qualifying	7	1	1	3	1	1	3	11	11	2	3	2	4	2	2	5
Race	1	1*	1*	3	–*	1*	2*	1*	7	1*	1	11	1*	1	1*	1*

	Bike	Pole positions		Wins		2nd Place		3rd Place		*Fastest laps		Points		Position	
Summary	Honda	4		11		1		1		10		325		**Champion**	

Key to Trigrams:

ARG = Argentina	CHN = China	INA = Indonesia	POR = Portugal
AUS = Australia	CZE = Czech Republic	ITA = Italy	QAT = Qatar
AUT = Austria	FRA = France	JPN = Japan	RSA = South Africa
BRA = Brazil	GBR = Great Britain	MAL = Malaysia	SPA = Spain
CAT = Catalonia	GER = Germany	MOT = Montegi	TUR = Turkey
	IMO = Imola	NED = Holland	VAL = Valencia

500cc — 2000

	RSA	MAL	JPN	SPA	FRA	ITA	CAT	NED	GBR	GER	CZE	POR	VAL	BRA	MOT	AUS
Qualifying	5	7	13	2	10	3	9	6	4	6	5	12	5	4	5	8
Race	–*	–	11	3	3*	12	3	6	1	2	2	3*	–	1*	2*	3

	Bike	Pole positions	Wins	2nd Place	3rd Place	*Fastest laps	Points	Position
Summary	Honda	–	2	3	5	5	209	Runner-up

250cc — 1999

	MAL	JPN	SPA	FRA	ITA	CAT	NED	GBR	GER	CZE	IMO	VAL	AUS	RSA	BRA	ARG
Qualifying	1	11	3	1	6	2	1	3	1	3	3	4	7	6	2	1
Race	5	7	1	–*	1*	1*	2*	1	1	1*	2	8	1*	1*	1*	3

	Bike	Pole positions	Wins	2nd Place	3rd Place	*Fastest laps	Points	Position
Summary	Aprilia	4	9	2	1	8	309	**Champion**

250cc — 1998

	JPN	MAL	SPA	ITA	FRA	MAD	NED	GBR	GER	CZE	IMO	CAT	AUS	ARG
Qualifying	7	2	3	4	3	4	3	2	4	2	5	2	2	3
Race	–	–*	2	2	2	–	1	–	3	–	1	1*	1	1*

	Bike	Pole positions	Wins	2nd Place	3rd Place	*Fastest laps	Points	Position
Summary	Aprilia	–	5	3	1	3	201	Runner-up

125cc — 1997

	MAL	JPN	SPA	ITA	AUT	FRA	NED	IMO	GER	BRA	GBR	CZE	CAT	INA	AUS
Qualifying	1	7	6	3	2	3	1	1	1	2	4	3	4	4	3
Race	1*	–	1*	1	2*	1	1	1*	1	1*	1*	3	1	1*	6

	Bike	Pole positions	Wins	2nd Place	3rd Place	*Fastest laps	Points	Position
Summary	Aprilia	4	11	1	1	7	321	**Champion**

125cc — 1996

	MAL	INA	JPN	SPA	ITA	FRA	NED	GER	GBR	AUT	CZE	IMO	CAT	BRA	AUS
Qualifying	13	18	10	7	8	13	8	4	9	3	1	2	5	11	12
Race	6	11	11	4	4	–*	–	5	–	3	1	5*	–	–	14

	Bike	Pole positions	Wins	2nd Place	3rd Place	*Fastest laps	Points	Position
Summary	Aprilia	1	1	–	1	2	111	Ninth

Key to Trigrams:

ARG = Argentina	CHN = China	INA = Indonesia	NED = Holland
AUS = Australia	CZE = Czech Republic	ITA = Italy	POR = Portugal
AUT = Austria	FRA = France	JPN = Japan	QAT = Qatar
BRA = Brazil	GBR = Great Britain	MAD = Madrid	RSA = South Africa
CAT = Catalonia	GER = Germany	MAL = Malaysia	SPA = Spain
	IMO = Imola	MOT = Montegi	VAL = Valencia